Culture and Sustainable Development in the Pacific

Culture and Sustainable Development in the Pacific

Antony Hooper (editor)

THE AUSTRALIAN NATIONAL UNIVERSITY

E PRESS

Asia Pacific Press at
The Australian National University

ANU

E PRESS

Co-published by ANU E Press and Asia Pacific Press
The Australian National University
Canberra ACT 0200, Australia
Email: anuepress@anu.edu.au
Web: http://epress.anu.edu.au
Previously published by Asia Pacific Press

The National Centre for Development Studies gratefully acknowledges
the contribution made by the Australian Agency for International
Development (AusAID) towards the publication of this series. The
financial support provided by UNESCO towards the publication of this
volume is also gratefully acknowledged.

ISSN   0817–0444

National Library of Australia Cataloguing-in-Publication entry

Culture and sustainable development in the Pacific.

ISBN 1 920942 23 8
ISBN 1 920942 22 X (Online document)

1. Sustainable development - Pacific Area. 2. Pacific Area - Social life
and customs. 3. Pacific Area - Civilization. I. Hooper, Antony.

909.09823

Series editor: Maree Tait
Editor: Elizabeth St George
Pagesetting: Jackie Lipsham and Matthew May

Cover design: Annie Di Nallo Design

First edition © 2000 Asia Pacific Press
This edition © 2005 ANU E Press and Asia Pacific Press

Contents

Tables   vii
Abbreviations   vii
Contributors   viii
Preface   xii

Introduction   1
Antony Hooper

1   Culture and sustainable development in the Pacific   22
     Langi Kavaliku

2   The ocean in us   32
     Epeli Hau'ofa

3   On the anthropology of modernity; or, some triumphs
     of culture over despondency theory   44
     Marshall Sahlins

4   Gender, culture and sustainable development—
     the Pacific Way   62
     Peggy Fairbairn-Dunlop

5   Governance, development and leadership in
     Polynesia: a microstudy from Samoa   76
     Malama Meleisea

6   Rumble in the jungle: land, culture and
     (un)sustainable logging in Solomon Islands   88
     Tarcisius Tara Kabutaulaka

7   Knowing about culture: the handling of social issues
     at resource projects in Papua New Guinea   98
     John Burton

8   Culture and sustainable marine resource development
     in the Pacific   111
     Philipp Muller

9   Fisheries resource-use culture in Fiji and its implications   116
     Joeli Veitayaki

10   Local hierarchies of authority and development   131
     Kerry James

11   A paradox of tradition in a modernising society:
     chiefs and political development in Fiji   142
     Robert Norton

12   Development and Maori society: building from
     the centre or the edge?   159
     Shane Jones

13   Culturally and ecologically sustainable tourism
     development through local community management   174
     Richard A. Engelhardt

14   Tourism and culture: a sustainable partnership   187
     Levani V. Tuinabua

15   Vaka Moana—a road map for the South Pacific
     economy   190
     Hana Ayala

16   Vaka Moana—the ocean roads   207
     Mali Voi

17   Afterword: after the World Decade   221
     Russell Marshall

Tables

Table 4.1   Micro-enterprises by type   69
Table 4.2   Pattern of multiple small enterprises and
             employment for family members   70

Abbreviations

CHOGM	Commonwealth Heads of Government Meeting
EEZ	Exclusive Economic Zone
ESCAP	Economic and Social Commission for Asia and the Pacific
FAO	Food and Agriculture Organisation
GDP	Gross Domestic Product
IMF	International Monetary Fund
MIRAB	Migration-Remittances-Aid-Bureaucracy
NAFTA	North American Free Trade Association
NGO	Non-government organisation
PPA	Pacific Platform of Action
SPC	South Pacific Commission
UN	United Nations
UNDP	United Nations Development Programme
UNESCO	United Nations Education Scientific and Cultural Organisation
UNICEF	United Nations Children's Fund
UPNG	University of Papua New Guinea
USP	University of the South Pacific
WOSED	Women's Social and Economic Development Program
WTO	World Tourism Organization

Contributors

Hana Ayala is President of EcoResorts International—Research and Development in Irvine, California, specialising in the planning of strategic alliances between tourism, conservation and research in the context of national and regional economies, with a special focus on concept design of hotel developments for heritage-centred sustainable tourism. She has a PhD from Masaryk University, and she was formerly on the faculty of the School of Social Ecology at UC Irvine.

John Burton is an ethnographer specialising in rural Papua New Guinean societies. He is a former lecturer in anthropology and sociology at the University of Papua New Guinea. He is a Visiting Fellow in geography at the Research School of Pacific and Asian Studies, Australian National University, and runs a small consultancy business in Canberra concerned with the social appraisal of mining and petroleum projects. He has a PhD from the Australian National University.

Richard Engelhardt is UNESCO Regional Adviser for Culture in Asia and the Pacific, based in Bangkok. Educated in anthropology, archaeology and history at both Harvard and Yale, he has worked extensively on culture and heritage projects throughout east, south and southeast Asia, specialising in urban conservation and the role of culture in development. Between 1991 and 1994 he was Director of the UNESCO office in Cambodia.

Peggy Fairbairn-Dunlop has played a leading role in Pacific women's research, training and policy identification. Formerly on the staff of the University of the South Pacific's School of Agriculture and Sustainable Human Development, Adviser for the UNDP in Suva, she has recently been appointed as Co-ordinator of Continuing Education at USP. She has an MA from Victoria University of Wellington and a PhD from Macquarie University.

Epeli Hau'ofa has recently been appointed as Director of the University of the South Pacific's Oceania Centre for Arts and Culture, after a period as Professor in USP's School of Social Science and Economic Development. He has a PhD from the Australian National

University and is well known for both his fiction and his extensive publications on Pacific regional issues.

Antony Hooper is Professor Emeritus at the University of Auckland. After leaving Auckland he was a Fellow in the Pacific Islands Development Program at the East West Centre in Honolulu for three years. He is now an independent consultant in Sydney, currently spending time as a Research Scholar at the Macmillan Brown Centre for Pacific Studies at the University of Canterbury, New Zealand. He has a PhD from Harvard.

Kerry James is an ethnographer specialising in Tonga and an independent consultant. Her PhD is from University College London. In recent years she has held research fellowships at the Macmillan Brown Centre, the Center for Pacific Islands Studies and the Pacific Islands Development Program at the East West Centre in Honolulu. She now lives in Sydney.

Shane Jones is chairman of the Poutama Trust and also a Commissioner for the Treaty of Waitangi Fisheries Commission.

Tarcisius Tara Kabutaulaka has an MA in Development Studies from the University of the South Pacific, and has been a lecturer in History and Politics there. In July 1996 he was awarded a USP scholarship for doctoral studies in Political Science and International Relations at the Australian National University, where his dissertation is concerned with the sociopolitical factors that affect the management of forestry in Solomon Islands. He has published papers in journals concerned with development, as well as short stories and feature and opinion articles in regional news magazines.

Langi Kavaliku is Deputy Prime Minister of Tonga and Minister of Education and Civil Aviation. Educated in Tonga, the United States, England and New Zealand, he has a BA from Harvard and a PhD from Victoria University of Wellington. He has served on the governing bodies of many regional organisations, including the Council of the University of the South Pacific and the Standing Committee of Pacific Islands Development Program in Honolulu. He is the author of several articles on education and development and has also published poetry. He is at present a member of the Executive Board of UNESCO.

Russell Marshall has been Chairman of the New Zealand National Commission for UNESCO since 1990, and is currently a member of the UNESCO Executive Board. He was a Member of Parliament from 1972 to 1990, and held several ministerial portfolios, including Education, Foreign Affairs and Pacific Island Affairs. He is a member of the Victoria University Council (Wellington), and has a BA in Anthropology and a Diploma in Teaching.

Malama Meleisea is Regional Adviser on Social Science for UNESCO in Bangkok. Educated in Samoa, the University of Papua New Guinea and Macquarie University, from where he has a PhD in History, he was the founding Director of the Macmillan Brown Centre for Pacific Studies in Christchurch before moving to Auckland University to be Director of the Centre for Pacific Studies there. He has published extensively on Samoa and has been President of the Pacific History Association.

Philipp Muller has had extensive experience in Pacific regional organisations, and his services have been recognised by awards of the Order of Australia (AM) and the Cross of Solomon Islands (CSI). Educated in science at the University of Auckland, he was Chairman of the Western Samoa Public Service Commission and a field expert in Hydrology for FAO in Apia before becoming Director of the South Pacific Forum Fisheries in Solomon Islands. He is currently Director of the South Pacific Applied Geoscience Commission in Suva.

Robert Norton is senior lecturer in Anthropology at Macquarie University and the author of *Race and Politics in Fiji*. He has been studying ethnic relations and politics in Fiji since 1966, and has also done field research on social change and local-level politics in both Samoa and Tonga. His PhD is from the University of Sydney.

Marshall Sahlins is Charles F. Grey Distinguished Service Professor at the University of Chicago. His PhD is from Columbia University and he has done extensive field and archival research on both Fiji and Hawaii. He is a member of the Academy of Sciences and the recipient of many international awards for his distinguished contributions to anthropology, social theory and Pacific scholarship.

Levani Tuinabua is Chief Executive of the Tourism Council of the South Pacific. Prior to taking this position in 1993 he was Director of Tourism in Fiji for many years. He has a BA from the University of the South Pacific and an MSc in Regional Planning from the University College of Swansea.

Joeli Veitayaki has an MA from the University of the South Pacific, and is a lecturer in that university's Marine Studies Program. He is at present on study leave for doctoral work at the National Centre for Development Studies, the Australian National University, which is concerned with development issues in artisanal fisheries.

Mali Voi is UNESCO's sub-regional adviser for Culture in the Pacific, based in Apia. Educated in Papua New Guinea and Australia, he has an MA from Macquarie University and was Registrar of the Papua New Guinea University of Technology before taking his present position. He has been awarded the OBE for cultural services in the Pacific, and a Long Distinguished Service Medal for Education and Cultural Services in Papua New Guinea.

Preface

The papers in this volume were presented at a UNESCO conference 'Culture and Sustainable Development in the Pacific' in Suva, Fiji, between 9–12 July, 1997. The conference was conceived as part of the *Vaka Moana* program, the UNESCO Pacific states' contribution to the United Nations sponsored 'World Decade for Cultural Development 1988–97'. It was financed by a UNESCO program grant to the New Zealand National Commission.

The conference had two main aims. The first, more general aim, was to explore the ways in which the two politically charged notions of culture and development are commonly conceived, talked about and argued in the region. Eighteen invited speakers addressed this broad theme, focusing on topics of their own choosing. Their papers make up the bulk of the volume. The second aim was to relate the issues raised in these papers to the *Vaka Moana* program and to the 1995 report of the World Commission on Culture and Development. Two of the papers presented here are concerned directly with the *Vaka Moana*. The two themes are brought together in three 'agreed-upon suggestions'. These are summarised in the Introduction.

Although UNESCO is known for its long-standing involvement with culture, it has not, at least until recently, been closely identified with development. The involvement came about through the UN sponsored 'World Decade for Cultural Development 1988–97,' which was founded in the context of the widespread critiques of development appearing since the early 1970s. Many projects had failed to achieve the broad goals of human betterment that were expected to be the outcome of international cooperation for material and technological advances throughout the developing countries of the world. The gap between rich and poor nations was not being significantly and uniformly closed, and within many of the developing countries themselves, projects were leading to political unrest and increasing misery of large numbers of people.

The World Decade for Cultural Development was an attempt to address these issues by shifting the emphasis within development paradigms from economic goals to cultural ones. As Perez de Cuellar, then Secretary General of the United Nations stated in launching the Decade in 1988, developments were failing 'because the importance of the human factor—that complex web of relationships and beliefs, values and motivations that lie at the very heart of a culture—had been underestimated in many development projects.' The responsibility for implementing the ideas of the World Decade and for bringing about this change of emphasis was then passed over to UNESCO.

In 1993 these issues were further addressed through another joint UNESCO/UN initiative—the World Commission on Culture and Development (chaired by Perez de Cuellar, by then no longer Secretary General)—which brought together a body of people 'eminent in diverse disciplines' to prepare a 'World Report' containing 'proposals for both urgent and long-term action to meet cultural needs in the context of development'. Although the notion of 'meeting cultural needs in the context of development' slides around the central contradiction, the Commission, according to its final report, did pay attention to the relationship between culture and development by considering problems such as the following: What are the cultural and socio-cultural factors that affect development? What is the cultural impact of social and economic development? How are cultures and models of development related to one another? How can valuable elements of a traditional culture be combined with modernisation? What are the cultural dimensions of individual and collective well-being?

The Commission's report was published in 1995 as *Our Creative Diversity: Report of the World Commission on Culture and Development.* Although it was hoped that it might achieve for culture and development what the Brundtland Report and the Rio Summit had done for environment and development, this does not appear to have happened.

The *Vaka Moana* program was the Pacific's reponse to UNESCO's World Decade. Conceived in 1991, it sought, among other things, to initiate projects that would demonstrate the importance and the practicality of 'taking account of the cultural dimension' in development. As one of the main themes of the World Decade, this was seen as particularly appropriate to Pacific countries, with their arrays of traditional institutions and cohesive local economic, social and value systems, many of which were seen to conflict with conventional strategies of economic development. Other related aims have been added as the *Vaka Moana* has evolved: the study and preservation of traditional bodies of knowledge about local environments; the reinforcement of traditional links and awareness of the common maritime heritage of Pacific peoples; and a host of other projects accommodated to what the governments of the region have seen as more obviously 'cultural' in nature, centred on archives, museums, crafts, oral history and traditions and cultural centres. The considerable accomplishments (and difficulties, mainly financial and bureaucratic) of *Vaka Moana* were canvassed during the course of the Suva meeting, and are fully described by Mali Voi in his paper in this volume.

The Suva meeting was happily unencumbered by such financial and bureaucratic constraints. Nor was it driven by the policy orientation that pervaded the work of the World Commission on Cultural Development. The immediate aim of the meeting was to address the conceptual issues involved in the relationship between culture and development, as these two protean terms are commonly understood and used in the Pacific region. Its second aim, as Russell Marshall expressed it in his conference paper, was 'to develop some philosophical basis from which we…[might] develop a more coherent strategy for UNESCO's cultural activities in the Pacific.' As convener, I was constrained only by these general goals and two suggestions from the office of the World Decade for Cultural Development in Paris: that not all the contributors should be anthropologists and that we should pay attention to the development (as I took it, the commercial exploitation) of natural resources. The invitations sent out to speakers reminded them of UNESCO's involvement with culture in both its humanistic and anthropological senses, and of the focus of the *Vaka Moana* program on 'the necessity of taking account of the cultural dimension' in development. No other particular meanings of either culture or development were mentioned and speakers were free to choose their own interpretations as well as the topics they applied them to in their prepared papers.

In particular, no mention was made of the World Commission's 1995 report, *Our Cultural Diversity*, or of that body's strong paradigm proclaiming what it saw as the essential meanings of the words and the ways they should (in an ideal world) be related to one another and applied to the goals of peace and the betterment of human kind. Since the conference was sponsored by UNESCO, this may appear to have been either an oversight or a deliberate affront. That was not the case. The aim was to explore the discourse of culture and development in the Pacific, not to relate the World Commission's recommendations and policies to the region.

Antony Hooper

Introduction

Antony Hooper

Throughout the South Pacific, as in many other places, notions of 'culture' and 'development' are very much alive, surfacing again and again in a wide variety of contexts—political debate, the news media, sermons and policy reports, as well as in the endless discourses of 'ordinary life', everywhere from outlying villages to gatherings of urban élites. Not infrequently the terms are counterposed, and development, along with 'economic rationality', 'good governance' and 'progress' is set against culture or 'custom', 'tradition' and 'identity'. The decay of custom and impoverishment of culture are often seen as wrought by development, while failures of development are haunted by the notion that they are due, somehow, to the darker, irrational influences of culture. Nevertheless, as Ron Crocombe has commented (1994:38), both are 'good' words throughout the Pacific, needing, and receiving, constant attention. The problem, as in other places, has been to resolve the contradictions between them so as to achieve the even greater good—access to material goods, welfare and the amenities of 'modern life' without the sacrifice of 'traditional' values and institutions that provide material security and sustain diverse social identities.

Many development economists are aware of these contradictions. The World Bank (1991:1–3) for example, acknowledges that '[p]rospects for economic development [in the Pacific] are conditioned to a large extent by the islands' social patterns', and that 'cultural endowments' exert a 'profound influence over the pattern...of development.' Wolfgang Kaspar (1991:49) makes the point that 'anthropological [by which he means cultural] facts matter in the South Pacific.' He gives a good account of them, but then, like the writers of the *World Bank Report*, he has not really sought to work out exactly how they matter, or what their implications may be for economic development. Nevertheless, he confidently reaches the general conclusion that South Pacific island countries could, if they really tried, emulate the growth of certain Asian economies, 'absorbing Western technology, management and economic modes of behaviour without giving up their Chinese, Malay, Korean, Japanese or Indian identities' (1991:790).

Development economists frequently draw comparisons between Asian and Pacific countries in much the same terms that Kaspar does (for example Cole and Tambunlertchai 1993), perhaps on the assumption that since they all belong in one Asia Pacific region, what goes for culture in the larger Asian part of it, goes for the remainder. This, I believe, is a false assumption, and one that I sought to question directly in my own contribution at the Suva meeting, by pointing out some of the less obvious ways that Pacific island countries are different, apart from scale and resources.

In general, what is construed as culture in the Pacific region is constructed in ways that are quite distinct from the kinds of construction prevalent in the larger Asian countries. Culture impinges on the 'harder' structures of political and economic organisation much more directly and effectively. There is, in every Pacific country, a large and vigorous traditional sector. It does not consist, as is the case in many other regions, of minorities or a few remnant groups in the hills with little influence on national economic and political affairs. In most cases, around 80 to 90 per cent of land resources are under customary tenure, and the traditional sector accounts for around 50 per cent of national GDP. Furthermore, the systems of customary tenure are commonly entrenched in constitutional or other legal structures which insulate them, either absolutely or in large degree, from the operation of market forces and state coercion. Custom thus controls a very large proportion of the economic resources that are basic for development in any of its conventional senses. In these circumstances development is not, as some would have it, simply a matter of engineering a transition from subsistence to dynamic monetary economies. The economic mode of Pacific traditional sectors is not 'subsistence' if by that is meant 'mere subsistence'—nor has it ever been. There is instead a wide variety of reciprocal exchanges and redistributions that integrate whole districts in networks of mutual obligation and concern going far beyond 'mere subsistence'. Such transactions are more than 'mere economics'. They are, in the well-worn phrase, 'embedded in the society', carrying within them a large moral and ideological force.

Culture also impinges on national politics. Pacific countries are democratic; most are wholly so, and the remainder at least to some degree. Politicians have to be elected, and where the electors derive a great proportion of their livelihoods from the traditional sectors, matters of custom and tradition carry considerable political clout. Again, most Pacific countries have constitutions which assert national legitimacy in terms of their distinctive culture and traditions, and these are given at least as much attention as universal notions of democracy and individual rights. In these ways, culture in one form or another is right at the heart of national economic and political life.

These basic facts clearly distinguish the region from the larger Asia Pacific conglomerate in which it is so often submerged. Culture plays a much more significant role in national economies and national life of Pacific countries than it does in most other regions of the world. One of the implications is that the national economies of the Pacific cannot be adequately encompassed by standard macroeconomic analyses. Economists do what they usefully can in charting the trends and fortunes of the private and public sectors, but they generally have little or nothing to say about what they call the traditional sector. This is understandable, given the nature of traditional economic transactions and their absence from national accounting systems. But where the traditional sector accounts for 50 per cent or more of GDP (according to what can only be gross estimates), such analyses can hardly be adequate as descriptions of what motivates people or what they are actually doing with their lives. In addition, since macroeconomic analyses commonly take little or no account of the constraints that the ideology of tradition places on the private and public sectors, recommendations for development take on an air of prescriptive unreality. Politicians and policymakers in Pacific countries do what they can to adapt the development recommendations to social and political realities (or, as some would insist, to their own ends), but it is often an inexact and disruptive process, beset by many unintended consequences.

There is, it seems, no widely agreed-upon way out of this situation—no general paradigm for economic development that does not, in the final analysis, involve getting people out of what is consistently called the subsistence economy and into a dynamic monetary economy. That, so they say, is an economic imperative. Be that as it may, it hardly contributes to an understanding of the contemporary economic, social and cultural reality in Pacific island countries. For that, the need is for a broader and more complex conceptualisation, made in socioeconomic rather than straightforward economic categories. A scheme that I have proposed involves three broad domains: a traditional domain, a private sector domain and a public sector domain. These are not simply sectors of economic activity but socioeconomic units, each with its own economic base, its own set of institutional structures and basic grounding ideas. They are present in every Pacific country, though differently constituted in each, according to the contingent historical and cultural structures which brought them into being. They have been there for generations, having been laid one over the other in the form of a palimpsest, each influencing what was there before and, in turn, acquiring a particular coloration of its own from what preceded it. Individuals may participate in several domains, as when a business person contributes profits to a traditional undertaking, or when traditional status is converted to political ends. Institutions, motivations and expectations may differ between separate domains. People know this, and can either keep them apart, or deliberately confuse them. The structure of domains may change, adapting to connections which are made with the outside world (as, for example, through emigration) and in this way influence the structure of other domains.

These chapters, in their diverse ways, pick up and elaborate on this general characterisation. They also cohere remarkably with one another in the following four ways. First, none of the contributors is at any pains to define either culture or development. They are instead concerned with the ways in which the terms are employed in common usage, with 'what is being accomplished socially, politically, discursively when the [concepts…are] used to describe, analyse, argue, justify and theorise' (Dominguez 1992:21). They are also very closely focused particularities, drawing on a variety of concrete examples and images: a two-storey house, Solbrew, centre and edge, a village band and so forth. Change is expected. Consistency is not an issue. What is characterised as culture appears sometimes as a weapon of the weak, sometimes as oppression by the strong. This produced no confusion, no dislocating sense of a ragbag of unrelated topics. Everyone present knew precisely what was at issue, drawing on a common fund of experience or what Dominguez has characterised as 'sameness and shared understanding'. This, I believe, is an important point which has clear implications for any plans for future action on behalf of culture in the Pacific.

Second, although the chapters show a common concern with what is understood as culture, there is no idealisation of it. That in itself is an accomplishment, since in the general Pacific discourse of 'culture and development' idealisation is pervasive—its nature neatly captured by Colin Filer's description of 'the village which is everywhere and nowhere',

> ...a community whose members lived in complete harmony with each other and with their natural environment, who jointly owned the land to which they had a mystical attachment, who chose their leaders by consensus, settled arguments by compromise, and redistributed the products of their labour to ensure that everyone enjoyed the same condition of subsistence affluence (1990:9).

Contributors to the conference were in general experienced enough to know that no traditional community exists entirely free from greed, self-seeking, treachery and disloyalty. The common regret that all the chapters express is simply the erosion of the traditional institutional forces that hold these forces in check, by the ideologies of development which are built on notions of cost accounting and bourgeois individualism. Pacific countries are all relatively small; social disruptions are not easily contained and can have very widespread and corrosive effects.

Third, it is obvious that traditional values and forms of social organisation have been remarkably resilient and persistent throughout the Pacific. Marshall Sahlins' chapter is the most powerful and eloquent statement of this point, drawing attention to the capacity of peoples to indigenise the forces of global modernity and turn them to their own ends. In the Pacific, this capacity depends not only on force of will, loyalty to kin, religion or respect for chiefs (though all these are important) but also upon a solid, and legally entrenched, economic infrastructure.

Culture and development in Pacific discourse

Culture

As a region of striking human diversity, the Pacific has attracted anthropologists ever since the halting beginnings of the subject as a separate field of social inquiry. Over the years, the anthropologists have produced a huge descriptive record of the region, couched in a wide variety of theoretical frameworks and including some of the classics of the discipline. 'Oceania' was thus built into a famous site of culture, with the descriptive record contributing significantly to the acceptance of culture in the anthropological sense, as an attribute of all peoples. This was in opposition to the restrictive German and French *kultur/culture*, 'high culture', or the possession of a privileged few, and also to the related notion of the equal worth of all cultural traditions which has passed into popular usage as vulgar cultural relativity.

Anthropologists established and retained what Linnekin (1992:255) has called 'narrative authority', if only because they were, for much of the time, the only ones to pay attention to 'culture' as such. The reaction of Pacific peoples themselves to these largely objectivist, positivist (Linnekin 1992:249) representations was highly varied—though, for complex and particular historical reasons, often muted. The situation was to change, however, as indigenous scholars and political leaders sought to construct their own versions of culture and tradition, as *kastom, pasim tumbuna, Maoritanga, fa'a Samoa, vaka vanua* and so forth, asserting their own narrative authority and defining for themselves the essential qualities by which they wished to be known to the outside world. None of these changes, of course, were peculiar to the Pacific. They were worldwide. The meaning of culture went through another historical transformation, becoming a self-conscious, objectified reality, a universally valorised marker of difference which could be used to good effect in struggles against colonial and other political oppressions and which directly reflected the ways in which multiculturalism in the industrial world used culture to refer to diverse collective social identities engaged in struggles for social equality. The background to this historical transformation of the meaning of culture is complex. Jocelyn Linnekin (1992:254) refers its intellectual genealogy to various postmodernists, while Terence Turner (1993:424) points to a great 'contemporary conjuncture' of the global organisation of capitalism, the suppression of the nation state and other changes such as consumerism and information technology.

Not unexpectedly, these moves led to a general excitation of the academic discourse on the region, with the result that there was a proliferation of the scholarly attention given to the general themes of tradition, nationalism and identity, often summarised under the label of the politics of tradition. This has provided fertile ground for continuing debates—impossible to summarise here, but whose leading ideas are well represented in a number of volumes of collected essays (Keesing and Tonkinson 1982; Linnekin and Poyer 1990; Jolly and Thomas 1992; Lindstrom and White 1993). Jolly and Thomas give a good summary of the issues that this literature addresses, several of which are relevant to an informed reading of this volume. The historically particular influences of colonialism, for example, have channelled broadly similar indigenous institutions in different ways. Thus there is a world of difference between what happened to 'chieftainship' in the Cook Islands under the New Zealand regime, and the way in which the British administration coopted chiefs into the mechanism of indirect rule in Fiji, as well as broad similarities in the fate of indigenous people in the white settler colonies of New Zealand, Hawaii and Australia. The nature of the indigenous societies was also relevant. There is an obvious difference in the way that culture has come to be constructed in more linguistically and politically unitary places like Fiji, Samoa and Tonga compared to the more diverse territories of Papua New Guinea, Solomon Islands and Vanuatu. What has come to be objectified and counted as culture (as distinct from 'church', 'business' or 'government') is thus extremely diverse.

Then there is the issue of authenticity, centred on the question of the extent to which representations of the past in indigenous constructions of tradition square, with 'historical facts'—the occasion of some notable disputes between Pacific peoples and academics. These have probably attracted much more attention in academic circles than among indigenous intellectuals and activists, most of whom have been preoccupied with more urgent, practical, political and legal concerns. A related issue here has been the extent to which all traditions, including the great European ones, have been ideologically constructed—a point neatly raised by Sahlins in his characterisation of the European Renaissance (1993:7–8).

Both of these issues are related to a third: the extent to which ideas of 'national culture' can be manipulated to serve the interests of westernised élites in control of the apparatus of government. This can give rise to accusations, justified or not, about 'politicians raised in urban settings and educated overseas [who] proclaim the virtues of a *kastom* they have never known' (Keesing 1982:299). In some places it can also give rise to the deeper, more complex and subtle ambiguities which appear when the culture that is extolled is no more than an analogue of 'high culture' in the Western sense, the attribute and possession of a privileged few. The well-known debate over 'The Pacific Way' illustrates aspects of this.

Development

A hundred and fifty or so years ago, when people of the Tokelau atolls began to have access to iron, European cordage and nautical goods, they set about acquiring it by whatever means available. They discarded their shell fishhooks and made their own out of iron, replaced their sennit lines with manufactured ones and their matting sails with canvas. They learned of *pulaka* (*Cytosperma chamissonis*) from what was then the Ellice Islands, labouriously dug up acres of their rough coral ground two metres down to the fresh-water lens and planted flourishing crops. When manufactured hooks and monofilament lines appeared they set upon those as well, and, much later, enthusiastically set about acquiring aluminium dinghies and Japanese outboard engines. Nobody in the atolls now refers to all this as 'development', however. It is regarded simply as common sense, what the people themselves did, for themselves, to make their production more efficient and to secure their food supply.

'Development' in the Pacific is commonly understood in a different sense, one whose hegemony effectively began with Harry Truman's acceptance speech on 20 January, 1949.

> We must embark [President Truman said] on a bold new program for making the benefits of our scientific advances and industrial progress available for the improvement and growth of underdeveloped areas. The old imperialism—exploitation for foreign profit—has no place in our plans. What we envisage is a program of development based on the concepts of democratic fair dealing (quoted in Esteva 1992:6).

As Esteva puts it, '[u]nderdevelopment began, then, on January 20, 1949. On that day, two billion people became underdeveloped. In a very real sense, from that time on, they ceased being what they were…' (1992:7). The old meanings of development, based on both religious and biological metaphors, faded in the popular mind. Development became a global project, directed from on high. It became even further impoverished through being taken over by economists who reduced it to economic growth, measured by indicators such as gross national product, launched by various international agencies in the 1950s. The failures were notable, with many projects having tragic consequences for the very people they were designed to assist.

Since then a variety of planning adjustments have been proposed and put into operation, all of them emphasising in one way or another the importance of integrating what was called the 'social and cultural' with the 'economic'. The list of the well-meaning initiatives is a long one: the 'unified approach', 'integrated development', 'another development', 'human-centred development', the 'basic needs approach', 'endogenous development', 'human development'—and so forth, down to the diverse current enthusiasms for 'sustainable development'—as the various international agencies have competed for attention and funding. There is no doubt about the sincerity of the efforts, yet the central contradictions remain.

Meanwhile in some parts of the Pacific at least, economic goals have been effectively integrated with local society by using the kinship and family loyalties which had long been a central feature of 'traditional culture.' Emigration from Tonga, Samoa and other 'MIRAB' (Bertram and Watters 1985) countries grew rapidly in importance, and, as it did so, not only did the volume of remittances sent back to sustain and improve the material situation of the home societies increase, but they also allowed the elaboration of 'culture,' feeding into the complex displays and ceremonial exchanges at the heart of traditional economics and status. This has involved a double irony. First, although the whole process has relied on essentially 'cultural' linkages, it has also been an exercise in pure textbook economic rationality, as people have simply deployed their labour resources to places where they can get the best return. Second, overseas remittances have come to be of great importance in the macroeconomic sense, greatly exceeding in some states the earnings from visible exports, and providing about half GDP.

Yet in spite of both the economic rationality of the process and the significant amounts of overseas exchange involved, remittances are nevertheless looked on as a suspect mechanism of development. The reason for this is not purely economic. As a 'global project' (usually, but not necessarily, involving aid, soft loans or foreign commercial investment) development operates within the context of nation states. It is thus inescapably a 'top down' process, driven and evaluated by macroeconomic principles—in whose light remittances are seen as entailing both high reservation wages (the wages at which people are willing to take up employment) and reductions in agricultural exports.

Development has also been affected by changing economic orthodoxies. From after the Second World War through to the end of the 1970s, development was essentially dependent on state planning. Programs were conceived and directed by economists of basically Keynesian outlook who placed heavy emphasis on infrastructure, capital formation and the expansion of public sectors. It was not until the early 1980s that the doctrines of free market and monetarism gained ascendence, with a profound effect on the reigning development paradigm. Since the mid 1980s the World Bank's advice and aid to Pacific countries has turned away from support for public enterprise and physical investment, towards human development (education and health), the dismantling of government economic controls, and support for the private sector.

The development programs before 1980 or so, brought about a number of significant changes throughout the Pacific. Although the general effect was to increase social welfare and induce some economic growth, the changes involved new social and regional inequalities and the results were not uniformly benign (Overton 1988:10). They also fuelled the emergence of a category, variously called 'middle class' or 'bureaucratic élite,' made up of people separated to some extent by education and economic interests from those in the 'traditional' rural sectors.

The new free-market, monetarist orthodoxy has prompted widespread anxieties and criticism. As Claire Slatter (1994) has pointed out, much of the World Bank's recent analyses of Pacific island economies (1991;1993) is confused and contradictory. While drawing attention to relatively high living standards and favourable social indicators that have been achieved in spite of constraints, the World Bank fails to attribute these facts to the overall success of the older development model. The developers' enthusiasm for private sector development and the opening of opportunities for foreign investment is also suspect, not only because of the likelihood that most of the profits will be repatriated overseas but also because, it is felt, social and economic inequalities will become more acute.

The papers

These chapters highlight various aspects of the broad contrast outlined above, but are so densely inter-related that they are difficult to sort into discrete thematic groups. They do, however, differ in what may termed their 'range', some deal with either basic conceptual issues or with the region as a whole, and others with specific examples and particular countries. On this basis I have made two groupings, the first 'general' and the second 'specific'. The third grouping, 'tourism', suggests itself not only because of the subject matter, but also because of the distinctive conceptualisation of culture which the subject involves.

General

Langi Kavaliku's chapter sets out the basic theme and offers a clear, principled stand on a number of issues. The perspective he brings is that of a political leader with long experience at the critical intersection of international development discourse and national policymaking. His address makes three significant points. First, that the majority of global conferences on development as well as the policies of major development agencies are overwhelmingly focused on economic issues. Culture generally appears as an afterthought, mentioned, if at all, 'only in dispatches.' While this was hardly news to his audience, his second point effectively stands the first on its head, drawing attention to the fact that,

> in spite of a seeming lack of concern with culture, their plans of action take matters of culture into account in any case. At the end of the day, I do not believe that any individual or group can act in a vacuum. They can only act as who they are, what they are, and what they want to be.

What this implies is that culture is not merely an afterthought, an impediment to development, and a contradiction of the basic premise of the universal rationality of economics. Economics cannot claim universal rationality. It was not created in a vacuum, but by a group acting from within the culture of capitalism. Thus Kavaliku's third point casts aside the conceptually flawed contrast between culture and development and replaces it with the much more potent rhetoric of modernisation and westernisation.

Given his identification with the powerful élite of a country with a notably stable and enduring national culture, it is understandable that Kavaliku does not dwell on the tensions, ambiguities and conflicts inherent in that culture. Many of the chapters in the following 'specific' group, however, address these issues directly in the context of other countries, using contrasts variously phrased as 'government and culture', 'centre and edge', 'rational/legal authority and traditional authority' as well as 'development and culture'.

The two following chapters have the same expansive theoretical sweep. Kavaliku used an image of Pacific countries as *lokua*, small fish living in reef ponds cut off from the sea at tidal lows, but periodically replenished by ocean waters. Epeli Hau'ofa's central concern is with the ocean ('our most wonderful metaphor for just about anything we can think of'), but his fish are hardly *lokua*; instead they are a much bigger, more confident species, ranging over the whole Pacific and its surrounding shores. Pacific emigrants have sustained their homelands independently of the world of official diplomacy and neocolonial dependency. The sea has been a pathway into the whole region, a common inheritance and a potent symbol of a common Oceanic identity—which, he points out, has the capacity to be the foundation on which to build a humane vision of the future free from the market economy and the 'homogenising force of the global juggernaut'.

Marshall Sahlins has little to say about the possibilities of regional unity, but much about the capacity of local cultures everywhere to seize the opportunities and the wealth provided by the global system for whatever good things make up the local conception of human existence. Culture is not disappearing, as predicted by the old 'Despondancy Theory'. Instead, 'global homogeneity and local differentiation have developed together'. The process, the 'indigenisation of modernity' echoes closely the distinction made by Kavaliku in his call for modernisation (of the local scheme of things) as against homogeneity and a disabling westernisation.

According to Peggy Fairbairn-Dunlop, although Pacific women generally argue that they have not been disadvantaged by the development process because they have been shielded by customary ways, the question remains as to whether those customary ways have in fact done enough to protect women's overall well-being. There is considerable evidence to show that this is not always the case: for example, despite generally having the same educational attainments as men, women participate much less in national decision-making;

family systems are weakening, marriages breaking down and households headed by women are increasing. Malama Meleisea, Tarcisius Tara Kabutaulaka and John Burton all lend weight to these general statements with their observations on how some women have been treated in development situations in Samoa, Solomon Islands and some Papua New Guinea societies.

Specific

Meleisea's chapter concerns governance in Samoa. It begins with the observation that 'values about governance are rooted in culture, and that not all cultures value the kind of openness and acceptance of individual rights that Western thinkers have argued to be the basis of human development'. His point is based on the well-known contrast between rational/legal authority underlying the constitution and government, and the traditional chiefly authority that is the basis of Samoan culture. This, he points out, 'gives us two system of legitimacy to draw upon', with the gloomy result that both systems are compromised and the sense of citizenship eroded. Meleisea's chapter resonates strongly with Kabutaulaka's account of the same sort of corrupting compromises in Solomon Islands, hinging on the interaction between the customary land tenure system and the logging industry. This, he points out, produces a hybrid culture—dynamic to be sure, and heavily influenced by the traditional patron-client political relationships, but in a situation which encourages and facilitates individual accumulation at the expense of traditional wealth redistribution. The resulting situation is one which has deleterious effects on social stratification, the position of women and the sustainability of resources.

Burton stresses the fundamentally political nature of the relationship between 'remote peoples', the central government of Papua New Guinea and the large foreign corporations involved in mining enterprises. His plea for sociocultural research is couched in terms which are disingenuously neutral and modest—namely 'the avoidance of risk for both investors and local communities'—but the wider implications, political catastrophes like Bougainville, are obvious. He lays some stress on the particularities of different situations: the nature of the traditional political organisation, the impact of mining, the corporate culture and the monitoring capacity of government. As his examples clearly show it is wrong to assume that 'remote peoples' have no power. They can, in certain situations, easily match the power of both central government and large corporations; but it is an enervating, and, in many cases, extremely combative process, which might be avoided to some extent if as much were spent on social and cultural monitoring as is spent on environmental impact studies.

Philipp Muller, like Kavaliku, writes from the perspective of a Pacific Islander with long experience of the management of development projects. Like Kavaliku, he has a clear idea of the contradictions involved when the 'educated privileged' (as he puts it, 'almost systematically desensitised to the needs of our own people') promote noble general goals such as job creation, foreign exchange earnings and improved balance of payments, in almost complete ignorance of what people on the ground consider to be important. Projects are directed by a faceless government, carried out by officials who are hard pressed and under-resourced—an unfortunate situation leading straight to what he calls two universal lies: 'that you can get useful information from a government department, and that a government official is there to help you'. Joeli Veitayaki has a keen awareness of the same contradictions. His experience, however, is shorter than Muller's, and, because his chapter on fisheries management deals with a situation in which cultural principles are taken into account, his perspective is a somewhat sunnier one. There are obviously good lessons to be learned from the way in which Fiji has endeavoured to take culture into account in its fisheries management, marrying it with research and grass-roots participation. Kerry James' chapter echoes many of the points about culture and participatory development made by Muller and Veitayaki. However, like Burton, she also stresses the particularities of local social organisations and authority structures and the dangers inherent in assuming that the 'educated privileged' have any greater understanding of them than the average foreign development project consultant.

Fiji can also apparently provide good lessons in the importance of 'taking cultural principles into account' in fields other than fisheries management. Robert Norton's chapter shows how the deep ethnic differences between Fijians and Indians have been successfully managed and negotiated in a way that, for the present at least, accommodates both groups. Again, it has depended on historical particularities rather than recourse to universalistic principles. Chiefs have retained their position as icons of traditional life, as against money-based lifestyles, and from this position of political and cultural strength they have been able to encourage acceptance among non-chiefly Fijians of the political and economic accommodations they have reached with Indian interests.

While virtually all the other chapters are concerned with relatively organised, relatively stable and ongoing 'traditional' cultures and their relationships to the forces of development, Shane Jones' chapter on the New Zealand Maori describes a situation where both 'culture' and 'development' are in the process of active construction. The question here is whether the natural resources transferred to Maori by the state are better developed from the centre (by building large commercial enterprises with growing capital bases, maintaining technical advances with profits dedicated to further Maori education and training) or from the edge, by having the resources developed by tribal bodies, the inheritors of the rights and resources denied to their ancestors. The New Zealand situation, as Jones describes it, is obviously a limiting case for any discussion of the relationships between culture and development, with conceptual, political and moral implications going far beyond the scope of this brief introduction.

Cultural tourism

Richard Englehardt, Levani Tuinabua and Hana Ayala deal with cultural tourism. All stress the spectacular, worldwide growth of the industry and its potential contribution to the economic development of countries like those of the South Pacific.

Englehardt reviews the hard questions that are commonly asked about the industry. Who actually benefits from the money that tourism generates? What are the effects of industry on the environment and the local cultures? Are children and women exploited on the fringes of affluent resorts? He stresses that there are no general answers since the necessary studies have not been done. He focuses on the lessons provided by two case studies, from Vietnam and Laos, stressing the importance of planning and exhaustive consultation with all the 'stakeholders' involved in tourism and heritage developments. He also makes the valuable and timely recommendation that properly prepared cultural impact assessments 'should be required by law prior to the approval of every (tourism) development activity.'

Tuinabua adds the valuable observation that tourism should not be held wholly responsible for drugs, immodesty and the trivialisation of sacred traditions, drugs and immodesty, which may be also be the result of other influences. He also draws attention to local cases in which tourism development has worked smoothly with traditional communities, to the obvious satisfaction of both sides.

Ayala writes from a planning, management perspective, but on a more ambitious and regional scale, stressing the possibilities open to Pacific countries through careful evaluation of their heritage resources, in particular for tourism, conservation and research. She points to the ways in which these activities might be mutually beneficial and the part that *Vaka Moana* might play in achieving their complementarity.

Together, these three papers all argue for a cautious approach to what is undoubtedly a contentious field of development. All are concerned that the process of development should not result in traditional cultures being destroyed. Their conception of culture is, however, less comprehensive than that embraced by any of the other conference chapters. What they stress is mainly the observable artefacts of culture, what Burton refers to as the 'feathers and paint', without exploring what is involved in translating these artefacts into commercial settings. This observation is not meant as a criticism. England, for example, has considerable industry in 'heritage tourism', but nobody would suggest that this does much to preserve the values, way of life and culture of Elizabethan times. Again, there are numerous Pacific examples of satisfactory accommodation between culture and commercialism of the kind referred to by Tuinabua.

'Further action'

Russell Marshall draws attention to the 'largely unrelated and *ad hoc* activities' of the *Vaka Moana* thus far, and expressed his hope that this project might lead to a more coherent strategy for UNESCO's cultural activities in the Pacific. His views on *ad hoc*-ery have been widely shared, not least by Mali Voi, who, as coordinator of *Vaka Moana* since 1992, has been caught between UNESCO's uncertainties about what culture is and what might be done about it, its bureaucratically-driven definitions and procedures, and the understandings of both political leaders and public servants in twelve very diverse small Pacific countries spread over a third of the earth. The management of *Vaka Moana* has been fraught with difficulties, and Voi's chapter is a detailed testimony as to how ad hocery has been the only coherent philosophical basis on which it has been possible to operate. The fact is that in spite its broad ideological proclamations, preambles and volumes such as *Our Creative Diversity*, UNESCO's international cultural program has in fact remained fairly firmly tied to specific activities such as museums, archives, folk art, crafts, festivals, traditional knowledge and so forth. These are all worthy and important, and within the funding limits, *Vaka Moana* has made notable contributions.

Proposals

The conference had no mandate to come up with resolutions for UNESCO as to what, if anything, might be done about the relationship between culture and development in the region. Freed from this requirement, the speakers and other participants were able to spend a couple of hours each day discussing exactly this point.

The discussions were lively and wide-ranging. From my own notes, there were three topics that provoked the most concern. First, how to bring about changes in the prevailing orthodoxies of development and so prevent, or at least mitigate, the kinds of injustice, victimisation and official indifference that were described in many of the chapters. Mention was made of the difficulties of persuading governments to articulate 'national visions', and all agreed that it was necessary to somehow gain access to those who actually make the decisions. Second, there was general agreement that the most industrial and influential nations of the world had no good grounds for urging smaller nations to follow the course that they had taken— given the evidence of crime, social injustice and general anomie in these countries. Third, corruption was the most delicate topic of all, and the one that perhaps provoked the most comments. The devolution of authority to small, localised social units was proposed as one remedy—and then dropped when it was pointed out that corruption was by no means confined to members of national power élites. There was also discussion of the difference between legal corruption, for which there was redress through the courts, and extra-legal or moral corruption, generally centred on money and its accumulation for individualistic ends, in contrast to the basic Pacific redistributive ethic.

The focus of these discussions was a series of 'agreed-upon suggestions'. None were formally set down in writing and voted on at the time, but there was a general consensus. The first was for a 'Bill of Cultural Rights', similar to 'Action 7' of the International Program of the World Commission on Cultural Development: 'Protecting Cultural Rights as Human Rights' (UNESCO 1995:281–84). The proposed bill involved an independent standing committee, perhaps with an ombudsperson empowered to set the parameters of cultural impact statements and hear complaints. The standing committee could assign particular projects to qualified people who would attempt to mediate cases of grievance.

The second proposal was for a '*Fono* of Wontok Peoples'. Like Action 9—'A People-Centred UN'—of the International Agenda (UNESCO 1995:285–87), this was based on the idea of gatherings, or a permanent forum, of elements of civil society, rather than government representatives. Such *fono* or assemblies would fit in with the well-established Pacific practice of touring parties from villages, islands or churches which raise funds for local projects and re-establish links with emigrants. An alternative scenario was to have the *fono* idea associated with the South Pacific Festival of Arts, providing a venue where traditional leaders rather than government representatives could meet.

The third proposal generally agreed was support for mandatory cultural impact assessments of development projects—which might be associated in some way with the standing committee envisaged by the first proposal. The idea had in fact already been put forward by Englehardt, though he carefully limited it to tourism projects. Burton's account also supports this idea in its discussion of the *realpolitik* of social impact studies of mining ventures in Papua New Guinea, and his statement that, in his experience, environmental impact assessments attracted approximately 100 times the financial support given to social impact assessments.

None of the participants would wish the agreed-upon suggestions to cut across any of the *Vaka Moana* projects already in train, or indeed any of those proposed by Voi. There was general agreement that these projects fit well with the way that culture has been institutionalised within UNESCO, and that they are of intrinsic value. The agreed-upon suggestions are based on a more holistic concept of culture, and more directly political in nature. The problem remains, however, as to how the three practical suggestions which arose might be translated into effective political action. One answer to this, I suggest, lies with the main regional development agencies. The World Bank and the Asian Development Bank have enormous influence in the region—not only in the aid-receiving countries, but also on the policies of the major bilateral donors. Both have attracted criticism for their economistic mind sets, and over the past few years, perhaps in response to this, they have begun to pay serious attention to social and cultural issues. The Asian Development Bank has published a commissioned volume on the topic (Schoeffel 1996) and the World Bank has published a series of 'Pacific Islands Discussion Chapters' devoted to the same issues (Hooper 1998; James 1998; Kabutaulaka 1998; Macdonald 1998; Sutherland 1998).

These initiatives might be usefully endorsed by UNESCO's Pacific agencies, with the aim of encouraging the banks to incorporate mandatory sociocultural impact reports into their own policy advice. In this manner, cultural issues could be brought to the attention of political leaders in Pacific countries, from where it is only a short step to bilateral donors and to the Pacific Forum, which might then be prepared to consider mandatory cultural impact studies for all development projects. Culture is not in any sense 'dying out' in the Pacific. It is adaptable, and is firmly entrenched in the structures of national life throughout the region. What is needed is a mechanism by which the principles on which it is based can be brought forward in the causes of equity and peace.

Notes

1 This scheme is based on a set of ideas which I first used in 1992 in a paper written for an audience of development economists (Hooper 1993) and later applied to an analysis of the course of development in Samoa (1998). Although conceived independently and for a different purpose, my notion of 'spheres' and 'domains' is strikingly similar to Ton Otto's use of the same terms to deliniate the manner in which Balauans (and other Pacific islanders) make a division between separate 'ways' in their own societies (Otto 1992).

2 There are many records of Pacific peoples objecting to the ways in which they were represented by anthropologists. But this was not the universal reaction. The story goes that, in the early 1970s, when Albert Henry, as Premier of the Cook Islands, called a meeting of traditional authorities from all the separate islands of the country with the object of compiling a kind of 'national compendium' of tradition, the representatives of Pukapuka proudly laid a copy of Ernest Beaglehole's *Ethnology of Pukapuka* on the table, announcing that their record was already complete.

3 Turner employs the useful distinction between 'critical multiculturalism' and the intellectually weaker 'difference multiculturalism' which simply fetishises difference without reference to economic and political contexts. Dominguez (1993) also draws attention to the ways in which multiculturalism as a

political policy can be used to justify the social, economic and political disadvantage of ethnic groups, making it appear as all the fault of 'their culture'. This situation is not unknown in the Pacific, particularly in the metropolitan white settler states.

References

Bertram, I.G., and Watters, R.F., 1985. 'The MIRAB economy in South Pacific microstates', *Pacific Viewpoint*, 26(3):497–519.

Cole, R. and Tambunlertchai, S. (eds), 1993. *The Future of Asia–Pacific Economies: Pacific Islands at the crossroads?*, Asian and Pacific Development Centre at the National Centre for Development Studies, The Australian National University, Canberra.

Crocombe, R., 1994. 'Cultural policies in the Pacific Islands', in L. Lindstrom and G.M. White (eds), *Culture, Kastom, Tradition: developing cultural policy in Melanesia*, Institute of Pacific Studies, University of the South Pacific, Suva:21–42.

Dominguez, V.R., 1992. 'Invoking culture: the messy side of cultural politics', *South Atlantic Quarterly*, 91(1):19–42.

Esteva, G., 1992. 'Development', in W. Sachs (ed.), *The Development Dictionary: a guide to knowledge and power*, Zed Books Ltd, London:6–25.

Hooper, A., 1993. 'Socio–cultural aspects of development in the South Pacific', in R. Cole and S. Tambunlertchai (eds), *The Future of Asia–Pacific Economies: Pacific Islands at the crossroads?*, Asian and Pacific Development Centre and the National Centre for Development Studies, The Australian National University, Canberra:314–42.

——, 1998. *Pacific Islands Stakeholder Participation in Development: Samoa*, Pacific Islands Discussion Paper Series 3, The World Bank, Washington, DC.

James, K., 1998. *Pacific Islands Stakeholder Participation in Development: Tonga*, Pacific Islands Discussion Paper Series 4, The World Bank, Washington, DC.

Jolly, M., and Thomas, N., 1992. 'Introduction', *Oceania*, 62(4):241–48.

Kabutaulaka, T., 1998. *Pacific Islands Stakeholder Participation in Development: Solomon Islands*, Pacific Islands Discussion Paper Series, The World Bank, Washington, DC.

Kasper, W., 1991. 'The economics and politics of South Pacific development: an outsider's view', in P. Bauer, S. Siwatibau and W. Kasper (eds), *Aid and development in the South Pacific*, Centre for Independent Studies, Sydney.

Keesing, R., 1982. 'Kastom in Melanesia: an overview', Mankind, 13(4):297–301.

——and Tonkinson, R. (eds), 1982. Reinventing Traditional Culture: the politics of Kastom in Island Melanesia, special issue of Mankind, 13(4).

Lindstrom, L, and White, G.M. (eds), 1993. Custom Today, special issue of Anthropological Forum, 6(4).

Linnekin, J., 1992. 'On the theory and politics of cultural construction in the Pacific', Oceania, 62(4):249–63.

——, and Poyer, L. (eds), 1990. Cultural Identity and Ethnic Identity in the Pacific, University of Hawaii Press, Honolulu.

Macdonald, B., 1998. Pacific Islands Stakeholder Participation in Development: Kiribati, Pacific Islands Discussion Paper Series 5, The World Bank, Washington, DC.

Otto, T., 1992. 'The ways of Kastam: tradition as category and practice in a Manus village', Oceania, 62(4):264–83.

Overton, J., 1998. 'The study of rural Fiji', in J.Overton (ed.), Rural Fiji, Institute of Pacific Studies, University of the South Pacific, Suva:1–11.

Sahlins, M., 1993. 'Goodbye to Tristes Tropes: ethnography in the context of the modern world system', The Journal of Modern History, 65:1–25.

Schoeffel, P., 1996. Sociocultural Issues and Economic Development in the Pacific Islands, Asian Development Bank, Manila.

Slatter, C., 1992. 'Banking on the growth model? The World Bank and market policies in the Pacific', in 'Atu Emberson–Bain (ed.), Sustainable Development of Malignant Growth? perspectives of Pacific Island women, Marama Publications, Suva:17–36.

Sutherland, W., 1998. Pacific Island Stakeholder Participation in Development: Fiji, Pacific Islands Discussion Paper Series, The World Bank, Washington, DC.

Turner, T., 1993. 'What is anthropology that multiculturalists should be mindful of it?', Cultural Anthropology, 8(4):411–29.

UNESCO, 1995. Our Creative Diversity: report of the World Commission on Culture and Development, UNESCO, Paris.

World Bank, 1991. Towards Higher Growth in Pacific Islands Economies: lessons from the 1980s, The World Bank, Washington, DC.

——, 1993. Pacific Island Economies: toward efficient and sustainable growth, The World Bank, Washington, DC.

1

Culture and sustainable development in the Pacific

Langi Kavaliku

The World Decade for Cultural Development was established by the United Nations in 1988, and UNESCO was given the mandate of being the lead agency for the program. One of the major objectives of the Cultural Decade is that the 'cultural dimension' must be taken into account in the consideration of policies, formulation of plans and the implementation of development plans and programs—in our case, in the Pacific island countries.

Our task is not so much to accept the call of the United Nations or UNESCO blindly, but rather to examine critically the objective to see whether there are any real relations of interdependence between culture and sustainable development—and if so why and how. Furthermore, if interdependence is established, to examine how this finding could help us in the understanding and framing of policies, plans, and programs for the development of peoples and nation states.

Culture

Culture has many definitions, but the one I have always preferred was succinctly spelled out in the Mexico Conference in 1982. According to that formulation, culture comprises the whole complex of distinctive spiritual, intellectual and emotional features that characterise society or social groups. It includes not only the arts and letters, but also different modes of life, the fundamental rights of human beings, value systems, traditions and beliefs.

Culture is both an instrument for decision-making and implementation as well as the end result of those policies and of the decisions implemented. Furthermore, culture is a dynamic reality. It changes, either gradually or rapidly, over time. Indeed, it is a system that changes with each new idea, new development, each new generation and each new interaction with other cultures and/or peoples. Past cultures lend themselves to conservation. Living cultures are based on legacies of the past, the ideas of the present and the hopes for the future. In trying to understand living cultures we must also understand their legacies from the past. As Kierkegaard once wrote, 'life can only be understood backwards, but it must be lived forwards'.

Sustainable development

Development, sustainable or otherwise, is the distinctive process of a society's movement through time, whether planned or unplanned. Since the Second World War and the Marshall Plan for Europe, however, development has become so closely associated with planning that the two terms have become almost synonymous. Global macroeconomic development models were created and studied, particularly by the United Kingdom, United States, Japan, Australia and the United Nations, amongst others, and were particularly fashionable in the 1970s and 1980s. Whatever development models were designed and/or adopted, the planning and implementation of the process meant primarily economic development and economic growth—and measurements of such development were made only in quantifiable, materialistic terms. The overriding context has been, and continues to be, economic.

Into this picture the concept of the 'sustainability' of development—the other half of the equation we are considering in this conference—was introduced. Sustainable development, especially as it was promulgated by the Brundland Commission, gained prominence because it added environmental and intergenerational dimensions to the original preoccupation with economic issues. The Rio Conference in 1992 gave it greater impetus. Today, in spite of the prevalence of its usage by the United Nations system as development that 'meets the needs of the present without compromising the ability of future generations to meet their needs', sustainable development is still an elusive term—not fully accepted by experts, policy and decision-makers or by the public.

Like culture, sustainable development is not a steady state-system but a dynamic one. Sustainability—whether of culture or development—changes form and levels with time and the use of resources available. As industrial countries went through stages of agricultural, industrial and now services and information revolution, so the basis and level of their sustainability changed. In the same way sustainability has different meanings and levels of expectations as we move from a fully subsistence economy to an increasingly cash-driven economy.

I regard sustainable development as development with a working rationale—one which stipulates that the interdependence of economic, intellectual, political, environmental and cultural dimensions must be considered together in the making of policies and plans for the future of peoples and nations. In essence it is development that can be sustained not only now but also in the future, given the social and physical resources available to a nation-state and the objectives it sets for itself.

Culture and sustainable development

The interrelationship between culture and sustainable development seems to be a matter of common sense. However, even though the UN system (and especially UNESCO) is pushing for recognition of it, the UN system has not in fact been very supportive. If we study the major global conferences of the 1990s—from Rio de Janeiro to Barbados, Cairo, Beijing, Copenhagen and Harare—their plans of action were concerned with sustainable development, but there was hardly a mention, even in despatches, of culture. The various Plans of Actions from Rio to the present have had very little to say about culture, but a lot about sustainable development. Even more tellingly for us in small developing island states, the plan of action approved at the Barbados conference—a conference designed to focus attention on the problems and needs of Small Island Developing States—culture was, I believe, mentioned only once as being an important aspect of sustainable development in the islands.

For those Pacific island countries which are members of the Commonwealth, the situation is just as confusing. Following the Barbados conference, Commonwealth leaders approved the establishment of a Ministerial Group and an Official Group to study and make recommendations to the Commonwealth Heads of

Government Meeting (CHOGM) on how best to meet the needs and solve the problems of Small Island Developing States in the Commonwealth. Culture was hardly mentioned at all in the reports of the 1996 CHOGM.

Sustainable development was certainly fashionable, but the reports of the various meetings and the programs which were adopted showed that it was not seen to be related to culture in any meaningful way. Development to the Commonwealth group concerned economic matters, crime, security, and human resource development, law and order, health and so on, but the cultural dimension was missing.

The question therefore arises as to whether UNESCO's commitment to 'culture as an integral part of development' is due only to the fact that culture is part of UNESCO's mandate. Even though I participated in many of these global conferences I cannot answer the question why culture was not considered one of the critical issues like environment, population, energy, women and so on. I can, however, answer for UNESCO's concern. The Director-General's commitment to the importance of culture and of culture in development is fully supported by the General Conference, Executive Board, Secretariat and the National Commissions. Furthermore, and thinking positively about a seemingly negative situation, I would like to believe that because so much of the concern of these conferences, of policymakers and decision-makers are matters of culture—as defined at the beginning—that in spite of a seeming lack of concern with culture, their plans of action take matters of culture into account in any case. At the end of the day, I do not believe that any individual or group can act in a vacuum. They can only act as who they are; what they are, and what they want to be.

The Pacific islands situation

In the early 1990s, the World Bank raised concerns about the low growth rate in the Pacific Island countries compared to other small island developing states of the Caribbean and Indian oceans, where development was subject to the same sorts of constraints (small internal markets, narrow production bases, high unit costs of infrastructure, heavy dependence on external trade, vulnerability to external shocks and natural disasters and isolation from large high-income markets) while enjoying the advantages of high levels of basic subsistence, favourable climate and sustainable concessional aid flows and remittances (World Bank 1993).

The World Bank experts called this phenomenon 'The Pacific Paradox'—simply an admission of their confusion. Indeed, the report went on to state that the Pacific Paradox did not yield to easy answers. It did, however, make suggestions on how the situation might be improved, pointing out that consideration should be given to 'the blend of customary practices and modern systems [which] has both inhibited development and helped provide some stability and social safety nets'. The implication was that 'culture' and 'customary practices' were important only as inhibitors of development and as a conservative social force. They did, however, end up recommending that 'the objective is not to impose some model derived elsewhere but to adopt new approaches'.

Since then, the growth rate in the Pacific has not shown any real improvement. The issue then for the Pacific island countries is whether or not there really is a 'Pacific Paradox'. In my view, there is no 'Pacific Paradox'. The paradox is solely in the eyes of the beholder who is blinkered against culture and sustainable development. It is not a reality.

A number of important questions were not raised such as: What is important to a Fijian, Solomon Islander, Tongan, Samoan and so on? Is it capital formation without other considerations or a balance of goods which are socially and culturally meaningful? What priority is given to meeting family and other social obligations? Is it wealth for the individual, or individual plus family, relatives and friends? What is wealth for anyway? Does it have the same meaning for a Pacific Islander as to a Westerner? Would a Tuvaluan, Ni Vanuatu or Ponapean accumulate wealth rather than help his family, relatives or neighbours?

For many experts the only remedy for the slow pace of agricultural development and therefore the growth in exports, is to change the land tenure system to allow for plantation-type agriculture. In many cases the theory may be correct, but in the Pacific island countries, one's soul and one's own identity is tied up with land and offshore resources. Do we then legislate for changing the basis of our destiny and identity? Or do we build on them? And if industrial agriculture and green revolution agriculture do not work too well in small island states, why not develop what is now called the Third Agricultural Revolution—the 'Crop Diversification Revolution'—which has long been practised throughout the Pacific.

The 'Pacific Paradox' provides a telling lesson because it shows that culture is an important aspect of development and will affect development and whatever we do. If we do not take culture into account and understand the interplay between it and development, we cannot move as surely as we should. If we are to participate in the global society we can only do so if we are Tongans, Papua New Guineans, I Kiribati, Fijians, Niueans and Samoans who are modern and not as modern men who happen to live in the Pacific islands. The importance of the culture and sustainability issue is that it points up the fact that what we want is the modernisation of the faa-Samoa, faka-Tonga and so on—modernisation of the Pacific Way, and not Westernisation or Asianisation or globalisation. The 'Pacific Paradox' exists only because of the influence of the concept of Westernisation.

The future

The Pacific island world is too complex for us to comprehend all its needs and problems fully, and to provide all the solutions. It is also too dynamic for any of us to assume that once problems and needs are identified and solutions provided that the solutions will last indefinitely. Neither culture nor sustainable development are steady-state phenomena. They both change, and new problems and new solutions call for continuous attention: the important thing is to understand the importance of both culture and sustainable development, as well as the relationship between the two.

There are many issues, problems and needs that we face. Gender issues, unemployment, institutions, the family and relatives, ethnic issues, hierarchical and status issues, equality, equitable distribution of income and resources, good governance, accountability, work ethics, values and social behaviour, technology, information, the media, drugs, law and order, religion, tourism, health, education, land tenure, ocean resources, regional cooperation are some of the major issues which we must address: these are the issues that challenge us in the Pacific islands as we move forward in our lives. In facing them I believe it is critical that the working inter-relationship between culture and sustainable development be understood and recognised.

In dealing with changes, the first step is to 'know thyself'. The rest of the steps are filled with the culture of the global ocean in which each of us must choose the course to take. As an example, let us take the case of women, and women and development. There are different interpretations of the position, status and role of women in Pacific island societies. Nevertheless, I believe there is one issue that we must agree upon and that is the equality of each and every human being. The issue facing us then, is the interpretation of what equality means. When the Secretary-General of the Tonga Women's Association came back from a conference on women in South Korea, one of her first comments was, 'Why do western women insist that we should be like them? Why do they think that their ideas are God's own and ours are backward?' Equality in the gender issue has become almost synonymous with 'same as men'. On the other hand, I was once heavily criticised by an officer in one of our regional organisations because in a report of a meeting which I chaired, 'women' was not listed as one of the major issues.

In considering culture and sustainable development, are we talking of equality as being 'same as men' or of 'two human beings who are equal but not the same'? If it is the latter, the issue then is the equity of the complementary relationship between two beings who are equal but not the same. Either way, the cultural dimension looms large and affects both development and culture.

Challenge of choice

The *lokua* is a small fish that lives in reef ponds cut off from the surrounding waters during low tides, but when the tides are high, they are periodically replenished by ocean waters. For people living in the Pacific islands, the issues are much the same as those faced by the *lokua*: whether to be an integral part of the larger ocean or to remain in our own little ponds, nurtured mainly by our own resources, but having them replenished from time to time by the regional and global environments.

If we want to become more and more a part of the global society, how much of the sheltering walls of our ponds do we want to knock down, in order to allow for a greater flow of ocean both at low tide and high tide? Can we be ourselves in a bigger world? What is our future among the bigger fish of the world's ocean? What resources will there be to allow us to live and participate in the global society? Questions of identity, culture, security and resources take on different dimension. Sustainability of both culture and development becomes paramount. Conversely, if each of us remains in our pond what would that mean? Could we survive?

No bystanders are allowed. The choice has to be made. The most challenging choices to be made concern cultural and environmental factors, social and physical resources. And we must face the ramifications of our past choices as well as the new ones arising from the global currents of the present.

Can we say that sustainable development, or indeed any sort of development, has no need to take into account the cultural dimension? In this regard I am reminded of the story of the tourist who went to a restaurant in a rather remote area. The restaurant had an impressive menu listing over a hundred dishes. After the tourist had made two orders and found that the restaurant in fact had neither of them, he asked the waiter to tell him what could be provided, and the waiter told him the two dishes they had. After he had ordered one of them he asked the waiter why they had such a menu when they could only produce two dishes. The waiter told him that the menu was planned and agreed in the capital, without regard for what was available locally. They were told it was the menu restaurant owners would have if they were running proper establishments which were both profitable and sustainable.

The experts and decision-makers agree on the formula. But is this really the way it should be? Is there any other way for a developing nation with limited resources to avoid being relegated to the bottom of the class because it hasn't got all the items required by the formula to be considered a success?

The question of what to do if you have limited resources is rarely touched on in discussions of culture and sustainable development. What standard of living and quality of life should you aim for? What sort of society? Who and what do you want to be? What pathways of development should many of us consider even with our being nurtured by the ocean of the global society. Asking these questions reminds me of a statement by Perez de Cuellar to the effect that development embraces not only access to goods and services but also the opportunity to choose a full, satisfying, valuable and valued way of living together, the flowering of human existence in all forms and as a whole. The choice can also be for a different style of development, a different path based on assessed resources and different values from those of the highest income countries. Different paths of development should be informed by a recognition of how cultural factors shaped the way in which societies conceive their own future and choose the means to achieve those futures.

Jacques Delors, the former President of the European Commission, stated that all-out economic growth can no longer be viewed as the ideal way of reconciling material progress with equity, respect for human conditions and respect for natural assets.

In fact we have choices and we face challenges that require a fundamental shift in our view on culture and sustainable development in order to be realistic in our objective and at the same time develop a life-style which each and every one will live with pride. The issue is not just the importance of culture in development but the issue of sustainability of our future in a global situation.

It is also necessary to keep in mind that both culture and sustainable development are dynamic processes. They are both instruments of change and the end results of change. What we are today is different in many ways from what we were 25 years ago and different from what our societies were 50 years ago. We should not be troubled by the lifestyle and livelihood changes all around us. We must make decisions about future directions and the goals. That is also why culture is a critical factor in development—sustainable or otherwise.

The challenge of choices will also be in development of ways and means of enlarging resources. In the same way that Israel and the Jews outside of Israel are interdependent, remittances are becoming increasingly important in the Pacific island countries and consequently the cultural dimension becomes significant. The Pacific island countries own, or have some control, over 3 million square miles of ocean and its resources. Why is it not possible for us to come together and work together in order to enlarge resources for ourselves? Is it because of cultural differences? Is it politics?

The world is rapidly reconfiguring itself into competing regional blocs, based on economic grounds. The European Union is expanding. North America now has NAFTA and the Organisation of American States. ASEAN is becoming a major player especially with the momentum of the new bloc, APEC, a reality recognised by Australia and New Zealand. This is an issue which the island states must address—sooner rather than later. The currents of the global ocean are shifting from the Atlantic to the Pacific Rim, and especially Asia. What do these shifting currents mean for us in the islands? What does it mean to be in the midst of the Pacific, yet forgotten?

I have raised these general issues because in my view they will affect us all. Do we in the islands take on these developments individually? Why is regionalism and regional cooperation a difficulty? Is it because of our cultures? Is it possible to build a regional identity to facilitate not only the development of regional cooperation but also of shared resources and allow island states, individually or together, to participate more fully in the global society? Perhaps our concern in islands should be more about the regional society in order for us to be better able to participate in and benefit from the global society. If we are successful, we may also give hope to youth and the population at large. The issues are social and cultural, as well as moral, political and economic. They also have intellectual dimensions, not only for the élite but also for Pacific people in general. Questions of development, regional cooperation, natural and human resources, gender issues, reaching the unreached (our youth) must also be considered by ordinary men and women. Perhaps after all there is a case for culture and sustainable development.

There is a Tongan saying, *Taumulivalea*, which roughly translated means that if you do not know where you come from, how can you hope to know where you are going? This proverb highlights the reasons why culture is important in any discussion of development and any hope for the future.

However, 'taking account of cultural dimensions' in sustainable development is not a panacea for all our problems. It is only a small but important part of the formula, which is all too often implied but not treated vigorously or seriously. It is a part of the process of development as well as the objective of that development. We need economic development in order to live. We need to consider the environment in order to be able to hand over with a clear conscience to future generations. We need to consider other social, political and intellectual dimensions in order to enhance our lifestyles and standards of living. We need to consider culture not only to achieve our objectives but also to achieve a quality of life befitting the integrity of each and all of us as human beings who are also Pacific islanders, as well as Fijians, Samoans, Nauruans and so on.

As the Director-General of UNESCO stated that we must be able to assimilate the best of the past in order to be able to better share the future with the help of a judicious application of knowledge. Cultural development is an instrument and an objective of sustainable development.

Reference

World Bank, 1993. *Pacific Island Economies: toward efficient and sustainable growth*, The World Bank, Washington, DC.

2

The Ocean in us

Epeli Hau'ofa

> *We sweat and cry salt water, so we know*
> *that the ocean is really in our blood*
> Teresia Teaiwa

I have advanced the notion of a much enlarged world of Oceania that
has emerged through the astounding mobility of Pacific peoples in the
last fifty years (Hau'ofa 1993). Most of us are part of this mobility
whether personally or through the movements of our relatives. This
expanded Oceania is a world of social networks that criss-cross the
ocean, all the way from Australia and New Zealand in the southwest,
to the United States and Canada in the northeast. It is a world that we
have created largely through our own efforts, and have kept vibrant,
and independent of the Pacific island world of official diplomacy and
neocolonial dependency. In portraying this new Oceania I wanted to
raise, especially among our emerging generations, the kind of
consciousness that would help free us from the prevailing, externally-
generated definitions of our past, present and future.

I wish now to take this issue further by suggesting the development
of a substantial regional identity that is anchored in our common
inheritance of a very considerable portion of Earth's largest body of
water, the Pacific Ocean. The notion of an identity for our region is not

new; and through much of the latter half of this century people have tried to instil a strong sense of belonging for the sake of sustained regional cooperation. So far these attempts have foundered on the reef of our diversity, on the requirements of international geopolitics, combined with assertions of narrow national self-interests on the part of our individual countries. I believe that a solid and effective regional identity can be forged and fostered. We have not been successful in our attempts so far because, while fishing for the elusive school of tuna, we have lost sight of the ocean that surrounds and sustains us.

A common identity that would help us act together for the advancement of our collective interests, including the protection of the ocean for the general good, is necessary for the quality of our survival in the so-called Pacific Century when important developments in the global economy will be concentrated in huge regions that encircle us. As individual, tiny countries created by colonial powers and acting alone, we could indeed 'fall off the map' or disappear into the black hole of a gigantic Pan-Pacific doughnut. Acting together as a region, for the interests of the region as a whole, and above those of our individual countries, we would enhance our chances of survival in the century that is already dawning upon us. Acting in unison for larger purposes and for the benefit of the wider community could help us to become more open-minded, idealistic, altruistic and generous, less self-absorbed and corrupt, in the conduct of our public affairs than we are today. In an age when our societies are preoccupied with the pursuit of material wealth, when the rampant market economy brings out unquenchable greed and amorality in us, it is necessary for our institutions of learning to develop corrective mechanisms if we are to retain our sense of humanity and of community.

An identity that is grounded on something so vast as the sea is, should exercise our minds and rekindle in us the spirit that sent our ancestors to explore the oceanic unknown and make it their home, our home.

I am not in any way suggesting cultural homogeneity for our region. Such a thing is neither possible nor desirable. Our diverse loyalties are much too strong to be erased by a regional identity and our diversity is necessary for the struggle against the homogenising forces of the global juggernaut. It is even more necessary for those of us who must focus on strengthening their ancestral cultures against seemingly overwhelming forces, to regain their lost sovereignty. This regional identity is supplementary to other identities that we already have, or will develop in the future, something that should serve to enrich our other selves.

A regional identity

The ideas for a regional identity that I express here have emerged from nearly twenty years of direct involvement with the University of the South Pacific (USP), an institution that caters for much of the tertiary education of the South Pacific islands region, and increasingly of countries north of the equator. Its size, its on-campus staff and student residential arrangements and its spread make the USP the premier hatchery for the regional identity. Nevertheless the sense of diversity there is much more palpable and tangible than that of a larger common identity. Not surprisingly students identify themselves more with their nationality, race and personal friendships across the cultural divide, than with a common Pacific Islander identity. Apart from primordial loyalties, students go to the university to obtain certificates for returning home to work for their respective countries. Ultimately they do not come to the USP in order to serve the region as such.

In the earliest stage of our interactions with the outside world, we were the South Sea paradise of noble savages living in harmony with a bountiful nature; we were simultaneously the lost and degraded souls to be pacified, Christianised, colonised and civilised. Then we became the South Pacific region of much importance for the security of Western interests in Asia. We were pampered by those whose real interests lay elsewhere, and those who conducted dangerous experiments on our islands. We have passed through that stage into the Pacific Islands Region of naked, neocolonial dependency. Our erstwhile suitors are now creating a new set of relationships along the rim of our ocean that excludes us totally. Had this been happening elsewhere, our exclusion would not have mattered much, however in this instance we are physically located at the centre of what is occurring. The development of APEC will affect our existence in fundamental ways whether we like it or not. We cannot afford to ignore our exclusion because what is involved here is our very survival.

The time has come for us to wake up to our modern history as a region. We cannot confront the issues of the Pacific Century individually as tiny countries, nor as the Pacific Islands Region of bogus independence. We must develop a stronger and genuinely independent regionalism than exists today. A new sense of the region that is our own creation, based on our perceptions of our realities, is necessary for our survival in the dawning era.

In the few instances when the region has stood united, we have been successful in achieving our common aims. It is of utmost significance for the strengthening of a regional identity to know that our region has achieved its greatest unity on threats to our common environment: the ocean. It should be noted that on these issues Australia and New Zealand often assumed the necessary leading role because of our common sharing of the ocean. It is on issues of this kind that the sense of a regional identity, of being Pacific Islanders, is felt most acutely. The movement toward a Nuclear Free and Independent Pacific, the protests against the wall-of-death driftnetting, against plans to dispose of nuclear waste in the ocean, the incineration of chemical weapons on Johnston Island, and the 1995 resumption of nuclear tests on Mururoa, and most ominously, the spectre of our atoll islands and low-lying coastal regions disappearing under the rising sea-level, are instances of a regional united front against threats to our environment. As these issues come to the fore only occasionally, and as success in protests has dissipated the immediate sense of threat, we have generally reverted to our normal state of disunity and the pursuit of national self-indulgence. The problems, especially of toxic waste disposal and destructive exploitation of ocean resources, still remain to haunt us. Nuclear powered ships and vessels carrying radioactive materials still ply the ocean; international business concerns are still looking for islands for the disposal of toxic industrial wastes; activities that contribute to the depletion of the ozone still continue; driftnetting has abated but not stopped, and the reefs of the Mururoa atoll may still crack and release radioactive materials. People who are concerned with these threats are trying hard to enlist region-wide support, but the level of their success is low as far as the general public is concerned. Witness the present region-wide silence while the plutonium laden Pacific Teal is about to sail or is already sailing through our territorial waters. There is, however, a trend in the region to move from mere protests to the stage of active protection of the environment. For this to succeed, regionalism has to be strengthened. No single country in the Pacific can, by itself, protect its own slice of the oceanic environment:

the very nature of that environment prescribes regional effort. To develop the ocean resources sustainably, regional unity is also required.

A Pacific islands regional identity means a Pacific Islander identity. But what or who is a Pacific Islander? The issue should not arise if we consider Oceania as comprising human beings with a common heritage and commitment, rather than as members of diverse nationalities and races. Oceania refers to a world of people connected to each other. The term Pacific Islands Region refers to an official world of states and nationalities. John and Mary cannot just be Pacific Islanders; they must first be Ni Vanuatu, or Tuvaluan, or Samoan. For my part, anyone who has lived in our region and is committed to Oceania, is an Oceanian. This view opens up the possibility of expanding Oceania progressively to cover larger areas and more peoples than is possible under the term Pacific Islands Region. Under this formulation the concepts Pacific Islands Region and Pacific Islanders are as redundant as South Seas and South Sea Islanders. We have to search for appropriate names for common identities that are more accommodating, inclusive and flexible than what we have today.

The Oceania Centre for Arts and Culture

In 1996, the University of the South Pacific finally acted on a decision made by its Council in 1992 to establish an arts and culture program. A centre for Pacific arts and culture was to start operation in 1997. As I was intimately involved in the planning for this centre, which deals directly with the issue of culture and identity, I became aware of two things. First, this new unit provides a rare opportunity for some of us at the university to realise the dreams that we have had for many years. We have talked and written about our ideas and hopes, but only now have we been presented with an opportunity to transform them into reality. Second, if we were not careful, the programs being conceived for the centre would become a loose collection of odds and ends that would merely reflect the diversity of our cultures.

I began searching for a theme or a central concept on which to hang the programs of the centre. I toyed with the idea of Our Sea of Islands that I had propounded a few years previously, but felt uneasy about it because I did not wish to appear to be riding a hobby horse. It is bad manners in many Oceanic societies to appear to push things for yourself, but it is a forgivable sin if someone else accidentally does it for you. So I kept the idea at the back of my mind and while in this condition, I came across the following passage in an article written by Sylvia Earle for the October 28 issue of *Time*.

> The sea shapes the character of this planet, governs weather and climate, stabilises moisture that falls back on the land, replenishing Earth's fresh water to rivers, lakes, streams—and us. Every breath we take is possible because of the life-filled life-giving sea; oxygen is generated there, carbon dioxide absorbed. Both in terms of the sheer mass of living things and genetic diversity, that's where the action is. Rain forests and other terrestrial systems are important too, of course, but without the living ocean there would be no life on land. Most of Earth's living space, the biosphere, is ocean—about 97 per cent. And not so coincidentally 97 per cent of Earth's water is Ocean. (1996:52)

After I read Earle's account, it became clear that the ocean, and our historical relationships with it, would be the core theme for the Centre. At about the same time, our journalism students produced the first issue of their newspaper, *WANSOLWARA*, a pidgin word which they translated as 'one ocean—one people'. Things started to fall into place, and we were able to persuade the university to call the new unit the Oceania Centre for Arts and Culture.

Oceania

Despite the sheer magnitude of the oceans, we are among a minute proportion of Earth's total human population which can truly be referred to as 'oceanic peoples'. All our cultures have been shaped in fundamental ways by the adaptive interactions between our people and the sea that surrounds our island communities. In general, the smaller the island the more intensive the interactions with the sea, and the more pronounced are its influences on the culture of the island. However one does not have to be in direct interaction with the sea to be influenced by it. Regular climatic patterns, together with such unpredictable natural phenomena as droughts, prolonged rains, floods, and cyclones that influence the systems of terrestrial activities are largely determined by the ocean. On the largest island of Oceania, Papua New Guinea, products of the sea, especially the much-valued shells, reached the most remote highlands societies, shaping their ceremonial and political systems. More importantly, inland people of our large islands are now citizens of Oceanic countries whose capitals and other urban centres are located on coastal areas, to where they are moving in large numbers to seek advancement. The sea is already part of their lives. Many of us today are not directly or personally dependent on the sea for our livelihood; and would probably get sea-sick as soon as we set foot on a rocking boat. This means only that we are no longer sea travellers or fisherfolk, but as long as we live on our islands we remain very much under the spell of the sea; we cannot avoid it.

Before the advent of Europeans into the Pacific, our cultures were truly oceanic, in the sense that the sea barrier shielded us for millennia from the great cultural influences that raged through continental land masses and adjacent islands. This prolonged period of isolation allowed for the emergence of distinctive oceanic cultures with the only non-oceanic influences being the original cultures that the earliest settlers brought with them when they entered the vast, uninhabited region. Scholars of antiquity may raise the issue of continental cultural influences on the western and northwestern border islands of Oceania, but these are exceptions, and the Asian mainland influences were largely absent until the modern era. On the eastern extremity of the region there were some influences from the Americas, but these were minimal. It is for these reasons that Pacific Ocean islands from Japan, through the Philippines and Indonesia, which are adjacent to the Asian mainland, do not have oceanic cultures, and are therefore not part of Oceania. This definition of our region delineates us clearly from Asia and the pre-Columbian Americas and is based on our own historical developments, rather than on other people's perceptions of us.

Although the sea shielded us from Asian and American influences, the nature of the spread of our islands allowed a great deal of mobility within the region. The sea provided waterways that connected neighbouring islands into regional exchange groups that tended to merge into one another, allowing the diffusion of cultural traits through most of Oceania. These common traits of bygone and changing traditions have so far provided many of the elements for the construction of regional identities. However, there are many people on our islands who do not share these common traits as part of their heritage, and there is an increasing number of true urbanities who are alienated from their ancient histories. In other words although our historical and cultural traditions are important elements of a regional identity, they are not in themselves sufficient to sustain that identity, for they exclude those whose ancestral heritage is elsewhere, and those who are growing up in non-traditional environments.

The ocean that surrounds us is the one physical entity that all of us in Oceania share. It is the inescapable fact of our lives. What we lack is the conscious awareness of it, its implications, and what we could do with it. The potential is enormous, exciting—as it has always been. When our leaders and planners say that our future lies in the sea, they are thinking only in economic terms, about the development of marine and sea-bed resources. When people talk of the importance of the oceans for the continuity of life on Earth, they are making scientific statements. But for the people of Oceania, the sea defines us, what we are and have always been. As the great Caribbean poet, Derek Walcott, puts it, the sea is history. This realisation could be the beginning of a very important chapter in our history. We could open it as we enter the third millennium.

All of us in Oceania today, whether indigenous or otherwise, can truly assert that the sea is our single common heritage. Because the ocean is ever-flowing, the sea that laps the coastlines of Fiji, is the same water that washes the shores of all the other countries of our region. Most of the dry land surfaces on our islands have been divided and allocated, and conflicting claims to land rights are at the root of some of the most intractable problems in virtually all our communities. Until recently, the sea beyond the horizon and the reefs that skirt our islands was open water that belonged to no one and everyone. Much of the conflict between the major ethnic groups in Fiji for example, is rooted in the issue of land rights, but the open sea beyond the near-shore areas is open to every Fiji citizen and free of disputes. Similarly, as far as ordinary people of Oceania are concerned, there are no national boundaries drawn across the sea between our countries. Just about every year, for example, lost Tongan fishermen, who might well have been fishing in the Fijian waters, wash up in their frail vessels on the shores of Fiji. So far they have always been taken very good care of, then flown back home loaded with tinned fish.

It is one of the great ironies of the Law of the Sea Convention, which enlarged our national boundaries, that it also extended the territorial instinct to where there was none before. Territoriality is probably the strongest spur for some of the most brutal acts of aggression and because of the resource potentials of the open sea and the ocean-bed, the water that has united subregions of Oceania in the past may become a major divisive factor in the future relationships between our countries. It is therefore essential that we ground any new regional identity in a belief in the common heritage of the sea.

Realisation of the fact that the ocean is uncontainable and pays no respect to territoriality should spur us to advance the notion based on physical reality and practices that date back to the initial settlements of Oceania—that the sea must remain open to all of us.

A regional identity anchored in our common heritage of the ocean does not mean an assertion of exclusive regional territorial rights, for the same water that washes and crashes on our shores does so on the coastlines of the whole Pacific rim from Antarctica, to New Zealand, Australia, Southeast and East Asia, and right around to the Americas. The Pacific Ocean also merges into the Atlantic and the Indian Oceans to encircle the entire planet. As the sea is an open and ever flowing reality, so should our oceanic identity transcend all forms of insularity, to become one that is openly searching, inventive, and welcoming. In a metaphorical sense the ocean that has been our waterway to each other should also be our route to the rest of the world. Our most important role should be that of custodians of the ocean, and as such we must reach out to similar people elsewhere for the common task of protecting the seas for the general welfare of all living things. This is no more grandiose than the growing international movements to implement the most urgent projects in the global environmental agenda: the protection of the ozone layer, the forests and the oceans. The formation of an oceanic identity is really an aspect of our awaking to things that are already happening around us.

The ocean is not merely our omnipresent, empirical reality; equally importantly it is our most wonderful metaphor for just about anything. Contemplation of its vastness and majesty, its allurement and fickleness, its regularities and unpredictability, its shoals and depths—its isolating and linking role in our histories—excites the imagination and kindles a sense of wonderment, curiosity and hope, that could set us on journeys to explore new regions of creative enterprise that we have not dreamt of before.

In short, in order to give substance to a common regional identity and animate it, we must tie history and culture to empirical reality and practical action. In much the same way our ancestors wrote our histories on the landscape and the seascape; carved, stencilled and wove our metaphors on objects of utility; and sang and danced in rituals and ceremonies for the propitiation of the awesome forces of nature and society.

Twenty years ago, Albert Wendt (1976) in his landmark paper,

'Toward a New Oceania,' wrote of his vision of the region and its first season of post-colonial cultural flowering.

I belong to Oceania—or, at least, I am rooted in a fertile part of it and it nourishes my spirit, helps to define me, and feeds my imagination. A detached objective analysis I will leave to sociologists and all the other 'ologists'…Objectivity is for such uncommitted gods. My commitment won't allow me to confine myself to such a narrow vision. So vast, so fabulously varied a scatter of islands, nations, cultures, mythologies and myths, so dazzling a creature, Oceania deserves more than an attempt at mundane fact; only the imagination in free flight can hope—if not to contain her—to grasp some of her shape, plumage, and pain. I will not pretend that I know her in all her manifestations. No one…ever did; no one does…; no one ever will because whenever we think we have captured her she has already assumed new guises—the love affair is endless, even her vital statistics…will change endlessly. In the final instance, our countries, cultures, nations, planets are what we imagine them to be. One human being's reality is another's fiction. Perhaps we ourselves exist only in each other's dreams (1976:49)

At the end of his rumination on the cultural revival in Oceania, partly through the words of the region's first generation of post-colonial writers and poets, Wendt concluded with this remark,

[t]his artistic renaissance is enriching our cultures further, reinforcing our identities, self-respect and pride, and taking us through a genuine decolonisation; it is also acting as a unifying force in our region. In their individual journeys into the Void, these artists, through their work, are explaining us to ourselves and creating a new Oceania (1976:60).

This is very true. For a new Oceania to take hold it must have a solid dimension of commonality that we can perceive with our senses. Culture and nature are inseparable. The Oceania that I see is a creation of countless people in all walks of life. Artists must work with others, for creativity lies in all fields, and besides, we need each other.

These were the thoughts that went through my mind as I searched for a thematic concept on which to focus a sufficient number of programs to give the Oceania Centre a clear, distinctive and unifying identity. The theme for the Centre and for us to pursue is the ocean—the interactions between us and the sea that have shaped and are shaping so much of our cultures. We begin with what we have in common, and draw inspirations from the diverse patterns that have emerged from the successes and failures of our adaptation to the influences of the sea. From there we can range beyond the tenth horizon, secure in the knowledge of the home-base to which we will always return for replenishment and to revise the purpose and the direction of our journeys. We shall visit our people who have gone to the lands of diaspora, and tell them that we have built something, a new home for all of us. Taking a cue from the ocean's ever-flowing and encircling nature, we will travel far and wide to connect with oceanic and maritime peoples elsewhere, and swap stories of voyages that we have taken and those yet to be embarked upon. We will show them what we have, and learn from them different kinds of music, dance, art, ceremonies, and other forms of cultural production. Together we may even make new sounds, new rhythms, new choreographies, and new songs and verses about how wonderful and terrible the sea is, and how we cannot live without it. We will talk about the good things the oceans have bestowed upon us, the damaging things that we have done to them, and how we must together try to heal their wounds and protect them forever.

I have said elsewhere that there are no more suitable people on earth to be the custodians of the oceans than those for whom the sea is their home. We seem to have forgotten that we are such a people. Our roots, our origins are embedded in the sea. All our ancestors, including those who came as recently as sixty years ago, were brought here by the sea. Some were driven here by war, famine and pestilence; some were brought by necessity, to toil for others; and some came seeking adventures and perhaps new homes. Some arrived in good health, others barely survived the traumas of passage. For whatever reasons, and through whatever experiences they endured, they came by sea to the Sea, and we have been here since. If we listen attentively to stories of ocean passage to new lands, and of other voyages of yore, our minds would open up to much that is profound in our histories, to much of what we are and what we have in common.

Contemporary developments are taking us away from our sea roots. Most of our modern economic activities are land-based. We travel mostly by air, flying miles above the oceans, completing our journeys in hours instead of days and weeks and months. We rear and educate our young on things that have scant relevance to the sea. Yet we are told that the future of most of our countries lies there. Have we forgotten so much that we will not easily find our way back to the ocean?

As a region, we are floundering because we have forgotten or spurned the study and contemplation of our pasts, even of our recent histories, as irrelevant for the understanding and conduct of our contemporary affairs. We have thereby allowed others who are well-equipped with the so-called objective knowledge of our historical development to continue reconstituting and reshaping our world and our selves with impunity, and in accordance with their shifting interests at any given moment in history. We have tagged along with this for so long that we have kept our silence even though we have been virtually defined out of existence. We have floundered, also, because we have considered regionalism mainly from the point of view of individual national interests rather than those of a wider collectivity; and we have failed to build any clear and enduring regional identity because we have continued to construct edifices with disconnected traits from traditional cultures and passing events, without basing them on concrete foundations.

The regional identity proposed here has been constructed on a base of concrete reality. The sea is as real as you and I, it shapes the character of this planet, it is a major source of our sustenance, and it is something that we all share in common wherever we are in Oceania: these are all statements of fact. Above that level of everyday experience, the sea is our pathway to each other and to everyone else, the sea is our endless saga, the sea is our most powerful metaphor, the ocean is in us.

Notes

This paper is an edited version of one with the same title published in *The Contemporary Pacific,* 10(2), 1998. We gratefully acknowledge the permission of both the author and the editor of *The Contemporary Pacific* for permission to reproduce this considerably shortened version here.

References

Earle, S., 1996. 'Oceans: the well of life', *Time,* 28 October:52–3.

Hau'ofa, E., 1993. 'Our sea of islands', in E. Waddel, V. Naidu and E. Hau'ofa (eds), *A New Oceania: rediscovering our sea of islands*, School of Social and Economic Development, University of the South Pacific, Suva:2–16.

Wendt, A., 1976. 'Towards a New Oceania', *Mana Review,* 1:1.

3

On the anthropology of modernity, or, some triumphs of culture over despondency theory

Marshall Sahlins

In the late 18th century, at the height of the European Enlightenment, the French philosophers invented the word 'civilisation' to refer to their own society—a usage that was quickly adopted in Britain. Among the other not too enlightening ideas that logically followed was the notion of a progressive series of evolutionary stages, beginning in 'savagery' and culminating in 'civilisation,' into which one could fit—and fix—the various non-Western peoples. The imperialism of the last two centuries has not reduced such enlightened contrasts between the West and the Rest. On the contrary the ideologies of 'modernisation' and 'development' that trailed in the wake of Western domination took their basic premises from the same philosophical regime. Even the critical arguments of the Left about indigenous 'dependency' and capitalist 'hegemony' could result in equally dim views of the historical capacities of non-Western peoples. As though these peoples had nothing to do with history, except to suffer from it.

What has not been too enlightening

In too many narratives of Western domination, the indigenous peoples appear merely as victims—neo-historyless peoples whose own agency disappeared more or less with their culture, the moment Europeans erupted on the scene. Indeed, as Margaret Jolly has pointed out, when Europeans change it is called 'progress', but when 'they' (the others) change, notably when they adopt some of our progressive attributes, it is a loss of their culture, some kind of adulteration. As the European folklore goes, before we came upon the inhabitants of the Americas, Asia, Australia or the Pacific islands, they were 'pristine' and 'aboriginal'. It is as if they had no historical relations with other societies, were never forced to adapt their existence. Rather, until Europeans appeared, they were 'isolated'—which just means that *we* were not there. They were 'remote' and 'unknown'—which means they were far from us, and we were unaware of them. Hence the history of these societies only began when Europeans appeared—an epiphanal moment, qualitatively different from anything that had gone before, and culturally devastating. The historical difference with everything pre-colonial was power. Exposed and subjected to Western domination, the less powerful peoples were destined to lose their cultural coherence, as well as the pristine innocence for which Europeans—incomplete and sinful progeny of Adam—so desired them.

Accordingly, one of the main academic consequences of the violence inflicted by the West was the 'despondency theory' that became popular in a variety of twentieth century literature relating to colonised peoples. Despondency theory was the logical precursor to dependency theory. But as it turned out—when the surviving victims of imperialism began to seize their own modern history—despondency was another not terribly enlightening idea of the power of Western 'civilisation'. Here is a good example from A.L. Kroeber's great 1948 textbook, *Anthropology.*

> With primitive tribes, the shock of culture contact is often sudden and severe. Their hunting lands or pastures may be taken away or broken under the plough, their immemorial customs of blood revenge, head-hunting, sacrifice, marriage by purchase or polygamy be suppressed, perhaps their holy places profaned or deliberately overthrown. Resistance is crushed by firearms. Despondency settles over the tribes. Under the blocking-out of all old established ideals, without provision for new values and opportunities to take their place, the resulting universal hopelessness will weigh doubly heavy because it seems to reaffirm inescapable frustration in personal life also (1948:438–39).

A corollary of despondency theory was that the others would now become just like us—if they survived. The Enlightenment had already prepared for this eventuality by insisting on the universality of human reason and progress: a course of development that would be good—in all senses of the term—for the human species as a whole. In his *Primitive Culture* of 1871, E.B. Tylor showed the doom that awaited appreciation of cultural diversity by these theories of unilineal evolution, by endorsing—as an appropriate procedure for classifying societies in evolutionary stages—the immortal observation of Dr. Johnson that 'one set of savages is just like another.' A late classic of the genre was Walt Rostow's *Stages of Economic Growth* (1957), with its unilinear sequence of five developmental stages from 'traditional societies' to 'the age of high mass consumption.' (Rostow must have been among the first to perceive that the culmination of human social evolution was shopping.) Explicitly argued as an alternative to Marxist stages of progress, Rostow's thesis appeared as a mirror image, with the added advantage of turning left into right twice over. Common to many theories of development was a cheerful sense of cultural tragedy: the necessary disintegration of traditional societies that functioned, in Rostow's scheme, as a precondition for 'economic take-off'. Foreign domination was needed to accomplish this salutary destruction, since otherwise the customary relations of traditional production would set a ceiling on economic growth. By its own providential history, Europe had been able to develop itself, but according to Rostow, other peoples would have to be shocked out of their backwardness by an intrusive alien force. No revolutionary himself, Rostow could agree with Marx that in order to make an omelette one must first crack the eggs. Interestingly many peoples now explicitly engaged in defending their culture against national and international domination—the Maya of Guatemala and the Tukanoans of Colombia, for example (Warren 1992; Watanabe 1995; Jackson 1995)—have distanced themselves both from the bourgeois Right and the proletarian Left, refusing the assimilation pressures that would sacrifice their ethnicity to either the construction of the nation or the struggle against capitalist imperialism. Contrary to the evolutionary destiny the West had foreseen for them, the so-called savages will neither be all alike nor just like us.

In this vein, and as the century wears on, Max Weber's comparative project concerning the possibilities for capitalist development afforded by different religious ideologies seems increasingly bizarre. Not that it is by any means bizarre to talk of the cosmological organisation of pragmatic action. What seems increasingly weird is the way Weberians became fixated on the question of why one society or another failed to achieve this *summum bonum* of human history:

capitalism. One American Sinologist said China during the Qing dynasty had come so very close. It is like asking why the New Guinea Highlanders failed to develop the spectacular potlach of the Kwakiutl people. A question the Kwakiutl social scientist might well ask, given how so close the New Guineans had come with their elaborate pig exchange ceremonies. Likewise the Christian missionaries' question of how Fijians in their natural state failed to recognise the true god. One might as well ask why European Christians did not develop the ritual cannibalism of Fijians. After all, they came so close.

What is perhaps more interesting, as it actually happened, is how Christianity was Fijianised. Local societies everywhere have attempted to organise the irresistible forces of the Western World System by something even more inclusive—their own system of the world, their own culture.

The indigenisation of modernity

This is a modern song of the Enga people of New Guinea, about capturing the power-knowledge of Europeans, the 'Red Men' in local parlance

> When the time comes,
> Our youngsters will feed upon their words,
> After the Red Men drift away from this land,
> Our youngsters, like honey birds,
> After the Reds have gone,
> Will suck the flowers,
> While standing back here.
> We will do like them,
> We shall feed upon their deeds
> Like honey-birds sucking flowers.
> (Talyaga 1975:n.p.)

Reversing the real relations of exploitation and domination, these verses could easily be mistaken for the wistful fantasies of the powerless. Yet it would be wrong to suppose them motivated by self-contempt or a sense of their impending doom. Everything about the modern ethnography of Highland New Guinea indicates that the sentiment of cultural usurpation—here so ambiguously figured as honey-birds feeding on the powers of banished White men—is the guiding principle of the Highlanders' historical action. Rather than despondency, it is a positive action towards modernity, premised on the Enga's assurance they will be able to harness the good things of

Europeans to the development of their own existence. 'Develop-man' is the neo-Melanesian term for 'development,' but it would not be wrong to re-pidginise it back to English as 'the development of man', since the project to which it refers is the use of foreign wealth in the expansion of feasting, politicking, subsidising kinship and other activities that make up the local conception of a human existence. These are the activities that the working and warrior youth of the Enga are being urged to undertake. Rather than the death of tradition, the Enga thus express their confidence in a living tradition, a tradition that serves as a means and measure of innovation.

In anthropological terms, which is to say perceiving great things in little ones, this active appropriation by the Enga of the European power imposed upon them, is a local manifestation of a new planetary organisation of culture. Unified by the expansion of Western capitalism over recent centuries, the world is also being re-diversified by indigenous adaptations to the global juggernaut. In some measure, global homogeneity and local differentiation have developed together, the latter as a response to the former, in the name of native cultural autonomy. The new planetary organisation has thus been described as a 'Culture of cultures,' a world cultural system made up of diverse forms of life. As Ulf Hannerz put it: 'There is now a world culture, but we had better make sure we understand what this means. It is marked by an organisation of diversity rather than a replication of uniformity' (1990:237). Thus one complement of the new global ecumenicism is the so-called culturalism of very recent decades: the self-consciousness of 'culture' as a value to be lived and defended, that has broken out all around the Third and Fourth worlds. Ojibway, Hawaiians, Inuit, Tibetans, Amazonian peoples, Australian Aborigines, Maori people, Senegalese: everyone now speaks of their 'culture,' or some local equivalent, precisely in the context of national or international threats to the existence to that culture. This does not mean a simple and nostalgic desire for tiki ornaments and war clubs, or some such fetishised repositories of a pristine identity. Such a 'naive attempt to hold peoples hostage to their own histories,' as one anthropologist has said, would thereby deprive them of history (Turner 1987:7). What the self-consciousness of 'culture' does signify, is the demand of different peoples for their own space within the world cultural order. The focus of the Enga song above is not so much a refusal of the commodities and relations of the world system, but rather a desire to indigenise them. The project is the indigenisation of modernity.

Tradition and change

The struggle of non-Western peoples to create their own cultural versions of modernity undermines the received Western dichotomy of tradition and change, custom and rationality—and most notably its twentieth century version of tradition and development. This tradition-change antithesis was already old by the time the philosophers of the Enlightenment took on the project of destroying entrenched superstition by progressive reason. It had been kicking around advanced European thought at least since Sir Francis Bacon proposed to smash the idols of the cave and the tribe by the exercise of rational-empirical wisdom—and thus rescue humanity from the metaphysical consequences of Original Sin. Modern versions of the same ideological hang-up notably include the theories of development economists in which, as we have seen, so-called tradition, supposedly burdened with irrationalities, appears as an obstacle to so-called development.

Paradoxically, almost all the cultures described as 'traditional' by anthropologists, were in fact neotraditional, already changed by Western expansion. In some cases this happened so long ago that no-one, not even anthropologists, now debate their cultural authenticity. The Iroquois confederacy was by all accounts a post-contact development, as were the Plains Indian cultures that flourished through the acquisition of the horse. For all that, were the Iroquois less Iroquoian or the Sioux less Souian? And nowadays, are not the Maori people Maori, the Fijians, Fijian? In Fiji today, Wesleyan Christianity is considered the 'custom of the land'. Margaret Jolly rightly wonders why church hymns and the Christian mass should not be considered 'part of Pacific tradition', given that they 'have been significantly remade by Pacific peoples, so that Christianity may appear today as more quintessentially a Pacific than a Western faith'. If Pacific peoples gloss over the distinction—so critical to the Western sensibility—between the colonial and the precolonial past, it is that they 'are more accepting of both indigenous and exogenous elements as constituting their culture' (Jolly 1992:53). Faced with this hybrid state of affairs, we might be advised to return to the indigenous daily routine of the average American man described some decades ago by Ralph Linton.

> After breakfast our good man settles down to read the news of the day 'imprinted in characters invented by the ancient Semites upon a material invented in China by a process invented in Germany. As he

absorbs the accounts of foreign troubles he will, if he is a good conservative citizen, thank a Hebrew deity in an Indo-European tongue that he is 100 percent American' (1936:329).

In *Europe and the Peoples without History*, Eric Wolf correctly pointed out that most of the world was a mix of the indigenous and the exogenous by the time Western anthropologists arrived. Imperialism had arrived first. Regrettably, in his effort to convince fellow-anthropologists that they had never really known the pristine peoples they hankered after, Wolf neglected to draw the complementary conclusion concerning the cultural differences the ethnographers had nonetheless discovered and described. If the indigenous peoples were not without history, it was because they were not without their culture—which is also why their modern histories have differed.

In the late 18th century, the Hawaiian chiefs largely monopolised trade with the British and American vessels stopping for provisions and sandalwood while en route to China with furs from Northwest America. The chiefs, however, had distinctive economic demands, mainly for unique adornments and domestic furnishings, flashy goods that linked their persons to the sky and overseas sources of divine power, fashionable goods that could also differentiate them from their aristocratic fellows and rivals. Their Kwakiutl counterparts on the Northwest Coast were beginning a long economic history of a contrasting kind, demanding standardised items from the fur traders by the tens of thousands, items which eventually became Hudson's Bay blankets. Moreover, rather than hoarding their treasures as Hawaiian chiefs did, the Kwakiutl distributed their blankets (in potlatches) in ways that allowed them to correlate and measure their otherwise distinct claims to superiority. In contrast to the rather mundane woollen blankets that Kwakiutl demanded, Honolulu traders of Boston firms sent to America for de luxe articles: 'Everything new and elegant will sell at a good profit. Coarse articles are of no use.' The letter books of these traders are full of orders for fine calicoes, silks, shawls, and scarves 'in handsome patterns', superfine broadcloths and cashmeres; a whole catalogue of Polynesian splendours in a European idiom—commodities, moreover, from which most people were excluded. Unlike the Kwakiutl chiefs who were fashioning their pre-eminence out of common cloth, the Hawaiian élite were bent on unique projects of economic aggrandisement. But then, the Hawaiian chiefs were all more or less closely descended from the gods, and the main issue between them was how to turn these quantitative differences of genealogy into qualitative distinctions of standing. By contrast, the Kwakiutl chiefs already represented distinct and unrelated lineages, with different divine origins and powers. As heirs of unique ancestors and treasures, they used stock European goods in public fashion to make comparative representations of their worth, to turn their qualitative differences in genealogy into quantitative measures of rank. Accordingly the politics, economics and destinies of the Hawaiians and the Kwakiutl acquired different forms and fates in the nineteenth century. Their respective cultural traditions survived in the different ways they changed. Tradition is not the opposite of change.

Corollary: money and markets, moralities and mentalities

Everyone thought native Americans were finished long ago and yet modern ethnographers of the Cree nation are now talking about a 'cultural enhancement' or an 'indigenous affluence' that has actually been funded by the use of the market economy. They speak of a culturally-oriented project of development, one that reflects certain customary Cree ideas of 'the good life' by an explicit promotion of Cree 'culture', although their classic situation of dependency could still eventually be their downfall. In the meantime, the trappings of dependency could also be an empirical critique of the orthodoxy that money and markets are incompatible with the customs and kinship relations of so-called traditional societies. Indeed, Cree people find two-way radios useful in sustaining customary relations between kinsmen. Colin Scott found that snowmobiles and trucks likewise 'have increased [the] opportunities for sharing'. Human sharing is only an aspect of a cosmic cycle of exchange—that includes the animals who give themselves to the hunters and receive in turn their ritual rebirth—and snowmobiles have become part of an even larger economy than is dreamed of in the capitalist philosophy: a world system that includes both human beings and nature in social relations of personhood and interdependence. Over the centuries of increasing engagement in commodity production and exchange, Scott writes

> [t]he structure and quality of sharing, of kinship, and of man-animal relations remain quite distinctively Cree and quite characteristically egalitarian. Generosity is normal and expected. The needs of an extended network of relatives are a primary and lifelong occupation. Social and personal renewal are found in the encounter of people and animals. Cree themselves take these relations to be fundamental definers of their humanity and their cultural identity (1984:77).

The Cree culture has not simply persisted in spite of capitalism or because the people have resisted it. This is not so much a culture of resistance as the resistance of culture. Since Cree act in the world as social-historical beings, with their own cultural consciousness of themselves and of the objects of their existence, their experience of capitalism is mediated by the practice of their own form of life. Culture inhabits action. In the event, the capitalist forces are played out in a different cultural universe.

According to Marx, money destroys the archaic community because money becomes the community. It is as if, Freud complained, a person suddenly got a psyche when he drew his first pay check. In a book called *Money and the Morality of Exchange*, however, Maurice Bloch and Jonathan Parry collect a number of ethnographic examples to refute the idea. As against the idea that money gives rise to a particular world view—the unsociable, impersonal and contractual one we associate with it—they emphasise 'how an existing world view gives rise to particular ways of representing money' (1989:19). Money can very well be the servant of custom not its master. The destructive effects of markets and money on communities presuppose a separate 'economic' domain, as Bloch and Parry point out, an amoral sphere of transaction separated from the generosities of kith and kin. Where there is no structural opposition between the relationships of economy and sociability, where material transactions are ordered by social relations rather than vice versa, then the amorality we attribute to money need not result. Where the economy is embedded in society, say Bloch and Parry, 'monetary relations are rather unlikely to be represented as the antithesis of bonds of kinship and friendship, and there is consequently nothing inappropriate about making gifts of money to cement such bonds' (1989:19).

It follows that in certain structural conditions, money could actually increase kinship bonds: it could 'develop' the so-called traditional societies in the sense that they understand develop-man—as obtaining more and better of what they consider to be good things, such as anthropological reports from the New Guinea Highlands since the 1960s have reported. Benefiting from the market returns to migratory labour, coffee production and other cash-cropping, the great inter-clan ceremonial exchanges have flourished in recent decades as never before. Among the Enga, Chimbu, Hagen, Mendi, and others, the ceremonies have increased in frequency as well as in the magnitude of people engaged and goods transacted in them. Accordingly big-men are more numerous and powerful. Old clan alliances that had lapsed have been revived. Interpersonal kinship networks have been widened and strengthened. Money has been the means, rather than the antithesis, of community. High-value bank notes replace pearl shells as key exchange valuables, gifts of Toyota land cruisers complement the usual pigs, and large quantities of beer function as initiatory presents (adding certain celebratory dimensions to the customary festivities). Captured in reciprocal obligations and bride-wealth payments, 'the money which circulates in exchanges is generally not "consumed" at all,' as Andrew Strathern noted of the Hageners, 'but keeps on circulating, through the momentum of debt and investment' (1979:546). Rena Lederman reports that among modern Mendi people the exchange obligations between clans and personal kin create 'a demand for modern currency far greater than the demand generated by existing market outlets' (1986:332). Hence the Mendi say *they* have the true exchange economy, by contrast to the mere 'subsistence economy' of white men (1986:236).

Reversing centre and peripheries

Cities are the favoured places of *merantu*, the customary journeys of the Menangkabau and other Indonesian men beyond the boundaries of their own culture, whence they return with booty and stories worthy of their manhood. The Malay community in Mecca is second in size only to that of the Arabs. Some remain on the haj for 10 years or more; some are delayed for years, returning via Africa or India (Provencher 1976). The Mexican villagers working in Redwood City, California, and the Samoans in San Francisco likewise intend to return, an eventuality for which they prepare by sending money back to relatives, telephone calls and periodic visits to their native places, by sending their children home for visits or schooling and otherwise maintaining their natal ties and building their status in their former and future home. Can Samoans, Malays, Oaxacans, Africans, Filipinos, Peruvians, Thais—the millions of people now cycling between the 'peripherae' and metropolitan centres of the modern world-system— be content to return to a bucolic existence 'after they've seen Paris'? Is it not true (as the medieval proverb goes) that *Stadt Luft macht Frei*? Or if not free, proletarians forever? However true in an earlier European history, today the huge phenomenon of circular migration is creating a new kind of cultural formation: a determinate community without entity, extending transculturally and often transnationally from a rural centre in the so-called Third World to 'homes abroad' in the metropolis, the whole united by the toing and-froing of goods, ideas and people on the move. 'The geographic village is small,' writes Uzzell of Oaxacan *campesinos*, 'the social village spreads over thousands of miles' (1979:343).

Taking shape as urban ethnic outposts of rural, 'tribal' or peasant homelands, these synthetic formations remained unrecognised as such by the Western social scientists studying them for a long time. Or rather in studying urbanisation, migration, remittance dependency, labour recruitment or ethnic formation, Western researchers presented a spectacle something like the blind men and the elephant, each satisfied to describe the cultural whole in terms of one or another of its aspects. No doubt the Euro-American history of urbanisation had a stranglehold on the anthropological imagination. The general presumption was that urbanisation must everywhere put an end to what Marx called the idiocy of rural life. Relations between people would become impersonal, utilitarian, secular, individualised and otherwise disenchanted and detribalised because of the very nature of the city as a complex social and industrial system,. Such was the trend in Robert Redfield's 'folk-urban continuum'. As the beginning and end of a qualitative change, countryside and city were structurally distinct and opposed ways of life. 'After the rise of cities,' Redfield wrote, 'men became something different from what they had been before' (1953:ix). British social anthropology of the period was hung up on the same dualist *a priori*. Max Gluckman was the father of the African version: 'The African in the rural areas and in town,' he said, ' is two different men' (1960:69).

Enlightenment was soon in coming. Explicitly taking on the folk-urban continuum, Edward Bruner demonstrated the continuity of identity, kinship and custom between Toba Batak villages of highland Sumatra and their urban relatives in Medan. 'Examined from the structural point of view, the Toba Batak communities in village and city are part of one social and ceremonial system' (1961:515). Speaking more widely of Southeast Asia, Bruner wrote that 'contrary to traditional theory, we find in many Asian cities that society does not become secularised, the individual does not become isolated, kinship organisations do not break down, nor do the social relationships in the urban environment become impersonal, superficial and utilitarian' (1961:508). By the mid 1970s such observations had become common in the Latin American homeland of the folk-urban continuum as well as in ethnographies by Gluckman's colleagues and others throughout sub-Saharan Africa. As the gestalt shifted from the antithesis of the rural-urban to the synthesis of the 'translocal' cultural order, study after study groped for a suitable terminology. The scholars spoke variously of 'a bilocal society', 'a single social and resource system', 'a non-territorial community network', a 'common social field' uniting countryside and city, a 'single community spanning a variety of sites on both sides of the border', 'a single social field in which there is a substantial circulation of members' or some new species of the like.

What any and all these descriptions express is the structural complementarity of the indigenous homeland and the metropolitan 'homes abroad,' their interdependence as sources of cultural value and means of social reproduction. Symbolically focused on the homeland, whence its members derive their identity and their destiny, the 'translocal' community is strategically dependent on its urban outliers for material wherewithal. The rural order itself extends into the city, inasmuch as the migrants associate with each other in the urban context on the basis of their relationships at home. Kinship, community and tribal affiliations acquire new functions, and perhaps new forms, in the relationship among migrants: they organise the movements of people and resources, the care of homeland dependents, the provision of urban housing and employment. Insofar as people conceive their social being and their future in their native place, the material flows generally favour the homeland people. The indigenous order is sustained by earnings and commodities acquired in the foreign-commercial sector. But should we speak of 'remittances' as the foreign economic experts do? Epeli Hau'ofa has argued on occasion that this flow of money and goods is better understood by the norms of 'reciprocity,' since it reflects the migrants' obligations to homeland kin, even as it secures their rights in their native place. 'Reciprocity' as opposed to 'remittances' appropriately shifts the analytic perspective from a geographic village that is small to a social village spread over thousands of miles. Rather than lament the fate of a village that lives on 'remittances' one might, with Graeme Hugo, commend its success in reversing 'the parasitic function traditionally ascribed to cities' (1978:264). In spanning the historic divide between traditional and modern, the developmental distance between centre and periphery and the structural opposition of townsmen and tribesmen, the translocal community deceives a considerable body of enlightened Western social science.

Indeed this capacity of indigenous peoples to move freely and improvise culturally obliges us to reconsider certain presuppositions about the precolonial order—presuppositions whose source, incidentally, could never have been ethnography but rather the folklore of the civilising mission. Typically the cultural scheme was universal, and in the spaces beyond, true human beings were other kinds of persons and powers, which need to be appropriated as a precondition of local society. From exploits that transcended the community borders, men—most often men—returned with trophies of war or the chase, with goods acquired in raid or trade, with visions, songs, amulets, potions and cults, things familiar or new that could be consumed, sacrificed, exchanged, given away or otherwise disposed of in order to reproduce and develop the indigenous form of life. If in spite of all this it could be thought these peoples were historyless or closed to innovation, it is probably because they sought novelty in the things they considered to have reproductive virtues, which might have been a new kind of valuable shell or magical formula, not exactly what a development-economist would consider a 'capital investment'. It follows that few if any of the peoples known to anthropology were culturally *sui generis*. Their supposed closure was, as I say, a myth that owes more to enlightened prejudices about their isolation than to any ethnographic observation. We have not been playing with amateurs, then, in games of construction-of-the-Other. This helps explain Marilyn Strathern's observation, regarding Melanesians: 'It has been something of a surprise for Europeans to realise that their advent was something less than a surprise' (1990:25).

It should not now come as a surprise that ethnographers working in New Guinea and Vanuatu, in Mexico, Indonesia and the Amazon Basin, have seen a certain continuity, or more precisely a develop-man, of ancient custom in the modern phenomenon of circular migration. Since 1858 certain Xhosa have been working in the mines and towns of southern Africa. Their crossing into the dangerous terrain is still explicitly conceived and ritually protected as an excursion of war—from which they return with the booty of civilisation, to be celebrated as 'good and moral men' (McAllister 1980). In highland New Guinea too: 'Just as the blind Homer sang of the journeys and heroes of Troy, so recent Enga poets have praised their heroes and immortalised their deeds through images of commemorative chants' (Lacey 1985:93). This travelling tradition has seen exponential growth through the colonial and post-colonial periods, and their journeys now take Enga men to coastal towns and foreign lands, but even in pre-colonial days the heroes returned with means of cultural innovation and transformation. The whole highlands culture, as presently constructed, is a few centuries old or less, following the European expansion that brought the sweet potato into the Pacific.

Culture is not disappearing

It is possible that the translocal community will soon disappear as a cultural form. If the migrants settle permanently abroad, the structure might have a generational half-life, the attachments to the homeland dissolving with each city-born or foreign-born generation. However, in parts of Indonesia, Africa and elsewhere, circular migration has been going on for many generations. Reports from Nairobi in the 1980s echo observations in Java from 1916: the migrants were not being proletarianised. From a large review of anthropological literature on culture and development, Michael Kearney recently came to precisely that conclusion: 'migrants have not been proletarianised in any deeply ideological sense' (1986:352). However, here I am not concerned with the longevity of the form. What is of more interest is the on-going creation of new forms in the modern world Culture of cultures. No-one can deny that the world has seen an overall decrease of cultural diversity in the past five centuries. Indeed, anthropology was born out of the consciousness of the decrease as much as the appreciation of the diversity. There is no special reason now to panic about the death of culture.

Suppose for argument's sake we agree that Branislow Malinowski's *Argonauts of the Western Pacific* was the beginning of modern professional ethnography. If so, it is sobering to reflect that it opens with these words

> [e]thnology is in the sadly ludicrous, not to say tragic, position, that at the very moment when it begins to put the workshop in order, to forge its proper tools, to start ready for work on its appointed task, the material of its study melts away with hopeless rapidity. Just now, when the methods and aims of scientific field ethnology have taken shape, when men [n.b.] fully trained for the work have begun to travel into savage countries and study their inhabitants—these die away under our very eyes (1922:xv).

History studies past objects, but how many academic disciplines other than high-energy physics originated as the study of disappearing objects? Yet anthropologists can take heart. Another set of cultural forms has developed since the fifteenth century: hybrid forms, some of them space-defying or using the latest technology in creative projects of indigenising modernity. The discipline seems as well off as it ever was, with cultures disappearing just as we were learning how to perceive them, and then reappearing in ways we had never imagined.

The best modern heirs of the Enlightenment philosophers know this. I mean for example the West African intellectuals who argue, with Paul Hountondji (1994), that 'culture is not only a heritage, it is a project'. It is, as Abdou Touré insists, an African project, or set of projects, and not the universal march of reason proclaimed by the eighteenth century and still worshipped in the development religions of the twentieth.

> That which the minority of [élite] leaders has voluntarily forgotten is Culture as a philosophy of life, and as an inexhaustible reservoir of responses to the world's challenges and it is because they brush aside this culture that they're able to reason lightly in terms of development while implying a scale of values, norms of conduct or models of behaviour transmissible from one society to another! (Touré 1994).

Touré's conclusion is that 'Africa is no longer subjected to the Western model of development for the simple reason that there is no longer a model of any worth.' Finally—enlightenment.

Notes

1 Another characteristic example

> A village that is inwardly alive is proof against a government policy as well as against natural cataclysms neither of which affects its spiritual energies; but it cannot withstand the disintegrating forces of trade and commercial development, the stealthy invasion of money economy, the gradual weakening of its agricultural basis, of the tie that binds it to the soil – a tie which is but a part of the bond that unites man with man, the contact with the rest of the world. For these latter are destructive forces that kill not only the physical 1 element in the communal bases—agriculture to supply domestic needs—but also the two spiritual elements which underlie the village community—religion and social unity—and with these kill the soul of the village (Boeke 1942:19).

2 As if in response to Rousseau's Second Discourse, Clifford Geertz writes: 'men unmotivated by the customs of particular places do not in fact exist, have never existed, and most important, could not in the very nature of the case exist' (1973:35; cf Sahlins 1993:12-13).

3   Here is a modern song of the Enga people

When I have taken possession of them,
Of the great books of the lowlands,
I'll happily stride back
To Wabag, that land of mine,
Where the quiet stars go by.
It's my heritage, the land of my proud fathers,
There I'd make my home,
And there I'd settle,
There I'll settle,
Where the stars will pass over me,
With books firm in my hand.
(Talyaga 1975: Song 21)

References

Bloch, M., and Parry, J. (eds), 1989. *Money and the Morality of Exchange,* Cambridge University Press, Cambridge.

Boeke, J.H., 1942. *The Structure of the Netherlands Indian Economy,* Institute of Pacific Relations, New York.

Bruner, E., 1961. 'Urbanization and ethnic identity in North Sumatra', *American Anthropologist,* 63:508–521.

Geertz, C., 1973. *The Interpretation of Cultures,* Basic Books, New York.

Gluckman, M., 1960. 'Tribalism in modern British Central Africa', *Cahiers d'Études africaines* 1:55–70.

Hannerz, U., 1990. 'Cosmopolitans and locals in world culture', *Theory, Culture and Society,* 7(2–3):237–51.

Hountondji, P., 1994, 'Culture and development in Africa: lifestyles, modes of thought and forms of social organization', Paper prepared for the World Commission on Culture and Development, CCD-IV/94/REG, INF.9, UNESCO, Paris.

Hugo, G. J., 1978. *Population Mobility in West Java,* Second edition 1981, Gadjah Mada University Press, Yogyakarta.

Jackson, J., 1995. 'Culture genuine and spurious: the politics of Indianness in the Vaupés, Columbia', *American Ethnologist,* 22:3–27.

Jolly, M., 1992. 'Specters of inauthenticity', *The Contemporary Pacific,* 4(1):49–72.

Kearney, M., 1986. 'From the invisible hand to the visible feet: anthropological studies of migration and development', *Annual Reviews of Anthropology,* 15:331–61.

Kroeber, A.L., 1948. *Anthropology*, Harcourt Brace, New York.

Lacey, R., 1985. 'Journeys and transformations: the process of innovation in Papua New Guinea', in M. Chapman (ed.), *Modernity and Identity in the Island Pacific*, Special issue of *Pacific Viewpoint* 26:81–105.

Lederman, R., 1986. *What Gifts Engender: social relations and politics in Mendi, highland Papua New Guinea*, Cambridge University Press, Cambridge.

Linton, R., 1936. *The Study of Man*, Appleton Century Crofts, New York.

Malinowski, B., 1922. *Argonauts of the Western Pacific*, Routledge and Kegan Paul, London.

McAllister, P.A., 1980. 'Work, homestead and the shades: the ritual interpretation of labour among the Gcaleka', in P. Mayer (ed.), *Black Villages in an Industrial Society*, Oxford University Press, Capetown.

Provencher, R., 1976. 'Shifts in the cycle of experience: Malay perceptions of migration', in D. Gullet and D. Uzzell (eds), *New Approaches to the Study of Migration*, Rice University Studies, Houston 62:63–71.

Redfield, R., 1953. *The Primitive World and its Transformations*, Cornell University Press, Cornell.

Sahlins, M., 1993. 'Goodbye to Tristes Tropes', *Journal of Modern History* 65:1–25.

Scott, C., 1984. 'Between "original affluence" and consumer affluence' in R.F. Salisbury and E. Tooker (eds), *Affluence and Cultural Survival*, The American Ethnological Society, Washington, DC:74–86.

Strathern, A., 1979. 'Gender, ideology and money in Mt Hagen', *Man* 14(3):530–48.

Strathern, M., 1990. 'Artefacts of history: events and the interpretation of images', in J. Sikala (ed.) *Culture and History in the Pacific*, The Finnish Anthropological Society, Transactions No.27, Helsinki:25–44.

Talyaga, K., 1975. *Modern Enga Songs*, Institute of Papua New Guinea Studies, Boroko, Port Moresby.

Touré, A., 1994. 'Minority culture, majority development' Paper prepared for the World Commission on Culture and Development, UNESCO CCD-IV/94/REG/INF.11, Paris.

Tylor, E.B., 1871. *Primitive Culture*, Murray, London.

Turner, T., 1987. 'The politics of cultural survival', in B. Spooner (ed.), *Conservation and Survival*, Oxford University Press, Oxford.

Uzzell, D.J. 1979. 'Conceptual fallacies in the rural-urban dichotomy', *Urban Anthropology* 8:333–350.

Warren, K.B. 1992. 'Transforming memories and histories: the meaning of ethnic resurgence for Mayan Indians', in A. Stepan (ed.), *Americas: new interpretive essays*, Oxford University Press, New York:189–219.

Watanabe, J.M., 1995. 'Unimagining the Maya: anthropologists, others and the inescapable hubris of authorship', *Bulletin of Latin American Research* 14:25–45.

Wolf, E., 1982. *Europe and the People Without History*, University of California Press, Berkeley and Los Angeles.

4

Gender, culture and sustainable development—the Pacific way

Peggy Fairbairn-Dunlop

Women's work in developing countries has usually been analysed in terms of economic growth models, each of which conclude that women have been adversely affected in the change from traditional to modern economic systems. Liberal-feminist women and development theorists (Boserup 1970; Rogers 1980) identify the decline of women's traditional roles in production, and the importation of Western concepts of women's inferiority as the cause of an erosion of women's status. Increased workloads in subsistence cash cropping, and informal trading, as well as the diminution of women's traditional rights in land, education and decision-making in the national institutions and policymaking bodies are used as evidence to underscore the worsening position of women. Marxist-feminist theorists, on the other hand, see women's low status as resulting from the sexual division of labour which emerges as an expression of women's roles in reproductive activities, and the articulation of these with production outside the home (Beneria and Sen 1981; Nash 1981). They draw attention to women being forced by economic circumstances to work long hours for very low wages, as well as the increasingly common practice of women working a 'double day'.

Pacific women argue that they have not been disadvantaged in the development process, because they have been shielded by customary ways. The case studies presented below show tremendous faith of Pacific women in the family system—the family systems that are central to both Pacific women's vision of what development should be (as documented in the Pacific Platform of Action for Sustainable Development) and to the strategies Pacific women are using to achieve their development goals. At the same time, while Pacific women are preserving the customary ways, the question must be raised of whether the customary ways, as they are practised, are ensuring women's physical, social, economic and spiritual well-being in these times of transition. Women's vulnerability in times of rapid change is briefly discussed.

Building on the customary systems

Case one—the vision of Pacific women

The Pacific Platform of Action (PPA) for Sustainable Development came into being as a direct result of the region's preparations for the Beijing Women's International Conference in 1995. The PPA represents a major milestone for Pacific women. Until the PPA was published, Pacific women did not have a regional policy document, and there were very few national policy statements or reports about the situation of women. As a result, government and NGO programs lacked an overall cohesion: they were often disjointed, fragmentary, and sometimes more externally than internally driven. The PPA gave Pacific women a mandate. This baseline document—produced by representatives from all Pacific nations—now serves as a guideline for national and regional planning.

Where did the drive to write this regional statement begin? In late 1994 I was asked by ESCAP to prepare a regional report on Pacific progress for forward looking strategies, information from which would be included in an Asia-Pacific Report for Beijing.[1] In the Decade for Women which followed (1985–95), Nairobi delegates were charged with addressing these goals, and then reporting their progress back to the 1995 Conference at Beijing.

This request from ESCAP for a regional Pacific report raised a number of questions
- were Pacific women aware of, or trying to implement the forward looking strategies (FLS)?
- were the forward looking strategies appropriate for the Pacific?

- did Pacific women want to be subsumed, yet again, into another Asia-Pacific paper?

All too often, as Pacific delegates attending conferences, we find that our input is 'lost' in Asia concerns, the assumption being that Pacific needs are but a microcosm of those of Asia, or that our 'smallness' (in comparison with Asia) makes our concerns insignificant. This is as partly our fault. We continually call attention to our 'uniqueness', but at the same time we have seldom examined or documented what makes us different, nor have we networked to present a unified Pacific voice on the global scene.

In discussions with the Pacific Women's Bureau of the South Pacific Commission (SPC), it was agreed that the real priority for Pacific women was a regional report which reflected women's present status, their vision for the future and ways to achieve this vision—in short, a sort of a Pacific FLS. Many of these goals and strategies would undoubtedly be similar to the global forward looking strategy, while others might be different. Such a report could be included in the proposed Asia-Pacific paper, but most importantly, it would also serve as a much needed strategy-guiding document for national women's machineries and for the SPC women's regional program.

The initial preparation years of the PPA in 1994–95 became an intensive, sometimes frenzied but always jam-packed learning time as Pacific women from all walks of life learnt about women's experiences globally and then applied these findings to their own situation. The substantial regional and national commitment to this program was backed by a tremendous spirit of good will from regional and national government organisations, NGOs, and donors. For many members of the national teams formed to gather cross sectional data for national reports, this was the first time they had read the forward looking strategy, and/or asked themselves the question, 'what do we want development to bring for ourselves, our children and our community?' Team members asked questions which were not often raised in national forums, and answered these with extreme honesty and fearlessness. They questioned the merits of planning driven wholly by economic concerns; the economic, social and physical vulnerability experienced by low-income families, and households headed by women today; the effects of unemployment and underemployment, illiteracy and increased violence against women and children; the concerns of youth, and the increasing incidence of poverty-related health issues in the Pacific.

When the national women's reports were completed, these materials were set with other regional data so as to identify the key issues of concern for Pacific women in a draft PPA. This draft was then presented to the Sixth Triennial Conference of Pacific Women, held in Noumea in May 1994, where it was reviewed and rewritten over four days (and nights) by nearly 200 delegates, until a regional document was agreed upon. In these workshop sessions, Pacific women learnt to listen to each other, to look beyond their own immediate concerns, recognise commonalities of experience and to accept different viewpoints. They learnt that ideas should be backed by data, to search for cause and effect relationships, and to lobby for their principles. In short, women learnt to work together to create a regional statement they could support.

The PPA is very much a Pacific document with culture at its centre. The Noumea Declaration—the preamble to the PPA—highlights the centrality of custom, tradition and family to Pacific women's vision of sustainable development, with the family as the basic block on which sustainable development must be built. The Declaration emphasises the uniqueness of the Pacific region

- the central role of custom and tradition
- the primacy of the family
- the strong affinity of our people with the land
- the unique challenges we face as a consequence of our history, demography and geography.

The 13 areas of critical concern identified in the PPA again directly reflect the Pacific social, economic and cultural context—the semi-subsistence nature of Pacific economies (as in the role of women in agriculture and fishing); shared decision-making, and the belief that the advancement of women would proceed within the context of environment, culture and the family mechanisms. The 13 areas of critical concern are

- health
- education and training
- economic empowerment
- agriculture and fishing
- legal and human rights
- shared decision-making
- environment
- culture and the family
- mechanisms to promote the advancement of women

- violence
- peace and justice
- poverty
- indigenous people's rights.

When the Pacific delegates presented the PPA to the Asia Pacific meeting at Jakarta in late 1994, they experienced the joy and power which comes with having the statement of a well-defined vision and presenting this vision as a unified regional voice. At Jakarta, Pacific women finetuned their skills in presenting a case, listening, negotiating and prioritising—with some success. Many of the Pacific concerns were included in the Jakarta Declaration—the Asia Pacific statement for Beijing. Others were not. Even issues that were not included in the Asia Pacific Report were still critical issues for the Pacific and a starting point for Pacific development interventions.

The areas of common concern included in both the Pacific Platform for Action and the Jakarta Declaration included

- the growing feminisation of poverty
- inequality in women's access to, and participation in economic activities
- inadequate recognition of the role and concerns of women in environment and natural resource management
- inequitable access to power and decision-making
- violation of women's human rights
- inadequate, or lack of access to health facilities
- lack of equality and access to education and literacy provision
- inadequate mechanisms for promoting the advancement of women
- inadequate recognition of women's role in peace-building.

The Pacific issues of concern that were not incorporated were

- indigenous women's rights
- insufficient support, recognition and promotion of women's participation in agriculture and fisheries, and in particular, women's roles in food security
- inadequate mechanisms to preserve customs, cultural and traditional values and social safety nets.

The PPA has become a manifesto of Pacific women, for them to use as a guide, to challenge, and to review. This baseline policy document stresses women's firm commitment to family systems and the belief that family systems are the key to sustainable development for Pacific women, their families, communities and nations.

Case two—the economic strategies of Pacific women

Family systems are often described in the development literature as being 'hindrances' to economic development. The following two examples show how Pacific women are using their family systems to encourage and enhance economic development options. Aggie Grey's enterprise is an example of a business which has used family systems to grow 'vertically' in size, to increase the numbers employed and capital outlay. The second example of women entrepreneurs shows women who prefer to run a number of small businesses at one time, following a 'lateral' pattern of business development, rather than increasing the size of a single business.

Building a large enterprise—Aggie Grey's, Samoa. Aggie's holds pride of place as the most well-known hotel in the South Pacific. For tourists it is a Pacific landmark, while to economic experts it is proof that an indigenous business enterprise can 'work'. Aggie reportedly went into business following the bankruptcy of her husband's business during the depression years of the 1930s, because she was determined that her younger children would enjoy the same education as her elder children. Aggie began by selling baskets of fruit and vegetables to the wives of New Zealand administrators. From this beginning, Aggie progressed to handicrafts sales, and then to hospitality. The modest two-roomed guesthouse Aggie opened in the 1930s has now grown into an internationally recognised multi-million dollar hotel, incorporating 154 rooms, a gift shop, tours and an extensive farm to supply fresh produce to the hotel kitchens. Each new 'development' represents a response to changing social conditions, such as the stationing of thousands of US military in Samoa in the 1940s; the growth of air travel—the introduction of three-day package TEAL flights, Pan-Am flights from Hawaii to American Samoa and the development of Polynesian Airlines as the national carrier—and the shooting of a major movie, *Return to Paradise,* in Samoa, featuring international box-office stars Gary Cooper and Roberta Haines.

A statement frequently heard is that 'Aggie's is run like a chiefly system with Aggie at the head'. The relationship between the Grey family and their staff is personal rather than directive: every worker feels they have a personal stake in the business. Alailima writes

> Aggie looked at her staff not as employees but as members of her own extended families. Many of them were really her kin…Though Aggie held no title, they thought of her as the chief of this large household. She assigned jobs, gave instruction, inspected progress and scolded

malingerers. She made very clear what she expected and was by no means easy to please. In return Aggie...provided more than wages. She acted like a parent, designing their clothes, sticking flowers over their ears, and dabbing her 'daughters' with perfume. She advised them about sex. When they were sick she nursed them, when they were in trouble she stuck by them and when they had a *faalavelave* [a special demand] she was generous (1988:294).

Aggie's business dealings are based on family, personal friendships and trust. For example, she always purchased handicrafts and other hotel supplies from certain villages and buyers, thus guaranteeing these producers a market. In many cases she gave higher prices than a piece of handicraft warranted, and/or created work for those urgently in need of cash. As in a family, staff members are adept at most of the jobs needed to keep the hotel running smoothly. The girls who clean rooms by day are the dancers at the floorshow in the evening, while the pool attendants and gardeners provide the musical back-up support for the *fiafia*, or party. It is the tradition also for a member of the Grey family to perform the *taualuga* (last dance—the most important) at the weekly *fiafias*. In the early days Aggie was the *taualuga*. Now her grand-daughter has this honour. The Grey family, as fitting its prominent chiefly status, give generously to national and local fund-raising efforts—particularly of the Apia village. These gifts reinforce the relationships between the enterprise and the people; as in traditional times true wealth is displayed in giving.

Aggie's continues to draw on family networks to build the business, and by doing so, is not only spreading the benefits of development more evenly, but strengthening family networks. Today Aggie's employs over 250 staff. A daughter-in-law commented that 'We could run the hotel with fewer...but you don't fire family.' **Economic security through a number of small family-based micro-enterprises, Fiji.** The uncertain economic situation in many Pacific countries has seen the increase of informal trade and small businesses, the majority of which are run by women. Many of these largely agriculturally based businesses have become the main source of family income for a growing number of families (see Appendix 1). The WOSED (Women's Social and Economic Development Program) micro-credit program is run by the Division of Women's Affairs, Fiji. It is based on the Grameen model of peer group support and the premise that credit and/or savings is the catalyst that will enable women to develop resources to effect change and thereby contribute to the fulfilment of their personal and family development. WOSED is designed to assist unemployed and underemployed women, who are usually unable to meet the collateral and equity required by the formal lending system to gain access to credit. One of the aims of WOSED is that women will learn skills and develop sufficient collateral to access a larger loan from a commercial bank, as they increase the size of their businesses.

A review of WOSED carried out in April 1997 showed that over 250 small loans of under F$1000 had been given out, and some women had taken a second loan. As seen in Table 1, a high percentage of the enterprises undertaken by the women borrowers were agriculturally based, and almost a third were weaving and handicraft production 'for our family living in town', 'for traditional use' and for sale. There were very few non-agricultural enterprises and two enterprises could be classified as 'services' (such as brush cutter and catering hire). All told, the enterprises were family based and physically located within the ambit of both family and community.

Interviews with the women borrowers revealed two further trends: a significant number of WOSED members were engaged in more than one income-earning venture, and, often when one enterprise was operating effectively, women gave this to the care of another family member and then started another small enterprise. For example, the multiple enterprises of a Savusavu solo mother of 8 included vegetable gardening, poultry (father now does this), a piggery (son

Table 4.1   Micro-enterprises by type

Agriculture related (95)	Sales (98)	Clothing related (39)	Service (2)
Weaving, handicrafts (32)	Canteen (43)	Sewing (19)	Brush-cutter (1)
Fishing (14)	Market vendor (35)	Fabric printing, tie dyeing (12)	Catering equipment hire (1)
Poultry (13)	Kava (8)	Embroidery (8)	
Vegetables (11)	Baking, cakes (3)		
Farming (8)	Retail shop (2)		
Pigs (5)	Wool (1)		
Ducks (6)	Second-hand clothing (1)		
Copra (3)	Snacks, sweets, peanuts (5)		
Rice (2)			
Bees (1)			

Source: Fairbairn-Dunlop P. and Struthers J., 1997. *Review of the Women's Social and Economic Development Program (WOSED)*, Ministry of Foreign Affairs and Trade, Wellington.

helps), and fishing. In addition to this, she and other family members sell produce at the market, at a roadside stall (built on the main road in front of their house) and at a siding on the main bus route to Labasa. This lateral development pattern which sees other family members absorbed into the businesses is seen in Table 4.2.

This lateral pattern of business development no doubt reflects factors such as the desire to spread risks, keep options open, an unwillingness to be burdened by a big debt, and a preference for keeping enterprises at a 'hands on' stage. This pattern is at odds with assumptions that people want to 'grow' a business in size, that larger businesses are 'better' or 'more successful' than smaller business and that people should progress from micro to larger-size loans.

These groups are practising an alternative development paradigm which is a viable strategy in today's rapidly changing social and economic conditions. It is a strategy which has implications for national development planning and service provision as well.

To conclude: are the family systems supporting women?

These cases have shown that women are choosing development options which build on the strengths of family systems, and therefore preserve the customary ways. Are the customary ways preserving the physical, social, economic and spiritual well-being of women, in these rapidly changing times?

Table 4.2   Pattern of multiple small enterprises and employment for family members

Case	District	Loan 1	Who helps?	Loan 2	Who helps?
1	Central	Catering	Daughter	Brush cutter	Son[a]
2	Central	Market vendor	Daughter	Canteen	Daughter[b]
3	North	Market vendor	Husband	Food parcels	Husband
4	North	Poultry/pigs	Father	Vegetables	Daughter
5	West	Fishing	Sister	Canteen	Daughter[b]
6	West	Crockery hire	Family	Video filming	Family
7	East	Bread baking	Husband	n.a.	n.a.
8	East	Mat weaving	Daughter[a]	n.a.	n.a.

n.a. not applicable
[a] presently unemployed
[b] child in school at present/ looking to next year.
Source: Fairbairn-Dunlop P. and Struthers J., 1997. *Review of the Women's Social and Economic Development Program (WOSED)*, Ministry of Foreign Affairs and Trade, Wellington.

Major economic and social transformations are occurring today, and are changing household formations and patterns of obligation rapidly and substantially. New data are showing areas where Pacific women do not enjoy equal chances with males, such as education. Educational equity is particularly critical because education is the key to every other aspect of personal and national development. It is linked with good health, widened employment options, and the sustainable use of natural resources. Education is also positively correlated with population growth, in that women with a higher level of education have fewer children. (Population growth is a critical development issue because Pacific countries have amongst the highest rates of population growth in the world. It is estimated that the region's population will double in 20 years. That over 50 per cent of our populations are aged 15 years and under presents a major challenge to every sustainable development strategy). The general pattern of educational participation and use in the region shows three trends. First, the higher the level of schooling the lower the female participation. For some countries, the major priority is getting and keeping girls in primary schools. In others, women's access to schooling equals males through to secondary schooling, and then there is a large drop out of females at that point. Second, women are grossly under-represented in the sciences. Third, women's educational achievements do not translate into equal participation in the economic, social or political spheres. The lack of participation of women in national decision-making means that the concerns women see as important, and the alternative strategies women's groups such as WOSED are trying, may not be discussed at these national planning forums.

What are the factors contributing to the present under-use of women's potential? It is probably true that the institutional structures are in place for women to have equal educational access to males, since education is compulsory in most Pacific countries. However, are there social attitudes and circumstances at play which work to prevent women from fully using these chances—are girls kept home from school to help in the home? Is it seen as a waste of time for girls to enrol in tertiary study, and, is science 'too hard' for girls? Or, is the belief still widely held that women do not need as much education as males because their brothers or their families will look after them?

Despite our protests to the contrary, family systems are not protecting Pacific women as in past. The disastrous effects of the weakening of family systems in these transition times is seen in the increased number of marriage breakdowns, households headed by women; land disputes and misuse of family land (as in logging contracts), unemployment and incipient poverty (overcrowded living conditions, poor nutrition), increased crime, increases in the reported incidence of violence against women and children, and the lack of care for the elderly, once the honoured members of society. The growth of households headed by women is clear in all our countries, and many of these families are living in conditions below the poverty line, as shown in Appendix 2.

Societies develop their own patterns of organisation to ensure that the social, economic physical and spiritual needs of their members are met. The communal systems—including the large subsistence sector, strong cultural identity and traditional values and the stable social fabric based on the village community and extended family systems— have prevented the onset of severe poverty on a large scale in every Pacific country. Sustainable progress in human development will depend on strengthening these systems to ensure that social, economic and structural changes will continue to improve people's lives and their well-being. It is time to review the customary systems and the gender roles these promote to see whether they are working in the interests of women and their families.

Appendix 1

The following data from the Solomon Islands and Vanuatu give some
idea of the extent of women's activities in the informal sector and their
importance to family security.
Solomon Islands, 1993. (Sample size: 323 randomly selected women.)
Vanuatu, 1994. (Sample size: 949 women market vendors from Efate,
Santo, Malekula and Ambae).
Two-thirds of a sample were self-employed at the time of the interviews.
Of this two thirds, 75 per cent said they spent 16 hours or more each
week on their income-generating ventures.

- More than one third of these women were sole income
  providers.
- Agriculture was the major enterprise—farm gardening (38
  per cent), food catering (21 per cent), crafts (15 per cent) and
  textiles (11 per cent).
- 40 per cent sold their products directly to consumers at the
  market, 34 per cent sold from their homes, and 16 per cent
  from shops.
- Over 75 per cent had not received any assistance to run their
  businesses, whether from relatives, banks or other sources.
- 75 per cent were married (average 5 children) and 25 per
  cent lived in households of more than seven people. More
  than 50 per cent had only a few years of primary school
  education and almost one-fifth had no formal education at
  all. 25 per cent were not able to write in any language and
  almost one-third could not do any calculations.

Source: Ward, M. and Arias, F., 1995. Employment for Women in
Solomon Islands, National Centre for Development Studies, The
Australian National University and ILO/UNDP, Canberra.

The survey found
- profits from these sales was the household's major source of
  income for 64 per cent of the sample—89 per cent of these
  profits was spent on household expenses including food, 37
  per cent on school fees
- agricultural goods were the major items sold. However,
  women did not specialise in any one item but engaged in
  multiple economic activities (MEA) thus spreading their
  risks over a number of options, and working at any activity

which would 'ensure our children have food on the table'
- the main source of loans to develop their business for 73 per cent, was from family members; 18 per cent obtained them from an unstated source, 12 per cent from commercial banks and credit unions; and 4 per cent borrowed from the Development Bank
- 28 per cent has attended a training course.

Source: Women's Business Unit of the Department of Cooperatives and Rural Business Development, and Statistics Department, Vanuatu.

Appendix 2

Some Pacific realities

- 50 children die each day
- 10,000 children do not reach their fifth birthday
- 1,100 women die from birth-related problems each year
- 1.4 million adults cannot read nor write—the majority of these are women
- 40 per cent of children have less than 8 years of schooling
- there are growing inequalities, poverty and human distress
- the region's rainforests will be gone in less than 20 years
- massive depletion of reef, lagoon and ocean resources is taking place
- the population of the region will double in 20 years, urban populations will reach 43 per cent
- an extra 3 million wage-earning jobs will be needed in the next 20 years.

Note

1   The Forward Looking Strategies derived from the 1985 Women's International Conference in Nairobi, which passed two major resolutions, CEDAW (Convention for the Elimination of Discrimination against Women) and the FLS.

References

Alailima, F., 1988. *Aggie Grey: a Samoan saga*, Mutual Publishing Company, Honolulu.

Beneria, L. and Sen, G., 1981. 'Accumulation, reproduction and women's roles in economic development: Boserup revisited', *Signs* 7(2):279–300.

Boserup, E., 1970. *Women's Roles in Economic Development*, George Allen and Unwin, London.

Fairbairn-Dunlop P., 1994. 'Gender, culture and tourism development in Western Samoa', in J. Momsen and Y. Kinnaird (eds), *Gender: the tourism dimension*, Boulder Press, Westview.

——, 1995. The road to Beijing: the path from Apia, Paper presented to the Seminar on Gender and Development Issues at the Asian Development Bank's 28th Annual Meeting of Governors in Auckland, New Zealand.

Fairbairn-Dunlop, P. and Struthers, J., 1997. *Review of the Women's Social and Economic Development Program (WOSED)*, Ministry of Foreign Affairs and Trade, Wellington.

Nash J., 1981. 'Ethnographic aspects of the world capitalist system', *Annual Review of Anthropology*, 10:94–119.

Rogers, B., 1980. *The Domestication of Women*, Tavistock, London.

South Pacific Commission, 1995. *Pacific Platform of Action: rethinking sustainable development for Pacific women towards the year 2000*, South Pacific Commission, Noumea.

UNDP, 1994. *The Pacific Human Development Report*, UNDP, Suva.

Ward, M. and Arias, F., 1995. *Employment for Women in Solomon Islands*, National Centre for Development Studies, The Australian National University and ILO/UNDP, Canberra.

5

Governance, development and leadership in Polynesia: a microstudy from Samoa

Malama Meleisea

One of the reasons that governance has become a fashionable topic for research is because it is now held by agencies such as the World Bank that successful 'development' is contingent on a certain manner of government. I am using the word development in the sense it is used by international agencies to refer to things like economic growth and rising standards of living which can be measured by statistics for education, health, life expectancy and so on. It is now increasingly argued that the kind of government that is needed to produce such development is one that operates in a transparent manner, so its actions are known to its citizens; in other words, government which is accountable for its actions. One aspect of this discussion is that values about governance are rooted in culture, and that not all cultures value the kind of openness and acceptance of individual rights that Western thinkers have argued to be the basis of human development. There is debate about whether the kind of cultural values which underlie modernisation in the West are really necessary for a country to be economically successful. For example, an interesting new book by Huntington (1997) argues that we are in the early stages of new global conflict over different pathways, with 'development' values competing between cultural regions.

Twenty years ago, we used to talk about the particular amalgam of political, economic and cultural features of our region as the 'Pacific

Way'. However this has become such a cliché that we are now embarrassed to use the term to refer to the set of attitudes and values that were supposed to characterise our region. Professor Hau'ofa demystified such slogans by pointing out that they were dreamt up by élites with more in common with each other than with the ordinary people of their countries. However lately it has again become popular for the Pacific to be considered in this collective way. The recent World Bank studies, and the Pacific 2010 series produced by the National Development Studies Centre at the Australian National University have all pointed out the 'paradox' of the Pacific islands—that despite high levels of aid, populations are growing but not economies. Predicting that aid is drying up, these books point out that without economic growth there cannot be continuing improvements in education, health, and public infrastructure—because there will be no money to pay for these things (World Bank 1993, Cole 1993).

The present recipe for solving this problem is the application of policy reforms, usually at the instigation of the International Monetary Fund, the Asian Development Bank and other donors. This is usually only done when the country has reached a financial crisis and can no longer pay its wages and bills, let alone its overseas debts. In 1997 it was the Solomon Islands. In 1998 the most celebrated victim was the Cook Islands, a few years ago Samoa was in the same situation and some gloomy forecasters say that Fiji will be next. In recent years Pacific island countries only seem to get into the news because the leaders of one of our countries have been caught with their hands in the till. There has been misappropriation of public money in Samoa and Fiji, involving politicians and heads of government agencies. There is an on-going saga of corruption in the forest industry in Solomon Islands and Papua New Guinea. The army of Vanuatu recently kidnapped their president to force the Government to pay wages owed to them. Finally, as a lesson to locals who are too critical, there was the recent imprisonment of outspoken journalists in Tonga, and the charges of sedition against members of the opposition in Samoa for criticising government policy.

In a recent analysis of government and tradition in the Pacific islands, Stephanie Lawson concludes that there is a lingering 'traditional' element in all this (Lawson 1996). To understand the problem, we need look no further than Max Weber's classic analysis. The different bases of legitimacy which characterise 'traditional' and 'rational legal' forms of political authority are that the latter is based on formal laws and regulations, while the former is based on hereditary privileges attached to leaders. In the discussion of the 'politics of tradition' anthropologists have been interested in the way in which Pacific leaders and authority in Pacific societies have invoked culture and tradition as a means of justifying their behaviour, and have recognised that the politics of tradition has some of its roots in colonial intervention. For example, institutions which we have been asked to revere because of their traditional nature such as the Samoan *matai* system, the Tongan Monarchy or the Fijian Great Council of Chiefs, were all colonial compromises between traditional and modern forms of government. The modern arbitrator of Samoan custom, the Land and Titles Court, was founded to enable the central government to become involved in questions of chiefly succession. The German administration hoped to do away with the whole basis of chiefly authority, and invented the Land and Titles Court. All these things happened such a long time ago that people today see them as features which make their society unique and different from others. Thus most Tongans feel some sort of pride in their King, Samoans feel that their *fa'amatai* is what makes them a particular sort of people, and so on.

When Samoa became independent in 1962 a constitution was adopted which, it was hoped, would give us the best of Samoan and Western political institutions. It gave us two systems of legitimacy to draw on. One was the Samoan system of chiefly authority, based on the idea that titleholders would represent the interests of the extended families who gave them their titles. The other was more vaguely defined as a set of Western liberal principles such as individual rights, religious freedom, equality under law and so on. The contradictions between these two sets of principles was not really a problem in 1962 because most people lived in villages in a semi-subsistence economy, and migration and influences from the outside world had minimal impacts on most of us. Since then we have experienced changes which have made us among the most 'globalised' of people. During the 1970s and 1980s about one third of our population moved overseas, forming communities in the United States, New Zealand and Australia. In a period of 20 years we became, in effect, a nation without geographic boundaries.

Inevitably this process has had an impact on our political system because the economic impact of emigration was towards individualism. The two village censuses carried out by my wife, Dr Penelope Schoeffel, in 1976 and 1986 showed that while the population had not grown, there had been a sharp increase in the number of households. The great increase in the practice of splitting titles between multiple incumbents during this period, also reflected the break-up of families into smaller units. Prior to the elections of 1991, and following a national referendum, the government amended the Electoral Act to give universal suffrage to all people over 21 (previously only registered *matai* voted). But at the same time, in a sort of trade-off for this democratic concession, parliament voted for an extension of the parliamentary term from three to five years, and passed an act giving greater powers to village councils to enact and enforce village by-laws. These changes were accompanied by a great deal of rhetoric about the transition to democracy. They came about under a ruling party calling itself the 'The Human Rights Protection Party'.

Despite this supposed transition to a more democratic system of government, it is commonly believed that there is high-level corruption in Samoa. Until 1994, it was persistently rumoured that certain ministers and heads of departments had formed companies headed by close relatives to which they were awarding uncontested government contracts involving very large sums of public money. When a local newspaper cautiously alluded to these goings on, our Prime Minister stood up in Parliament and compared the local press to 'a lot of little stones rolling in the gutter'. We must recognise that rumour-mongering has been a popular local pastime for a long time, but these rumours were given more substance in 1994 when the Auditor General presented his report to parliament. This document gave details of massive official corruption. While nobody was surprised at the contents of his report, many were surprised and relieved that the Auditor General had found the courage to speak out. Samoa is a small country, with few senior jobs, so outspokenness is bad for one's career. In response to these revelations the Government appointed a commission of enquiry. After many months had passed, the findings of the Commission were presented in a document so strangely written that nobody could really understand its contents.

But one thing stood out. While the Commission's report vaguely acknowledged that most of the Auditor General's allegations had substance, its main finding was that he was at fault for exceeding his mandate. In short, the Auditor General was suspended from his position and, after two years, had not been reinstated. In the latest election which was held this year, the ruling Human Rights Protection Party was returned to office. Although it did not have a clear majority, it was able to persuade a number of independents to help form a government. Several parliamentarians named in the Auditor General's report have been re-elected and re-appointed to cabinet. Similarly, many of the heads of departments implicated still hold their positions.

Why has this sort of public dishonour caused so little concern in my country? I suggest that the problems are linked to the fact that we are living in two worlds, a situation which is breeding a kind of moral confusion. It is not that there are contradictions between new and old principles, but that these two sets of principles can be selectively invoked to justify our actions as it suits us. For example, our cultural principles disapprove of questioning, challenging or criticising our chiefs, and by extension our government. At the same time, we learn that in today's world, prestige and power come from the possession of money, and to obtain it we must be determined individualists.

The case of the two-storey house

The village that I grew up in has a population of between two and three hundred people. It is governed by a council of *matai* who are the holders of about 21 village titles. Some of the village titles are held by more than one person, so altogether there are about thirty *matai*. Of these, two titles are the most senior in ranking, both in the village and in the surrounding district. When I was growing up there, these two titles were each held by one person, but now both of them have been split, so there are several holders of each.

My story concerns two holders of these senior titles, Va'a and Samoa. They are both middle-aged men with adult children living away from the village in town or overseas. One has a small but not very successful store run by his wife, and until recently he earned his living as a Member of Parliament. The other is a subsistence farmer who lived for most of his life in a small *fale Samoa*, but who recently, with the help of his children overseas, built himself a small modern style house (*fale palagi*).

About two years ago these two chiefs filed a petition in the Lands and Titles Court to stop a junior chief called Solomona from completing his two-storey house which he had built beside the main road behind the village. The Lands and Titles Court, in response to the petition of the two high chiefs, sent an order notifying Solomona about the objection, and asking him to stop building the house. Solomona obeyed the order and continues to live in rooms behind his shop. After two years the court case is still pending and the house still stands half completed. It is quite common in Samoan custom for titles to carry with them certain privileges, especially if the titles are of high rank. High ranking titles usually carry special rights to be addressed in certain ways, to confer certain titles, to wear a headdress (*tuiga*) on certain occasions, to build a house in a certain location, and so on. It is not uncommon for modern versions of particular privileges to be added to titles as well. For example it is common for important titles to carry with them the right to be served tea out of a separate teapot while everyone else drinks from a common pot.

Solomona, the owner of the unfinished two-storey house, is in his late thirties and is regarded as one of the most successful businessmen in our district. Unlike most other well-off people in Samoa, he did not earn his capital by working overseas. He began about twelve years ago with a small store on his family land in the village. A few years later he took advantage of a government fisheries development project, which enabled him to buy a fishing boat. Then, assisted by his younger brothers in running the fishing boat, he built up a successful enterprise, fishing twice a day and selling the catch at the Apia market. After a year he bought a second boat and recently bought a third. With his fishing income, he extended his store, bought a truck and a small van, and also a small herd of cattle which he grazed on family coconut land. He soon dominated trading in the village, and became one of the leading traders in the district. The only other store in the village belonged to one of the high chiefs, Va'a.

Determined to expand his business, he abandoned the old store and relocated it on the main road where he was able to attract more customers from the traffic passing through the district. He also started a small banana plantation nearby, and a year later began work on his two-storey house. The land to which he relocated is regarded as *tuamaota*, referring to the fact that it is at the back of the village, and distinguishing it from the important sites round the *malae*. The site has no chiefly connotations; indeed Solomona's house is being built on the site once occupied by the village pig sty.

Solomona has always lived in the village, which is unusual since the emigration rate is very high. He went to primary, intermediate and junior high school there and then became a subsistence farmer and fisherman, gradually accumulating the means to start his businesses. He left school after Form 5. People say he is like his mother's late father, who was known in the village for his hard work and throughout the district as a master fisherman (*tautai*). Solomona's grandfather was also the first Samoan in the district to own and operate a bus, which was not only very useful for the village, but very much admired. So, in the 1960s, when Solomona's grandfather was very old, one of the previous holders of the two high titles of the village split the title he held, and bestowed the title on Solomona's grandfather. He did this to reward him for his service and achievement. However, because the old man's genealogical links to the title were somewhat tenuous, at the time this was a very controversial action. Of the two chiefs opposing Solomona's two-storey house, one came from a very well known family, but the other had acquired his high title in a manner that was just a tenuous as that of Solomona's grandfather.

There have been more dramatic cases of chiefs resisting innovation and change in their villages than my story of Solomona's two-storey house. For example in a case which occurred in Falelatai in 1986, a village entrepreneur was attacked, his business boycotted, and he was eventually expelled from the village because he disobeyed its village conventions. At one point his fellow *matai* were prepared to sentence him to an ancient punishment which involved trussing him to a pole like a pig and cooking him on the fire. Fortunately the village pastor intervened to save him. Another village entrepreneur in Fagaloa was less fortunate. He was shot dead, after which his house, store and truck were burned by village youths acting on the order of the *fono*. The man they executed defied the evening curfew for prayers required by the village, and had joined the cricket team of a rival village.

Both these cases, as I have said, involved small business operators who had accumulated the capital for their businesses from many years of working in New Zealand. They returned and tried to do things differently, challenging the rules of their villages. Typically the agents of change have been returning emigrants who have wanted to do things differently, but Solomona was different. Although his case involves the same clash between conflicting constitutional principles and customary and individual rights, Solomona never left the village. His behaviour was correct by customary principles; as a young man he worked for the village youth group, and when he got his title he became a member of the *fono*. He is a dutiful member of the church. The unconventional aspect is that he has more money and status, in the modern sense, than the high chiefs of the village. Perhaps we could say that this case illustrates an uncomfortable disjunction between class and rank.

As stated above, since the 1960s there has been an increasing trend toward economic individuality in most villages, which has been accelerated by new farming technologies which reduce labour requirements, by emigration and remittances, urbanisation and changing values, and a greater emphasis on nuclear families as distinct economic units. This has tended to weaken the solidarity of descent groups and extended families, and it has contributed to fragmentation where rival branches of families are contesting and splitting titles and the assets attached to them. Allegiance and service to chiefs has become more tokenistic as functional economic and political interdependencies have been increasingly weakened by the emergence of new economic and political institutions. At the same time, high-ranking chiefs continue to invoke traditional privilege to try to prevent those who have achieved status through the agency of the modern market economy from overshadowing them.

While important chiefs continue to demand their traditional rights and privileges, there are signs all around us in Samoa today that they are no longer willing to carry out their communal responsibilities. For example, during most of this century our villages have had a particular tradition of self-reliance, in which the village builds and maintains its own schools, and groups of villages—working through district councils of representatives—have built and maintained their own health centres. Villages even provided the food for teachers and doctors working at village levels, to supplement their salaries (although this practice was discontinued when public service salaries were increased in the early 1960s).

Although village and district leaders are still expected to organise the maintenance of public facilities, the junior high school in my district has been gradually deteriorating since the early 1970s, and about six years ago the leading chiefs of each village decided to go on a fundraising expedition to New Zealand to pay for the renovation of the school—but when the fundraising group returned no work was ever carried out. The money vanished and remains unaccounted for to this day. There are many other examples of public funds disappearing into the pockets of local leaders in similar circumstances, even where the government provides funds for public works in villages. In recent years, under the provisions that give greater powers to local village councils, the government allocated funds to each village council for the maintenance of local plantation access roads. The amount is determined by the number of roads per village, with the average grant

for each road being WS$4000. In one well known incident recently—
although this was not in my village—the village council donated
almost the entire road maintenance grant for the year to a new
conference centre being built by the Catholic church in another
district. Why? Because this village is associated with one of the
paramount chiefs of Samoa, and the paramount chief in question
asked the village council to raise a donation to be given in his name.
Rather than go to the trouble of raising the funds in the usual manner,
the village council decided to allocate most of their road maintenance
grant for the year.

My village has only one access road and it has been the practice in
recent years for the road maintenance money to be divided among the
three high ranking *ali'i* and the pastors, with far smaller amounts to
the other village *matai*. Not only is there no work done on the access
road, the purpose of which is to assist agricultural production, but the
money seems to be spent on card games, beer and food, with little (if
any) of the money reaching the youth, women and children of the
village.

The district health centre was once maintained by a consortium of
village women's committees who raised funds, took it in turns to
provide voluntary labour to help the nurses and doctor, and to weed
and clean the compound. Today the health centre is deteriorating with
minimal community support because the leading families have pick-
up trucks and are able to go to town to obtain medical care.

We hear much today about the environmental fragility of the
Pacific islands, and the problem of shoreline erosion. This has always
been a problem in my village, and in the past each household
prevented erosion of the sea on the foreshore near their houses, by
collecting large rocks and constructing breakwaters. However today it
is left to the central government to address this problem, and the
central government takes the problem to international aid donors. The
high ranking chiefs try to get the government to pay for a sea wall
with aid to stop erosion, but families did this themselves in the old
days.

What I find interesting—and sad—about the leadership decline
that I have been talking about is how cynical rural people have
become. One way in which people have responded is to become more
individualistic, but individualism only works well for those who are
reasonably prosperous. Families with few material possessions were
major beneficiaries of community provision of services in the past and

it is obvious that the gap between the haves and the have-nots is increasing in rural areas as well as in town. Village *matai* control the churches of Samoa as well as local government, and have the power to fine people who show their cynicism by not attending church. While the Village Fono Act of 1991 was heralded as a move to reinforce and strengthen rural self reliance, it has in fact formalised the power of *matai* and local hierarchies. The Act allows *matai* to force compliance with their dictates through the means of fines or even expulsion from the village. Increasingly rural people see *fa'asamoa* as another word for oppression.

Conclusion

My story of Solomona and his two-storey house is a parable of the situation in contemporary Samoa. It illustrates my contention that the political rhetoric about rural development and self-reliance which accompanied the introduction of universal suffrage in 1991 has little substance. These changes have in fact disguised the potential for the abuse of chiefly power. Although we may now elect our Parliament, the *matai* who run the country have given themselves a five year term of office, and increased powers at village level. There are few checks on the abuse of rank privilege, which allow leaders to invoke their rank privileges to suppress dissent or competition.

I do not accept that this has always been a feature of our political system. My earlier example of Solomona's grandfather was just one of many that I can give to show how achievement was recognised and rewarded. I think what is occurring is symptomatic of a moral vacuum which has arisen among a people who are trying to live in two worlds. We have two concurrent sets of social and political values, either of which may be appealed to as it suits us.

In Western Polynesia, we are no longer small nations of people belonging to a few small islands. Today we are nations of people without borders. We extend, as Hau'ofa has pointed out, across seas; operating, as Bertam and Watters (1985:511) have put it, as transnational corporations of kin. We now draw unconscious distinctions between society and the state. People are both citizens of the state and members of society, but the rules of being a citizen and a member of society are not always the same. Take the case of the two chiefs in my story. They were attempting to defend traditional principles of society and the rank order of their village, even though, paradoxically, they were appealing to an agency of the state, in the form of the Lands and Titles Court. However, Solomona might equally well appeal to the state to uphold his rights as a citizen and his rights as an individual to build the house of his choice. The outcome of my story is still not known.

The idea of the state, of the common good on a national scale, was introduced at independence. Before that, the state was seen as the possession of the colonial power. Government was what they controlled, and families and villages were what we controlled. Before we had time to develop a consensus about what it was to be a citizen, as distinct to being the member of an extended family or a village polity, there was mass emigration. This led to the further objectification, for want of a better word, of Samoan-ness, to defend against outsiders. Emigration increased this process as we formed little islands of Samoan-ness in seas of *palagi* society around the world. Thus the petition of the two chiefs against Solomona's house is based on the convention that no one in the village—other than the holders of its paramount titles—may build a two-storey house. Since none of the high chiefs had ever owned a two-storey house, in effect the rule is that no one in the village of lower rank may build a house of greater height than the houses of its high chiefs. Two-storey houses of course are not 'traditional' but they have been common in Samoa for the past century and are generally seen as being more prestigious than one-storey houses. In the past, Samoan houses displayed the rank of the occupant by the number if tiers (or the height) of the stone foundations (*paepae*) on which the house was built. Therefore the modern status equivalent to a house built on a high foundation would be a two-storey house, and thus this indicator of rank was reserved for the high chiefs of the village. Local by-laws to protect the dignity of the high chiefs are quite common. For example, in my mother's village in the 1970s, only chiefs were allowed to use umbrellas, carry brief cases, or to use fans in church.

In the case of Solomona's two-storey house, the village council of *matai*, the *fono*, did not take action against him. It could have ordered him to stop building his house, or it could have fined him, as is usually done when someone breaks a village convention. It was noteworthy that the two high chiefs did not appeal to the *fono*, but took their case against Solomona to the Land and Titles Court themselves and in so doing they were shifting the grounds for complaint. If Solomona was in breach of local convention, then the matter should have been for the *fono* to adjudicate, but by taking the case to the Land and Titles Court, the two high chiefs were, in effect, asserting that the building of a two-storey house is a traditional perquisite attached to the defence of those elements of culture that have come to be seen as a virtue. The questioning of them is seen to be an attack on our integrity as a people. For those of us who live in Samoa, this has retarded the evolution of a sense of citizenship, with the ill-effects on governance that I have discussed previously.

References

Bertram, I.G. and Watters, R.F., 1985. 'The MIRAB economy in South Pacific microstates', *Pacific Viewpoint*, 26(3):497–519.

Cole, R. (ed.), 1993. *Pacific 2010: challenging the future*, National Centre for Development Studies, The Australian National University, Canberra.

Huntington, S.P., 1997. *The Clash of Cultures and the Restructuring of the World Order*, Simon and Schuster, New York.

Lawson, S., 1996. *Tradition Versus Democracy in the South Pacific: Fiji, Tonga and Western Samoa*, Cambridge University Press, Cambridge.

World Bank, 1993. *Pacific Island Economies: toward efficient and sustainable growth*, World Bank, Washington DC.

6

Rumble in the jungle: land, culture and (un)sustainable logging in Solomon Islands

Tarcisius Tara Kabutaulaka

As a landowner from Malaita gulped down the *Solbrew* to quench his thirst, with a sigh of relief he made it clear where the money came from to finance his favourite pastime: *Lif blong akwa nomoa tok* (it's the leaf of the *akwa* tree that talks). In another incident, a Guadalcanal man who went on a drinking spree with his son told him: *Inu ko inu dalequ, inau a lani ona* (drink, drink my son, I'm a landowner). I recount these incidents not because there is any particular connection between logging in Solomon Islands and the beer company *Solbrew*. Rather, the statements demonstrate the ties between land, forest resources, landowners and the kinship bond between people. It signifies the power landowners have, or at least think they have, over resources such as forest.

I have chosen alcohol and drinking—a substance and an activity which are normally found far from rain forests, logging trucks and chainsaws—as the starting point around which to build my exploration of the relationship between land, culture and logging. It illustrates that in the process of resource exploitation and increasing commercialisation, there is also a process of cultural construction and deconstruction taking place. The eventual product is a hybrid culture which has a profound impact on the issue of sustainable forest management. In this case, the beer shifts from the bar and home to the forest. In some instances, the alcohol becomes the commodity around which the logging industry revolves—it dictates the nature of logging negotiations, state policies, and the relationship between landowners and the different stakeholders in the forest industry. This affects sustainability. It is when this happens that the rumble in the jungle begins.

Sustainable logging in Solomon Islands has been difficult, not only because of poor state policies, but also because (i) the land tenure system, and (ii) the logging industry, produce a culture characterised by the rapid monetisation of certain sectors of society, increasing corruption at the political level, and the emergence of a new élite group in the villages. This new élite group is nearly always financed by logging money and backed by logging companies.

Logging and cultural production

An old man from Guadalcanal once said to me: *logging hemi spoelem ples en kastom blong iumi* 'logging spoils our place and custom'. Implicit in this statement is the conception of culture, not only as rules, norms or customs that regulate society, but also as the social and physical environment around which culture is produced and sustained through time. The forest, therefore, is not just an economic commodity with the potential of generating monetary income. Rather, it is part of the physical and social existence of society.

Antony Hooper, in discussing the sociocultural aspects of development in the South Pacific, defines culture as 'the body of shared understandings in terms of which social interactions take place' (1993:315). Culture also includes the means by which shared understandings are produced and sustained through time. Tradition, on the other hand, is used here to refer to a model of a past way of life. It does not imply something which has existed unchanged since contact with the outside world, even though it is sometimes represented as being unchanging. Rather, the term is used here to refer to the sets of social behaviour and 'ways of doing things' that have emerged, and continue to have a connection to the past. According to Erchak, 'culture is shared symbolic knowledge which people draw on as they make their way through life. It provides its bearers pathways to a satisfying life—or at least survival' (1992:3). This is a useful definition when discussing the impact of large-scale resource exploitation on society, and the production of a hybrid culture which often has a significant impact on both the industry and society. In nearly all large-scale resource development projects such as mining, forest and fisheries, there are usually a number of stakeholders involved. Often, the most dominant are the state, multinational companies, landowners, non-government organisations, politicians, and local entrepreneurs. These stakeholders usually have different interests in participating in an industry such as forestry. Each stakeholder attempts to maximise its monetary benefit from the resource at stake. In such a situation, 'the body of shared understandings' is usually embodied in the contract signed between the stakeholders. This contract is, in nearly every case, surrounded by a culture of intense competition between stakeholders which often is subsequently accepted as the norm.

Logging in Solomon Islands: a background

In the past ten years, logging in Solomon Islands has attracted considerable debate, both nationally and internationally. The discussions have centred around (i) the unsustainable rate of log harvests; (ii) the country's increasing economic dependence on log exports; and (iii) allegations of corruption—especially in relation to politicians and public officers receiving bribes from logging companies.

Large-scale commercial logging started in Solomon Islands over thirty years ago. From 1963 to the early 1980s most logging took place on government land or customary land leased by the government, and the industry was then monopolised by Levers Pacific Timber, which accounted for around 75 per cent of log production. However, from the early 1980s there was a shift from government land to customary land (which makes up around 87 per cent of the total land area in the country). This period was also characterised by an influx of logging industry multinationals, mostly from Southeast Asia. During the period from 1981 to 1983, the number of logging licences given to foreign companies increased fourfold (Fraser 1997:41). This sets to rest the argument that communally-owned land or customary land is less likely to guarantee security of access, and therefore less likely to attract foreign investors. The fact that foreign logging companies swamped Solomon Islands at a time when logging was mostly on customary land is an indication that they have established a means of acquiring 'security of access' and maintaining it for a period long enough for them to accumulate substantial profit.

The increase in the number of logging licenses issued to foreign companies resulted in a rapid increase in log production, and by 1981 it had gone beyond sustainable levels (Fraser 1997:42; Montgomery 1995:75). By the mid l990s timber was being exploited at a rate that significantly exceeded the potential sustainable yield, which in 1995 was about 325,000 cubic metres per year (Solomon Islands Government 1995). Log exports in 1994 and 1995, for example, were 659,000 and 748,500 cubic metres respectively (Central Bank of Solomon Islands 1996:16). This was more than double the potential sustainable yield at that time. Consequently, it has been estimated that if current levels of log production continue, commercial trees may be depleted in less than a decade (Fraser 1997:51; Dauvergne 1997:6).

The increasing log production was exacerbated by the fact that by the beginning of the l990s Solomon Islands had become economically almost entirely dependent on logging. In 1990, for example, timber contributed 34.5 per cent of the country's total exports. This increased to 54.9 per cent in 1993. In 1994, it contributed 56 per cent of the country's export revenue and 31 per cent of all government revenues (Montgomery 1995; Fraser 1997). In 1995 it made up for 49.4 per cent of principal exports (Central Bank of Solomon Islands 1996:16).

Furthermore, insufficient finance, and the lack of technical and human resources to monitor logging operations has meant that it is difficult to implement state forest policies, and in particular environmental rules. Consequently, many multinationals in the industry break the regulations and get away with it. The Solomon Islands Division of Inland Revenue, for example, does not have the financial, technical and manpower capability to prevent or counteract corporate schemes to evade taxes (Price Waterhouse 1995:78). Dauvergne also noted that structural defects in Solomon Islands' forest management policies have enabled 'multinational investors to operate with remarkably poor harvesting and environmental standards, and make windfall profits' (1997:8). The problem was further exacerbated by the withdrawal in 1996 of the AusAID-funded Timber Control Unit. This unit, set up to monitor logging operations and the activities of corporate powers, had its funding withdrawn after relations between the Solomon Mamaloni-led government and the Australian government went sour (*Solomon Star,* 2 April 1996). This means that Solomon Islands lost out on millions of dollars worth of potential income from forestry. Further potential income was lost because of government policy to exempt some logging companies from paying export tax. In 1994 it was estimated that SI$34 million was lost through the government's decision to exempt some logging companies from paying export tax (Duncan 1994:10). This was particularly the case for 'locally owned' companies such as the Prime Minister's own Somma Ltd. Also, under-reporting of log volumes is estimated to have cost Solomon Islands SI$96 million in revenues evaded and foregone in 1993 (Duncan 1994:16). It is these situations in the forest industry that have raised widespread alarm both locally and internationally. However, so far, the campaign to slow down the rate of logging has been unsuccessful. Unsustainable logging continues unabated.

Hence, one is confronted with the questions (i) why is it that the unsustainable logging continues unabated despite evidence of its negative environmental, social and economic impact on Solomon Islands? and (ii) what is/are the solution(s)? So far, most literature on logging in Solomon Islands is either historical (Bennett 1995), or focuses on discussing forest as an economic commodity (Duncan 1994; Montgomery 1995). This is not surprising given that the logging industry was indeed viewed by the state and others as a resource of economic value to the country. However, the problem with such an emphasis on the economics of forestry is that often it fails to acknowledge the social factors that influence people's decisions. It is, therefore, necessary to discuss (i) the impact of land tenure on sustainable forest management and (ii) how social organisations affect decision-making on logging.

Land tenure and logging

Ballard, in discussing the moral economy of resource ownership in Papua New Guinea states that

> ...for those of us for whom ties to land consist of casual contacts with small and often infrequently tended suburban gardens, one of the more difficult exercises in imagination is to conceive of the relationship between rural communities and the lands and the resources that they consider theirs (1997:47).

Often this is also a problem for policymakers for whom land and the resources on it are primarily economic commodities—to bring in much needed monetary income for state wealth—and only secondarily as part of an environment around which a society constructs its culture and lives its life.

In Solomon Islands land-based resource developments such as logging and mining are usually influenced by a land tenure system where about 87 per cent of the land is owned according to custom, leaving only about nine per cent to government ownership and the rest to individual Solomon Islanders. Only two per cent of the land is leased to foreigners. However, what is important to consider in the relationship between logging and land tenure is the nature of the politics of land ownership, the interactions within and between landowning groups that has affected, and been affected by, the logging industry.

Today, logging and land disputes are interrelated. Many logging companies come to Solomon Islands from Southeast Asia, especially from Indonesia and Malaysia where the state owns the land. Hence, they find it much easier to deal with the state or individuals rather than the tribe or clan. Consequently, they create individual landowners. On the island of Rendova, in the Western Province, for example, I found an individual who had left a job in the public service to become a full-time 'landowner' because, with logging companies around, it is a much more financially lucrative profession. In such a situation, the tribe is usually marginalised and denied access to the wealth accumulated through logging.

There are also cases where the state has found itself at the centre of land disputes. A classic example is the case of Pavuvu in the Russell Islands in the Central Province. Here, the British colonial government in 1905 leased Pavuvu Island to Levers Pacific Plantations. The original owners of the island, the Lavukal people of the Russell Islands had, for many years, demanded that the island be restored to them. However, their demands were ignored (Rose 1995:10). On 10 March 1995, the executive of Central Province granted Marving Brothers, a Malaysian registered logging company, a business license that allowed the central government to issue a logging permit for Pavuvu Island. The island's forest was worth about US$120 million (Roughan 1997:160). The Lavukal people, assisted by non-government organisations such as the Solomon Islands Development Trust (SIDT), Soltrust, Greenpeace and Development Services Exchange (DSE) resisted the logging of Pavuvu. Company machines were sabotaged and workers were threatened. However, the central government sent in police officers to protect the company that is currently still logging on 'government land' (Roughan 1997; Tuhanuku 1995). Today, Pavuvu Island is still at the centre of intense confrontation between landowners, the central government, Central Province and Marving Brothers. In November 1995, Martin Apa, a Russell Island anti-logging campaigner, was murdered. So far police investigations have failed to find his killers although many suspect that the murder was connected to the Pavuvu Island logging issue.

This is only one example of land and boundaries disputes over that are now common throughout Solomon Islands, and particularly in areas where there are large-scale resource developments such as logging, mining, and plantation development. There's a need to take landowners and traditional land tenure systems seriously when planning national development programs. The large percentage of customary control of land also has implications for the state's capacity to manage land-based resource developments. One of the major arguments in the logging industry is that the government in reality does not have control over landowners' decisions to exploit the forest resource in the way they wish. In the case of the forestry industry, first, it signifies the fact that in Solomon Islands the state is weak in comparison to civil society (Kabutaulaka and Dauvergne 1997). The state does not possess the kind of power and authority over society that one would find in, for example, the hierarchical chiefly system of Tonga. Second, the nature of current logging practices in Solomon Islands indicates that 'people's' control over resources does not necessarily mean that it will be well managed. In fact, the case of forestry in Solomon Islands proves the opposite.

Another factor that characterises the relationship between logging and land tenure is the alienation of women, not only as land users, but as custodians of land. In the matrilineal societies of Guadalcanal, Ysabel and Roviana (on New Georgia island) women traditionally had authority as custodians of land. However, throughout Solomon Islands I have not yet found a logging agreement in which women have been included as signatories. This is because men have always been promoted as landowners and income earners.

Logging and a political culture

In Solomon Islands, logging has given rise to a political culture often characterised by the increasing participation of state leaders in the forest industry, and the adoption by state leaders of a double identity, as state leaders and landowners—a kind of schizophrenic professional commitment. The most well known of these state leaders was the former Prime Minister who owns a logging company, Somma Ltd. His company also enjoys a 100 per cent export tax exemption on round log exports. It is interesting that in August 1998, when I asked the then

Finance Minister why he awarded a tax exemption to the Prime Minister, he replied that he did not give it to the Prime Minister, but to a landowner.

Corruption has also been widespread in the logging industry, from the village level to the highest offices of the state. In November 1995, five government ministers were alleged to have received SI$7 million in bribery money from a logging company and this has resulted in court proceedings which are currently under way (*Solomon Star*, 19 November 1995). In another case, two government ministers were charged with receiving favours from Marving Brothers, the logging company involved in the controversial Pavuvu logging disputes. In 1995, a local newspaper, the *Solomon Star*, reported that an accountancy firm had uncovered an internal report that a Malaysian company had paid SI$17 million to government ministers and officials, and named the then Minister for Commerce, Employment and Trade, the Minister for Finance and the Minister for Home Affairs, as well as the former secretary to the Foreign Investment Board (*Pacific Report* 8(21) November 20, 1995). The Ombudsman cited the funding of election expenses by timber companies and evidence that members of Area Councils deciding on applications from logging companies were given 'Negotiation Fees', employment and hotel stays when in Honiara (Solomon Islands 1989:10–11). There is also increasing concern over the distribution of logging revenues and whether it has contributed to socioeconomic development in the country.

Corruption in the forest industry has become a major concern in Solomon Islands today. The concern centres around the fact that corruption may become the culture of the forest industry. There are fears that we may reach a situation where we can no longer talk about getting rid of corruption from the system because it may become the system.

For politicians, what is regarded as corruption in the conventional sense is, in fact, the essence of survival. In a society where a Bigman's wealth is measured, not so much in what he accumulates as in what he distributes, it is important that a Bigman finds a means of acquiring wealth for distribution. Logging provides that means. A politician needs the logging money in order to stay in power. This is because of the nature of patron/client relationships that characterise our traditional culture—a norm that has suddenly been labelled as corruption. Wealth accumulated and kept.

Conclusion

What is obvious from the case of logging in Solomon Islands is that in large-scale resource exploitation there is a continuous process of cultural construction and deconstruction. These have an important impact on sustainable forest management—the ability to maintain the forest's capacity to produce timber at a specified rate. The concern is the maintenance of sufficient stocks to last for a defined period of time. It is conspicuous that in order to address the issue of sustainable forest management, there is a need to be aware of the sociocultural factors that influence decisions on forest development. For now, the rumbles in our jungles continue.

References

Ballard, C., 1997. 'It's the land stupid!: the moral economy of resource ownership in Papua New Guinea', in P. Lamour (ed.), *The Governance of Common Property in the Pacific Region,* National Centre for Development Studies and Resource Management in Asia-Pacific, Research School of Pacific and Asian Studies, The Australian National University, Canberra:47–65.

Bennett, J., 1995, 'Forestry, public land and the colonial legacy in Solomon Islands', *The Contemporary Pacific,* 7(2):243–75.

Central Bank of Solomon Islands, 1996. *1995 Annual Report,* Central Bank of Solomon Islands, Honiara.

Dauvergne, P., 1997. *Corporate Power in the Forests of the Solomon Islands,* Working Paper 1997/6, Department of International Relations, Research School of Pacific and Asian Studies, The Australian National University, Canberra.

Duncan, R.C., 1994. *Melanesian Forestry Sector Study,* International Development Issues No.36, Australian International Development Assistance Bureau, Canberra.

Erchak, G.M., 1992. *The Anthropology of Self and Behaviour,* Rutgers University Press, New Jersey.

Fraser, I., 1997. 'The struggle for control of Solomon Island forests', *The Contemporary Pacific,* 9(1):39–72.

Hooper, A., 1993. 'Socio-cultural aspects of development in the South Pacific', in R.V. Cole and S. Tambunlertchai (eds), *The Future of Asia-Pacific Economies: Pacific islands at the crossroads?* Asian and Pacific Development Centre and National Centre for Development Studies, The Australian National University, Canberra:314–42.

Kabutaulaka, T.T. and Dauvergne, P., 1997. 'The weak state in Solomon Islands', paper presented at the workshop entitled Weak and Strong States in Melanesia and Southeast Asia, 12–14 August, 1997, Research School of Pacific and Asian Studies, The Australian National University, Canberra.

Migdal, J., 1988. *Strong Societies and Weak States: state-society relations and state capabilities in the third world*, Princeton University Press, Princeton.

Montgomery, P., 1995. 'Forestry in Solomon Islands', *Pacific Economic Bulletin*, 10(2):74–76.

Price Waterhouse, 1995. *Forestry, Taxation, and Domestic Processing Study*, Consultancy Report for the Solomon Islands Government, Ministry of Finance and the Ministry of Forests, Environment and Conservation.

Rose, A., 1995. *Petition of the Lavakal People to the Solomon Islands Government*, Privately published, Honiara.

Roughan, J., 1997. 'Solomon Islands nongovernment organizations: major environmental actors', *The Contemporary Pacific*, 9(1):157–166.

Solomon Islands Government, 1995. *Forest Review*, Ministry of Forests, Environment and Conservation, Honiara.

Tuhanuku, J., 1995. *Report of the Opposition Delegation Mission to Pavuvu*, Office of the Leader of the Opposition, Honiara.

7

Knowing about culture: the handling of social issues at resource projects in Papua New Guinea

John Burton

Ethnography is a controversial activity when applied to development issues, notably the 'mineral policy process' in Papua New Guinea. This chapter concerns the kind of development where huge investments are involved—the Papua New Guinea minerals sector has been worth K2.2–2.4 billion in the last few years. The minimal view presented is that investors with hundreds of millions of kina to risk should adopt the precautionary principle of doing the best social impact appraisals they can, and continue to evaluate their own performance in relation to social issues and impact for the length of the mining projects. This is a minimal view: hopefully developers would wish to do considerably more than this and have corporate policies placing culturally appropriate management techniques in a more central position, but it is not necessary to my argument.

Within the mining industry, the kinds of skills and knowledge to handle social issues have been referred to as the 'new competencies' of mining, the 'soft skills that are, in fact, hard skills' as a landmark speech from the chairman of CRA described them (Davis 1995). At the level of executive corporate policy statements, other major resource companies echo this sentiment, with frequent reference to the concept of 'world's best practice in environmental care'.

The importance of sociocultural research is that in this narrow context, using suitably appropriate ethnographic techniques and inventing new ones where necessary can avoid risk for both investors and local communities. A loftier ambition is to head off more serious political crisis, such as occurred in Bougainville and more recently at Ok Tedi. Unfortunately, attainment of the 'new competencies' leaves much to be desired.

Mine impact studies in Papua New Guinea after Bougainville

In September 1989 at a Bougainville crisis workshop held at the University of Papua New Guinea, I commented that little research into the land and social organisational matters that sparked the Bougainville crisis was carried out prior to the opening of the mine, and no studies were done afterwards. Further, sustained fieldwork-intensive studies were not being carried out in any of the new mining areas. I called for a reprioritisation of funding arrangements for applied social research in Papua New Guinea (Burton 1989).

Nothing meaningful eventuated from the workshop, although many prominent Bougainvilleans attended, including the now rebel-aligned Premier Joseph Kabui. It was also ironic that institutional research funds were cut to nothing in the following budget year as part of the government's austerity measures.

A turning-point for mine impact studies in 1989 was a seminar given at the University of Papua New Guinea (UPNG) by Stuart Kirsch, a doctoral student in anthropology then returning from a long stay among the Yonggom people. Kirsch was able to detail at first hand the issues which were, five years later, to lead a group of Yonggom spokesmen to instigate law-suits in the Supreme Court of Victoria, in Melbourne, seeking reparations of A$4 billion for environmental damage. The seminar and its subsequent publication, notably in the *Times of Papua New Guinea* under the headline 'Ok Tedi a sewer' (Kirsch 1989a; 1989b), was treated by the mine operators and government officials as nuisance academic commentary. Photocopies of Kirsch's second article, published a little later in *Research in Melanesia*, circulated among the mining management in Tabubil and Port Moresby during 1990 and 1991, at the same time as the Papua

New Guinea government approved the Sixth Supplemental Agreement at Ok Tedi, which allowed, after three years of environmental studies, the permanent discharge of mine wastes into the Ok Tedi and Fly River systems.

In respect of Ok Tedi, a decade earlier, Richard Jackson (and his student Budai Tapari), were seconded to Papua New Guinea's National Planning Office for six months to do a planning study of the North Fly area, where the mine was then being negotiated. However, after the mine opened Jackson was only able to find a few thousand dollars for follow-up studies, and monitoring of the social environment ceased in 1984. Throughout the 1980s, starved of institutional funds, with intermittent international grants, and with a weak ability to market its expertise, mine monitoring work from the University of Papua New Guinea was limited to the environmental investigations in water bodies off the Fly River more than 250km from the mine site (Pernetta 1988).

Ok Tedi

From about 1990, consultancy work at UPNG received much stronger support from an administration keen to bring income to the university. A new program of company-sponsored social monitoring studies began in mid 1991 at Ok Tedi, focusing on the downstream communities, including those in the Lower Ok Tedi where Yonggom and Awin villagers were taking the brunt of environmental problems after the signing of the Sixth Supplemental Agreement.

The Alice villagers lodged writs in Australia in 1994 and, after two years of legal argument costing an estimated A$20 million, secured an out-of-court settlement with the company comprising various compensation packages worth about A$100 million to the year 2010. The company is committed to a river dredging trial costing A$60 million to the end of 1998 and will adopt further clean-up schemes after this, costed at a further several hundred million dollars.

How then should the spectacular success of the plaintiffs in the law suit be seen? First, it is worth bearing in mind that the litigation could not have been launched in the absence of a law firm prepared to carry its expenses until a settlement had been reached, and to write them off if it lost. The assistance of international NGOs, for example in extending invitations to meetings in Holland, Germany and Canada, was extremely important in helping the two principal actors, Rex Dagi and Alex Maun, reshape and express their ideas in the forms that would be most efficacious in attracting and keeping hold of international attention.

Nevertheless, the key may be that much of their success was due, not to the surmounting of traditional culture—for example, to form wider, stronger neighbourhood alliances or to make use of modern legal tactics—but from its use of traditional culture to resist being suborned by partisan political power and the intense pressure brought to bear on them by their adversaries. At the height of the crisis, for example, the national government passed the Prevention of Foreign Legal Proceedings Act just to outlaw the efforts of Dagi, Maun, and their less well-known associates Moses Oti and Robin Mokin, to seek redress in the courts. Kirsch reveals that the four were members of the same *kaget won*, or initiation cohort, some twenty years ago, and thus were not susceptible to wavering or division. This was not true of the interest block formed by the affected Alice villages in the course of the political process; a split emerged during the crisis between the east bank Awins and the west bank Yonggoms led by Dagi and Maun. Nor was there ever a rapprochement between the downstream Alice people and the Faiwol and Wopkaimin mine-lease landowners of the Star Mountains, who watched the litigation crisis with only the concern of rentiers concerned that their source of income would be cut off were the mine to close.

How did our social monitoring reports fit in? Could it be that we were instrumental in effecting a turnabout in the handling of the downstream landowners and of compensation claims along the Alice? An internal company document *Strategic Plan—Social Issues* dating from late 1992 attempted to rank risks to the company's operations mentioned our program in the following terms: 'The impact of development on the social structure of the people in the region is currently under study by anthropologists. Ranking—problems arising from the introduction of the new cultures are viewed as presenting a *relatively low long-term threat to Ok Tedi* [my emphasis]'.

Unfortunately, the rather quaint thought that we were studying the 'impact of development on the social structure of the people' failed to reflect the content of our (or anyone else's) reports. It is not surprising that a low risk assessment was made, given that the organisation lacked the ability to process messages carrying tell-tale warning signs that may have been received from time to time, either from our specialist reports or from the company's own field officers. A case in point is my re-discovery in 1997 of internal documents showing that a junior staffer had visited the Yonggom village of Dome in late 1988 and had reported to his superiors in detail the petition that later became the basis of the 1994 writs. His report was 'lost' to management by becoming buried in internal departmental files.

The signs that we and the key decision-makers did not share the same language and were not able to communicate properly were the least of our worries. We came to realise that one section of company management had hired us to stir another section—asleep at the helm in spite of Bougainville—into action. The first of our results, showing the seriousness of damage to land, crops and bush resources—and the extremely high risk of procrastination—appeared three years before the lawsuit started. Unfortunately, all twelve of our reports were denied to the company's Community Relations officers from 1991 to 1996 highlighting our overall ineffectiveness. Our creation of knowledge at the behest of the company was politically neutralised by forces within the company that were beyond our reach.

Misconceptions which were beyond our ability to control also sprang up. I remember a question from a senior official asking whether or not enquiries at village level provoked the political activism we were hired to assess and advise the company on. It seemed a common conviction. Logically it betrayed a raft of ill-articulated beliefs (a) that villagers possessed no independent powers of observation (b) that ethnographers are fumbling naifs easily misled by tricksters or, alternatively (c) that they have amazing superpowers enabling them to 'plant' misleading information on gullible villagers.

The mining industry was willing to spend money on monitoring of the physical environment but unable to understand and draw up policies for the social environment. In Ok Tedi's case, company expenditure on environmental monitoring in the decade after the opening of the mine amounted to over K50 million, but barely K0.5 million on social monitoring. This amounts to a spending ratio of about 100:1.

Despite this, some basic answers about the workings of the river system were not forthcoming from the scientific program. Two key examples were its inability to explain the unrelenting decline of fish biomass in the river system, below levels predicted in the studies used by government to authorise riverine tailings discharge; and the faulty computer models that led to the assertion that sediment build-up in the Middle Fly would be negligible, also taken into account in the government's decision. In the latter case, villagers were adamant in 1994 that the build-up of mine wastes was blocking their canoe passages and lagoon entrances. They were right; a re-study published in 1996 finally showed 2 metres of river bed aggradation, now modelled to rise to 3.5–4.5 metres in future years.

Porgera

At Porgera, in the Papua New Guinea highlands, an unprecedented level of economic benefits has flowed to the community: housing for over 500 families, about K60 million in business contracts, about K30 million in compensation for land clearance, and sundry other benefits, including mine employment for about eight hundred (Banks 1997). At the same time staff deployed in community relations functions has grown to about 85 people across the Enga Province, a far greater number than had ever been used in any other resource project in the country (Bonnell 1994:112).

The Porgerans invented what is termed the 'Development Forum': a series of round-table meetings in which the would-be developers, in this case Placer, and the various levels of government respond to a position paper presented by landowner representatives. The invention of the Forum reflects a substantially greater level of activism on the part of Porgera leaders; unlike the Faiwol, Awin and Yonggom, their society supplies a political style of leadership.

The other side of the story is the question of who has received this substantial income and what problems of distribution, so notorious in contributing to the cause of the Bougainville crisis have arisen (Filer 1990). I recently reviewed the ways in which company management at Porgera has sought to acquire knowledge about the social impact on the Ipili, the ethnic group surrounding the mine at Porgera (Burton n.d.). The Environmental Management and Monitoring Plan (EMMP), an essential part of the documentation required for mine approvals, noted the establishment of a socioeconomic liaison committee in 1991 (Porgera Joint Venture 1991:para 8.13). However, two years elapsed before this committee held a meeting, chaired by an official of the Department of the Environment and Conservation, the relevant government regulatory body. This meeting set my colleagues and I the task of writing a plan for what was termed the 'Porgera Social Monitoring Program', completed in June 1993 (Burton *et al.* 1993).

Since our document was laboriously put together by consulting with the other parties to the committee and building from earlier documents that had dealt with similar issues, it was unlikely to have been technically defective. At least, no other party responded by saying so, however—no other party responded at all! The state regulator proved incapable of effective comment because of the conflict of interest arising from the government's financial involvement in mining (Bonnell 1994:118).

A series of monitoring reports was produced over an eighteen month period in 1993–94 (for example, Banks 1994; Bonnell 1994), but the program lapsed thereafter.

Two conclusions are notable here. The first is that although the company had a large community relations staff, only a handful were in managerial positions and perhaps only two or three incumbents held tertiary qualifications, none at higher than bachelor degree or diploma level. Outside Porgera, in particular, the numbers are made up of assistants with a typical Grade 6–10 education. This means that their ability to make basic investigations at community level was extremely limited; even if information were collected, no member of staff had the time to analyse it or to write policy documents of greater-than-memo length.

The second conclusion is that the patterns of secondary distribution and investment of compensation money remain unknown, as systematic research to find this out has not been done. There are grounds for suspecting the compensation passed from the company to the community without sufficient measures to protect the latter's weaker members, such as women, infants, the aged, the children of single mothers, and people absent during assessments, such as those working outside the province. Documentation for a payment of K100,880 for clearance of an eight hectare land block shows members of a family received amounts ranging from K25,220 down to K140 (Department of Enga 1992). The beneficiary of the smallest amount, an infant, received 1/180th of the recipient of the greatest amount, a senior man. Does this mean that of the land compensated for, in adulthood the infant will be satisfied with only 1/180th of its inheritance? No, such a thing is ridiculous. Both company and provincial lands officers declined to use available legislation, such as the Land Groups Incorporation Act, to maximise fairness and accountability in decision-making over the pay-outs.

Even if suspicions of this nature are waved away, since the Porgera mine entered production in 1990, annual compliance reports for the Department of Environment and Conservation, mandatory under government guidelines, have not been submitted in respect of social impacts. Even if the activity reports of 1993 and 1994 count as compliance, this still leaves five years out of seven, 1990–96, with none submitted. If the Department of Environment and Conservation never asks for such reports, forgets to ask for them, or cannot read them if they are provided, the principle of best practice insists that a modern company acts as if it does. There is no excuse for failing in this; equally seriously, shareholders should be alarmed when any company fails to make a proper account of its activities to them. My full arguments run to some length, but assert that the company has blindfolded itself by failing to collect the kinds of knowledge that it requires to head off a serious crisis, a repetition of Ok Tedi's example.

Lihir

The Lihir mine in the New Ireland Province began production in 1997. In this case the current operator, Rio Tinto, adopted the objectively 'worst practice' of buying the prospect from another company, Kennecott, complete with a time-expired social impact study—and did not update it or attend to the limitations pointed out at the time.

> [Our report is limited by] the absence of any substantial documentation of Lihir society by anthropologists or other writers who have spent long periods of time there...research conducted on a 'fly-in-fly-out' basis can only produce particular kinds of information, and cannot do more than scratch the surface of village society (Filer and Jackson 1989:2).

A social impact review was finally ordered by the Australian government's Export Finance Insurance Corporation (EFIC) as a condition of loan guarantees—but the review was confidential to EFIC, an unacceptable practice in our field. In the 50 page summary *'Environmental Plan'* (EP), the social environment is dealt with in just three paragraphs.

Lihir landowners bettered their Porgeran brethren with still more generous compensation and royalty provisions, 12.35 per cent equity in Lihir Gold which may eventually be worth a couple of hundred million dollars, and a seat on the board.

In Australia, political conservatives claim uncertainty over native title poses a threat to the development of resources. At Lihir a preliminary understanding to proceed with mining was signed in 1984. It established the ownership of different clans of the approximately 600 hectares between the two principal creeks of the Luise Caldera. By 1995 when final approvals were granted, a little over half of the area changed hands following rulings in the Provincial Lands Court or was subject to ongoing litigation between customary owners. This is a clear example of 'uncertainty over native title'. When Lihir Gold was floated on the Sydney Stock Exchange in mid-year, it was not thought significant to mention this in the share prospectus, a serious non-disclosure.

The compensation and royalty provisions are generous, but insufficient measures have been taken to give a correspondingly greater level of accountability to their distribution. I have no doubt at all that complaints based on this will emerge in Lihir in years to come.

Conclusions

While my colleagues and I have certainly been able to generate a lot more information in the 1990s than in the 1980s, we have not been capable of prompting lasting reform within the corporations. In each instance, the companies are industry leaders—BHP, Placer and Rio Tinto—and each espouses best practice principles at the level of boardroom. At the 'coalface', that is to say at the middle management levels where their organisations interact with the village societies hosting their projects, these ideals are discarded and a reversion to type occurs.

What is this 'type'? I recently described what I called the 'discovery' paradigm, a package of concepts validating the enterprises of geological exploration and mining in—using the paradigm's own words—'remote' areas of the world (Burton 1997). The mission statement for the discovery paradigm, was Forbes Wilson's 1981 book *The Conquest of Copper Mountain*, about the discovery of the Freeport mine in Irian Jaya. Wilson described the overcoming of apparently insurmountable physical obstacles in 'the mountainous interior of the world's most trackless wilderness' (Wilson 1981:10). An additive is the cliché 'remote', still making almost daily appearances in mining-related literature on Papua New Guinea and seen in press reports such as 'the Ok Tedi project, on a mountain's edge in the remote… highlands of Papua New Guinea', which appeared in *The Sydney*

Morning Herald on the day the Ok Tedi court settlement was announced. I added the companion concept of *terra nugax*, which has one meaning of land that, not being used for anything else, or having 'trifling other uses', is a promising candidate for mineral extraction, and the fulfilment of national developmental goals through the exploitation of nationally appropriated resources.

But is this not a cultural landscape populated by tribes and customary landowners? Unfortunately, the qualities of being 'remote' and 'undiscovered', in the special sense of not having had a mining industry culture hero traverse the landscape, brings a second and key meaning to *terra nugax*; land that, though it is 'of someone', lies untouched by the political process of metropolitan society: it is invisible to the politically empowered citizenry of that society. The political connections of this land are believed 'trifling, of no consequence, nugatory' and that decisions can happily be made about it with few repercussions.

These attitudes centralise the metropolitan actors thought to be the 'real' political players and relegate the resident societies to being peripheral. Since they are all 'much the same', the ethnographer, whose job is often about difference and diversity, is out of work, or at best occupies an ornamental position. When our work closes in on something of real importance, as it occasionally does, we typically find ourselves, ostensibly the holders of key areas of knowledge, side-lined or neutralised.

However, the outcome of the Ok Tedi litigation, the extremely favourable compensation and royalty packages negotiated at Lihir and Porgera destroy the fundamental assumptions of the discovery paradigm, namely that the political connections of *terra nugax* to metropolitan political structures are not 'trifling, of no consequence, nugatory'. In fact they are extraordinarily powerful. In all of these examples, indigenous interest groups easily matched or surpassed both central government and the largest corporations in the court room and at the bargaining table.

Is what I have described about culture or about politics? 'Culture' is often discussed as a kind of thing separated from political affairs, governance, business and development. In Papua New Guinea, miners, often encouraged by government agencies, have consistently faced problems by believing that culture is something people put on with the feathers and paint they dance with. In Papua New Guinea, politics, whether inside the men's house or out on the hustings, is culture. Landowner representatives who bargain harder than others are doing it because their culture supplies them with better tools to do so—they are using their culture to elevate their profile as stakeholders.

It is frustrating to find that the thorough analysis of social issues—despite the sobering experiences of Bougainville and Ok Tedi—still has no more than an ephemeral, discontinuously-funded presence in the management structures of the resource companies. The 'new competencies' of mining may have been heralded by their chief executives, but they are definitely still to take root lower down their organisations.

Acknowledgments

I owe a debt to many, among academic colleagues, the mining industry, as well as in village communities. Let me thank them as a whole and apologise to any on whom critical comments, intended constructively, impinge.

References

Applied Geology Associates, 1989. *Environmental, Socio-economic and Public Health Review of Bougainville Copper Mine, Panguna*, A report for Bougainville Copper Limited, Wellington.

Banks, G.A., 1994. *Porgera Business Study*, PSMP Report No.5, Unisearch PNG Pty Ltd for Porgera Joint Venture, Port Moresby.

——, 1997. Mountain of desire: mining company and indigenous community at the Porgera Gold Mine, Papua New Guinea, PhD thesis, The Australian National University, Canberra.

Bonnell, S., 1994. *Dilemmas of Development: Social Change in Porgera 1989-93*, PSMP Report No.4, Subada Consulting for Porgera Joint Venture, Thornlands.

Burton, J. E., 1989. The land tenure system of the Nasioi people, and the bare cupboard of sustained research in mining areas, Paper presented at Bougainville Crisis Workshop, University of Papua New Guinea, September 1989 (unpublished).

——, 1991. *The Ningerum LGC Area*, Ok-Fly Social Monitoring Project Report No. 2, Unisearch PNG Pty Ltd, Port Moresby.

——, 1993. *Development in the North Fly and Ningerum-Awin Area Study*, Ok-Fly Social Monitoring Project Report No. 6, Unisearch PNG Pty Ltd Pacific Social Mapping, Port Moresby and Canberra.

——, 'Knowing the Ipili: evidence of the 'new competencies' at the Porgera gold mine', in C. Filer (ed.), *Social monitoring at Porgera*, National Research Institute, Port Moresby (forthcoming).

——, 1997. '*Terra nugax* and the discovery paradigm: how Ok Tedi was shaped by the way it was found and how the rise of political process in the North Fly took the company by surprise' in C. Ballard and G. Banks (eds), *The Ok Tedi settlement: issues, outcomes and implications*, National Centre for Development Studies and Resource Management in Asia-Pacific, Research School of Pacific and Asian Studies, The Australian National University, Canberra.

Burton, J.E., Filer, C., Banks, G., Bonnell, S., 1993. *Porgera Social Monitoring Program: plan and objectives*, Unisearch PNG Pty Ltd for Department of Environment and Conservation and Porgera Social Monitoring Steering Committee, Port Moresby.

Corren, A.G., 1989. Compensation for damage to land as a result of mining operations, Papua New Guinea Law Society Conference (unpublished).

Davis, L.A., 1995. New competencies in mining, Paper presented to Australian Institute of Directors, Melbourne (unpublished).

Department of Enga, 1992. Compensation claim [unnumbered], 26 May 1992, Division of District Administration and Mine Site Office, Porgera.

Filer, C., and Jackson, R., 1989. *The Social and Economic Impact of a Gold Mine in Lihir*. University of Papua New Guinea, Department of Anthropology and Sociology, Port Moresby (revised and expanded).

——, 1990. 'The Bougainville rebellion, the mining industry and the process of social disintegration in Papua New Guinea' in R.J. May and M. Spriggs (eds), *The Bougainville Crisis*, Crawford Press, Bathurst:73–112.

Kirsch, S., 1989a. 'Ok Tedi a sewer', *Times of Papua New Guinea*, 1 June:3.

——, 1989b. The Yonggom, the refugee camps along the border, and the impact of the Ok Tedi mine, *Research in Melanesia*, 13:30–61.

——, 1993. *The Yonggom people of the Ok Tedi and Moian Census Divisions: An area study*, Ok-Fly Social Monitoring Project Report No. 5, Unisearch PNG Pty Ltd and Canberra, Pacific Social Mapping, Port Moresby.

——, 1997. 'The Yonggom and the Ok Tedi', in C. Ballard and G. Banks (eds), *The Ok Tedi Settlement: issues, outcomes and implications*,

National Centre for Development Studies and Resource Management in Asia-Pacific, Research School of Pacific and Asian Studies, The Australian National University, Canberra.

Momis, J., 1974. 'Taming the Dragon', in P.G. Sack (ed.), *Problem of Choice: land in Papua New Guinea's future*, Australian National University Press, Canberra:190–99.

Oliver, D., 1991. *Black Islanders: a personal perspective of Bougainville, 1937–1991*, Hyland House, Canberra.

Pernetta, J.C. (ed.), 1988. *Potential Impacts of Mining on the Fly River*, UNEP Regional Seas Report and Studies No. 99 and SPREP Topic Review No.33, Nairobi.

Porgera Joint Venture, 1991. Environmental management and monitoring program for Porgera gold mine, Port Moresby, July (unpublished).

Wilson, F., 1981. *The Conquest of Copper Mountain*, Athenaeum, New York.

8

Culture and sustainable marine resource development in the Pacific

Philipp Muller

This chapter focuses on resource utilisation in the marine environment. I will draw largely from my own experiences, and my approach will be mainly anecdotal. It will also become obvious that I am not proposing any solutions. This is not because I think that there are no solutions. They are in fact fairly widely known, but if there is anything I have learned, it is that the solutions require action—and that is a different question.

The importance of the cultural aspects of development was brought home to me quite early in my career when it appeared that national developmental objectives were not being met. However, there were at the time enough reasons and excuses to confuse the real causes; and besides, the lessons were not easily learned. I was closely associated with efforts to improve the general well-being of our villagers by a variety of projects and programs in agriculture, forestry and fisheries. There were ever-present efforts to rehabilitate the copra, cocoa and banana export industries, which, for whatever reason, were directed towards harnessing the efforts of village smallholders. Very soon a mentality of providing incentives arose, where support was provided in bush-clearing, planting, weeding, fertilising, spraying, and whatever else was needed. Access roads, transport and centralised produce marketing soon followed. In fact, it almost seemed that the incentives were all set in place to prevent any sort of entrepreneurship from developing. Our planning had forgotten why villagers expended effort, and if it was for earning money, for what that money was going to be used.

In fisheries it was more boats, more outboard engines, bigger boats, bigger engines, ice plants, marketing incentives and development bank loans. At least in fisheries what remains is a thriving oceanic long-line fishery for export and a fairly effective fishing platform in the *alia* fishing vessels. Which is more than I can say for the banana export industry, where there is now not even a sign of a packing shed remaining.

Another early lesson I learned was that we, the educated privileged, were almost systematically desensitised to the needs of our people. Planners often neglected the needs of all the stakeholders, and at their own peril. We often enunciated noble goals such as job creation, foreign exchange earnings, improved balance of payments, and even a more equitable distribution or redistribution of wealth and involvement in development. We should have been attempting to understand motivating factors, such as family dignity, the pressure of politics, the community and the church, education, and events such as Children's Sunday and other matters of relevance to the individual and extended family. Everything was coming from a faceless government that was progressively becoming distressed by its lack of success, and being carried out by officials who were hard-pressed and under-resourced. Yet all that people wanted to know was what to produce, how to produce more, and how to get the best from markets. This brings to mind two universal lies: that you can get useful information from a government department and that a government official is out to help you.

Information (and the research that is needed to obtain such information) has generally been devoid of any consideration of how the result would be transferred to the final users, the people. The classic example is that of fisheries research in which total catch information has to be obtained, and maintained, and if over-exploitation is proven, or even suspected, then some way of reducing the quantity of fishing effort has to be found. The question is then how to do this. The fishermen know their catches are declining, but any form of regulation will mean that they will be committed to defeating the controls. Surely the fishermen who are most affected must be brought into a self-regulatory position. Traditional controls such as fishing closure in particular seasons, timeframes or areas, are easy to self police. Research should be geared towards culturally acceptable solutions and not the other way round.

This is not to say that there have not been traditional fishing methods which have had a disastrous effect on the fish stock or their environment. These include fish-drives, fish traps and fish poisoning. In the past, the resources could generally recover with time, but now, population pressures mean that the degradation continues at an almost irreversible rate. The fishermen need to be brought into the decision-making process and to take responsibility for policing any agreed-upon and culturally acceptable solutions. There are many examples of good management, such as the harvesting of trochus shells on only one day in Aitutaki, and the exclusion of fishing within the lagoons in Tokelau. The idea of marine sanctuaries and parks is also an excellent way of ensuring the maintenance of marine stocks in neighbouring areas.

The harvesting of trochus shells only on one day a year in Aitutaki lagoon meant that some adult stock and juveniles were allowed a year to spawn and grow. Minimum effort was expended and it was easy to identify anyone harvesting trochus out of season. Recently the harvest period has been extended and it will be interesting to find out the long-term effects.

Tokelau has maintained a closure on fishing within the lagoons. This has allowed a constant restocking on the ocean side, and the congregation of fish near out-flowing channels where a focused and sustainable fishery can be maintained. Lagoonal fish stocks are held in reserve against long periods of rough weather when fishing on the ocean side is not possible.

Subsistence fishing has always been in equilibrium so that catches were able to sustain the people. Windfall catches were normally distributed freely, and that in itself reduced the demand. It is a mistake, though, to think that subsistence fishing can be safely commercialised. The evidence shows that where this happens, increased catches are sold and the money is either accumulated as cash, dispersed for status, or even converted into capital investment in bigger vessels and equipment requiring larger catches, further stressing the fragile fish stock.

Development has brought widespread social changes, many of which can have indirect consequences for the marine environment. Population increases (despite heavy out migration), have increased demand, and as a consequence, severely affected and depleted fish stock. Urbanisation has also had the effect of concentrating the fishing of migrants in the neighbouring waters, which can rapidly become depleted and degraded. There are clear examples of this happening in Tuvalu and Vanuatu. The introduction of efficient new technologies such as scuba, hooker, netting and, on the industrial scale, super-seiners, has created further over-exploitation problems. Solutions need to be culturally sound and then science can monitor the status of the stock and support rehabilitation rather than the other way round.

We have embraced certain elements of technological development with open arms and without any reserve or caution. This is in stark contrast to our thinking when we considered the development of tourism in 1950s and 1960s, when there was strong opposition, mainly due to fear of negative effects for our culture and traditions. High technology heavy engineering has been used to effect development and infrastructure projects with little thought to the broader environmental effects. Beach-mining and land reclamation is commonly and widely practiced without being screened by our traditional leaders. In many cases our leaders are the instigators. In many villages a blind eye is turned to destructive methods such as dynamiting, to the point of achieving a form of traditional acceptance.

Finally, I give the most tragic example relating to the harvesting of pearl and trochus shell and, most recently, bêche-de-mer. Harvesting was previously limited to free diving to allow for brood stock to survive at depth, preventing total depletion. However, in a study of a small group of islands in the western province of Solomon Islands it was found that the pearl and trochus stock was almost completely depleted down to a depth of over 70 metres. This was accomplished by hooker gear confiscated from apprehended Taiwanese clam boats and disposed of by public tender. The population involved was a migrant group which was at the end of a harvesting bonanza but fighting for survival. The ranks of the young divers were severely reduced by death and paralysis from bends, and there was an air of defiance and bravado by the few remaining divers to go deeper and for longer. The survival of the community was threatened.

In Fiji, the number of cases of death and disability from the use of hooker diving as well as scuba diving for bêche-de-mer has steeply increased, and the government is trying to do something about it. This is happening everywhere in the Pacific as the original sources become depleted and the prices of these items increase dramatically. We are paying for our resources with the lives of our young men. When our resources are finished the prices will continue to increase out of hand and we will have nothing to sell. Does it not make sense to limit our catch, save the lives of our most valuable resource, our young people, and benefit for ever?

Because of my involvement in the Forum Fisheries Agency and the South Pacific Applied Geoscience Commission, I am interested in regional cooperation in the marine sector. For a whole range of reasons, more cultural than economic, Pacific Island countries were able to mount a coordinated approach to oceanic fisheries development. They were able to put forward a very bold and resolute front against the plundering foreign fishing fleets of America and Asia. Control measures have been adopted in the form of licences with minimum terms and conditions, and a regional register of fishing vessels with a black-listing of renegades, and have increased licensing revenues. The negotiated US Treaty not only circumvented the United States Magnuson Act, which had legitimised the US fleet stealing our fish, but extracted very high rent and made the United States assume responsibility for the behaviour of its fleet. Destructive drift-net fishing was also halted, even though the fishing was almost entirely in the high seas.

The question that now needs to be asked is why these gains were not consolidated into regional licensing and controls. National self-interest, self-assertion and pride must accept the responsibility. Some countries felt that they were worse off under regional arrangements despite receiving greater than five-fold returns under the US Treaty. Some made special arrangements with individual deep water fishing nations rather than sticking with the regional arrangements. The very same adversaries that the region had confronted were able to convince individual countries that it was in their national interest to accept bilateral arrangements which ended any hope of regional arrangements for the management and development of oceanic fisheries, the only truly shared resource. The real end to solidarity was that the countries with the fish felt that the others were there only for the ride. Little account was taken of the opportunity costs and the essential contribution of solidarity to establishing control over the fleets in the first place.

9

Fisheries resource-use culture in Fiji and its implications

Joeli Veitayaki

Like other Pacific Islanders, most Fijians are maritime people, with ongoing fishing traditions that are continually retold to the younger generations. Skilled fishers and seafarers are highly regarded. In coastal areas, fish provide an important component of the people's diet, and are of considerable cultural significance. The way in which people use their fishery resources is still influenced to some degree by these cultural factors. Although they may no longer believe literally in all the supernatural aspects involved, or, indeed, slavishly observe all the traditional prohibitions, they are generally aware of them and make reference to their usefulness.

The current consciousness surrounding the significance of traditional fishing practices has made it important that people today understand the culture that was part of traditional resource use. Traditional resource-use practices were based on empirical knowledge of localised natural and cultural systems. Although resource-use methods are rapidly changing, contemporary practices include features that were once part of the traditional system, and these often provide knowledge that can be usefully employed to enhance the sustainable utilisation of fishery resources.

There is an on-going debate as to whether the management practices of traditional fishery resource can be introduced as part of contemporary resource management arrangements (Johannes 1978; Hviding 1994; Ruddle 1994; Veitayaki 1995), but it is beyond the scope of this chapter, which is limited to considering how elements of traditional practice influence the contemporary resource-use system. The system of resource-use now observed in many parts of the country is a combination of the traditional system of resource-use and contemporary methods, that take into consideration the changes in Fijian communities. Understanding how the changes in resource use culture takes place and their implications on future fisheries resource-use will influence the successful implementation of sustainable fisheries development and the effective involvement of local communities.

Coastal communities in Fiji today are undergoing socioeconomic and technological modernisation. Commercial exploitation has given most communities the capability to deplete coastal resources rapidly. With the economic demands to which the people are subjected and their increased capacity and productivity levels, the sustainable use of marine resources has become a major issue. The situation has become so serious that one of the main contemporary challenges is the sustainability of fisheries development projects (Carleton 1983; Johannes 1989; David 1990; Dolman 1990; Liew 1990; Munro and Fakahau 1993). Meanwhile, most coastal fisheries development continues to be characterised by the periodic boom and bust cycles which are associated with the peaks and troughs of trade in marine commodities.

The changes that have taken place in most communities in Fiji call for modern management input. Most traditional communities have not fully understood the environmental issues and the scientific base of inter-relationships in the ecosystem. Science is required to provide information on the nature of the resources and ecosystems. Furthermore, the impact of modern fishing technology on the resource base is important because fishers now have the capability to overfish distant areas where they have never gone before. The increase in the number of fishers makes it critical that every fisher is familiar with the need to keep production levels well within the stock's capacity to replenish itself. The scenario is made more complicated by the deteriorating state of the marine environment.

In some areas of Fiji, the traditional owners of fishing grounds and fishing rights have become passive observers, allowing government officials and external experts to make all the resource-use decisions. In these instances, the traditional owners of fishing grounds and fishing rights are instructed in new ways to use their resources. In others, traditional fishing ground and right owners are suspicious of the government's motives because they do not fully understand them. The short lifetime of most fishery development projects, which have been introduced to increase productivity, income-earning opportunities and employment, has often negatively affected the state of the resources and the people's enthusiasm to be part of projects. In some cases, the people are burdened by the failure of projects that were doomed from the beginning because they did not accommodate the sociocultural reality of Fijian communities.

Fishery exploitation in Fiji involves five discrete sectors: subsistence, artisanal, aquaculture, recreational and industrial. The different sectors vary in nature, characteristics and associated issues. Interesting developments are now taking place as coastal Fijian communities are addressing the ecological problems associated with dwindling resources. The people have initiated various attempts to identify more sustainable ways of using their fishery resources and are incorporating traditional and community-based resource-use methods into contemporary arrangements.

Traditional resource-use culture

The most significant traditional practice still followed in Fiji is the customary ownership of rights to fishing grounds, which extend to the outer reef slope (Iwakiri 1983; Kunatuba 1983; Fong 1994; Waqairatu 1994; Veitayaki 1995). Like land rights, traditional fishing area rights are defined and owned by *vanua* or *tikina* (social units that include a number of villages in a district) which regulate their use and exploitation. People are expected to use their own allocations, and those seeking to use grounds belonging to others are expected to get permission from the owners. From time to time fishing ground owners may declare a portion of their grounds out of bounds to preserve the resources for a special purpose such as a wedding, birth or a death ceremony (Ravuvu 1983). On other occasions, the people can place restrictions on fishing methods to protect the resource (Fong 1994).

Traditional management arrangements were embedded in the wider social system, in which traditional authority prevailed, and the systems of retribution ensured compliance. In some parts of Fiji people were killed or banished for serious offences relating to fishing practices (Tippett 1959). The traditional notion of 'sacred ground' is still prominent in many parts of Fiji. The sacred fishing grounds were special areas where special rules were strictly adhered to. In such cases 'a close association was perceived between the living and the dead, whose spirits inhabited sacred areas, who showed offence when customary taboos and rituals were not adhered to' (Siwatibau 1984:366). Fishing at such sites was conducted only with the permission of a *bete*, or traditional priest, or when special requirements were met. In Qoma today, the people going to Cakau Davui, the sacred fishing ground, are expected to obtain special permission, to perform the rituals of an arrival party at the reef, and to fish according to the rules. Among the turtle fishermen of Qoma, the belief is that their gods will provide a catch sufficient for the purpose for which the fishing was asked. The fishers know that once a turtle swims through their net they have caught enough and they will not catch any more. To be successful in their fishing, the people need to please their gods by doing the correct and expected things. In Kaba, the traditional swimming spot for the paramount chief is fished only at the request of the chief.

This association with the supernatural ensures that the 'sacred grounds' are respected and protected at all times, and not only when enforcement officers are around. The supernatural associations can also lead to incidents that seem to defy normal logic and rational thought (Koroi 1989). Fijians accept these special cases because they embody their traditional culture and beliefs. The close ties between the people of Cakaudrove and sharks is one such example. In this part of Fiji, sharks are revered by the people, who in turn are protected by them while at sea. During a trip to one of the islands on the edge of Fiji's Economic Exclusion Zone (EEZ), a naval vessel with the former president and high chief of Cakaudrove on board was caught in a freak storm. At the height of the storm, the listing vessel was propped up by a shark as large as the boat that stationed itself alongside the vessel until the storm passed (*Fiji Times*, 1 June 1985). In a similar incident, a barracuda which had stationed itself at the Suva Wharf before the Royal yacht Britannia berthed only swam away after the same chief arrived and communicated with it (*Sunday Times*, 31 October 1982).

On Naigani island, trevally are traditionally fished and eaten according to certain prescribed rules. Fishing is decided by the traditional priest. People would only take home fish sufficient for the day. No fish was to be kept overnight at home, and the unsevered bones are returned to the sea in the morning, where they again become a live fish (Veitayaki 1990). In Vanua Balavu, the inland lagoon at Masomo is fished by the community only when the traditional priest authorises it (Koroi 1989). During the fishing, which normally takes around six hours, fishers are not allowed to wear anything other than grass skirts specially made for the occasion. The people should also oil their bodies well. Failure to follow the rules will anger the gods and is a recipe for trouble. Penalties which reflect the severity of the offence are meted out by the spirits.

The thought of retribution by the ever-vigilant gods are a continuous reminder to the people of the need to adhere to tradition, and expected behaviour. The fishing grounds in Fiji, like the land, are associated with the spirits that protected them. Siwatibau explains that in such societies the environment is not something separate 'but an integral part of one's self, providing the physical manifestation of the vital link between the living and the dead' (1984:367). Outsiders, therefore, must observe the protocol and code of conduct in any area they are visiting. For instance, visitors are expected to make an offering to publicise their arrival at a place. This practice ensures that the members of the community are aware of the presence of visitors among them and also protects the visitors from the wrath of the spirits who show offence when customary protocol is not followed (Siwatibau 1984). The tradition also ensures that the customary owners of fishing grounds and rights are consulted every time outsiders want to fish in their area.

Totemic beliefs may also contribute to conservation goals. All Fijians have a plant, a bird and a fish totem (Cappell and Lester 1953; Ravuvu 1983; Veitayaki 1995). The taboo associated with totems restricts particular clans, families, age groups or sexes from catching or eating the species concerned. Exploitation is thus restricted to a certain extent because the fishers are always careful not to harm their totem. In Qoma, for example, the fishers would abandon their nets if their totem fish was caught. Fishing was also a highly specialised activity, carried on by only a relatively few members of the community. This in itself limited the catches and contributed to the general maintenance of stock and the protection of the marine environment.

The contemporary resource-use culture

Fiji is presently self-sufficient in fish and earns F$66.54 million (representing 2.8 per cent of GDP in 1995) through its export of fishery products (Ministry of Agriculture, Fisheries and Forests 1995). The estimated value of the inshore commodities during the same period was around F$58.32 million. The Fisheries Division has the responsibility for the exploitation and management of all fishery resources, formulating plans for the development of all the various sectors, and monitoring on-going programs. The development of infrastructure and capacity is resulting in a continued increase in the exploitation of inshore resources.

Of the different fishery sectors in Fiji, the industrial sector and the recreational fisheries are predominantly conducted offshore and are associated with high capital inputs. These two sectors are adequately managed and are sufficiently covered in the literature. The development of offshore industrial fishing is beneficial both for the exports that it generates, and the relief that it gives to inshore resources. The inshore fisheries consist of subsistence, artisanal, commercial sectors and aquaculture that are mostly small-scale and operated cheaply by local people. Variations within the inshore fisheries are evident in spite of the use of the same resource base.

Since the establishment of the Fiji Fisheries Division in 1968, the national five year plans have emphasised the development of small-scale artisanal fishery through the introduction of new, motorised fishing boats, improved fishing gear and methods, the processing of traditional export items, the establishment of marketing and transportation systems, ice-making and cold storage plants, and the improvement of landing and berthing facilities in the main fishing centres.

The developments taking place in the management of inshore resources illustrate the incorporation of traditional practices into contemporary resource-use arrangements. The government, for instance, has recorded, surveyed and registered customary fishing ground boundaries that were previously based on oral claims. Some 406 customary fishing grounds have already been established. The government has involved the customary owners in the award of commercial fishing licenses within their areas (Kunatuba 1983; Cavuilati 1994), and is planning to return to the communities the ownership of their traditional fishing grounds, which currently rest with the state, a direct result of Fiji's colonial experience (Waqairatu 1994).

Commercial fishers operating within customary fishing areas in Fiji are required by law to have a licence which is renewable every year (Ministry of Agriculture Fisheries and Forests 1994; 1995). The licences are not transferable and are issued by the Fisheries Division on receipt of the approval of the head of the customary units owning the fishing area. Fishers seeking fishing licenses within the customary fishing areas are expected to pay goodwill money. Though open to abuse, this system effectively restricts the number of users in any customary fishing area and removes open access conditions. Fishing licenses offered in this way, although not rationally decided upon (as the traditional owners offer their consent to nearly everyone who asks and pays for them), can be improved if some scientific basis for permit allocation is used.

It is government policy that the customary fishing areas (inside demarcated area—IDA) be reserved as much as possible for local owners and other residents. The Fisheries Division is thus encouraging commercial fishing operators to go to outside demarcated areas (ODA) and exploit resources in those areas that are not traditionally important to people. The government's intention to develop specific ODA sectors are well illustrated by the placement of Fish Aggregation Devices (FADs) and the promotion of half cabin FAO-designed fishing boats; both of which enhance the movement away from the exploitation of inshore fisheries.

There are other examples that illustrate the incorporation of traditional and community-based marine resources management systems in Fiji. In Kaba Point the people, who were fed up with poorly planned fishery projects that they had been part of, decided that any future marine-based development, involving the use of their coastal resources within their customary fishing areas, required thorough evaluation (Veitayaki et al. 1996). They invited researchers from the local university and government to scientifically assess the viability of their proposed fisheries project. The study findings indicated that local fishery resources were extensively used and that further intensification of current fishing practices could not be viable. As a result of the study the villagers are redefining their goals and options for using and managing their coastal resources.

In a related development, the people approached their paramount chief and briefed her on the disturbed natural situation. The chief responded by initiating a six month ban on gillnet fishing within the Kaba Point areas. In 1995, the chief decided not to renew the seventeen permits for the commercial fishers within their customary fishing grounds and to restrict fishing to only the people of Kaba Point for a year. In May 1996, the villagers hosted a marine awareness workshop where they invited government representatives, non-government organisations and researchers to discuss the management of their coastal resources. The villagers are now pursing other alternatives such as aquaculture and deep-sea fishing to allow for the recovery of their fishing grounds. The people of Kaba Point are aware of the issues facing them and are using the opportunities available through traditional management arrangements to address them.

Similar developments are taking place in other parts of Fiji as customary fishing ground owners determine the exploitation of their resources. In Lau, the paramount chief of the province in the late 1980s banned the commercial exploitation of fisheries in his domain. According to the chief, commercial fishing makes a mockery of customary fishing tenure and therefore promotes a system of marine resource use that is detrimental to people and the proper utilisation of fishery resources (Veitayaki 1990).

In Verata, Tailevu, the people have banned the use of driftnets in their customary fishing grounds for about two years now. This decision was taken by the owners of the customary fishing area after observing the deteriorating status of their fisheries. A year after the moratorium on gillnet fishing, there was much celebration when the big fish that the people claimed to have missed for years returned to the fishing grounds. The chief and the people of Verata have decided to extend the moratorium and are thinking of making the ban a permanent management arrangement. A similar arrangement is being observed within Macuata in Vanua Levu, where the chiefs have testified to the value of a moratorium on gillnet fishing, huka gear use and Sunday fishing (Fong 1994).

In some other parts of Fiji, customary fishing ground owners have refused the building of roads and the use of coastal resources by tourists because of the pressure on fishery resources. The chief and people of Kiuva, Tailevu, for instance, have repeatedly opposed the construction of a road to their village because it would involve clearing and draining extensive mangrove areas on their land. The mangrove areas provide the people's main fishery resources. According to the chief and the people of Kiuva, it is better to travel by punts and have a good productive fishery than to travel by road and be left with badly destroyed resources.

On many occasions the owners of customary fishing areas have confronted fishers and tourist operators they believed were abusing their coastal resources. Although this situation is not conducive to the economic reputation of the country, it shows that the owners of customary fishing areas are serious about the proper use of their coastal resources. In some instances, fishing gear has been destroyed and lives threatened as customary owners exert control within their areas.

In some parts of Fiji, owners of customary fishing areas have employed fish wardens to patrol their territory. These people undertake surveillance work within their customary areas on behalf of the owners of customary fishing areas and the Fisheries Division. Although fish wardens are not paid, their involvement illustrates the commitment of coastal communities to the proper use of their customary fishing areas.

There is an increasing interest throughout Fiji in the declaration and development of marine reserves and protected areas. This is a direct result of the deteriorating state of fisheries, public education initiatives, and the realisation that a great deal of money can be earned through the display of properly managed marine environments and fishery resources. The development of protected marine areas and reserves in Fiji will be easy, as the ownership of the customary fishing areas is already held by the people, who only need to agree as a group to have a portion of their fishing ground declared a marine reserve or protected area. In some districts such as Tacilevu in Savusavu on Vanua Levu, the people have decided to prohibit fishing at all times in some portion of their fishing grounds. Fish do not respect human-drawn boundaries and so the effects of the fishing ban on a portion of the fishery is expected to have a positive influence on the whole fishery. The lifting of the prohibition period on a given portion of the fishing ground is decided on by the people depending on the feedback received by the fishers. Once a prohibited area is opened another portion is closed to all fishing. According to the people, they are enjoying good catches and are happy with their arrangements.

In collaboration with government departments and some non-government organisations, such as the Fiji Dive Operators Association, the International Ocean Institute, the World Wide Fund and the University of the South Pacific, some owners of customary fishing areas are participating in marine public education workshops to educate people who use the fisheries to consider the impact of their activities and to appreciate the importance of having a healthy, productive and vibrant marine environment. Judging from the current interest in these workshops the message appears to be getting through and is being well received by people.

Issues of fisheries resource-use culture

Although the traditional system of resource use was formulated for a time long gone, contemporary experience in Fiji has shown the usefulness of some traditional practices. Customary Marine Tenure and the involvement of customary ground owners in the management of fishery resources today, illustrate the amicable amalgamation of the two systems. In addition, some of the activities of those involved in fishery resource management are possible only because of the traditional rights people have over fishery resources. The traditional ownership of fishing areas, for instance, alleviates most of the problems associated with open access. On the other hand, custom is often quoted as a reason why people are still having difficulty managing their fishery business.

The development of fishery resources is a major undertaking because of the importance of fish to people and the significance of the marine environment. The uncertainties within the marine environment require that careful planning be conducted to ensure the amicable development of all sectors. An emphasis on maximising production and development should be pursued cautiously because of the need to ensure that resources are sustainably exploited and that the environment is not overly degraded. Other users of the sea should be consulted so that they are included in management decisions to conserve the resources and the marine environment.

Major contemporary fishery development issues are associated with the increasing commercial exploitation of the resources and the continued degradation of the marine environment. The major issues associated with the commercial exploitation of inshore fisheries include: the successful development of small-scale or artisanal fisheries; the management of fisheries and fishing grounds; the use of appropriate fishing technology; the importance of fish and fishing income; marketing and the distribution systems; uncertainty over what constitutes the resource, and the loss of traditional management practices.

Issues relating to the degradation of the marine environment include: the changing availability of fishery stock; the difficulties of conducting resource assessments, changes in environmental conditions, pollution and the pressures of land based activities.

The sustainable utilisation of fisheries in the future will depend on how well these issues are addressed. The present low number of successful fishery projects seems to indicate our failure to find the magical formula. The fact that the technology or the capital is available from an external source should not be allowed to drive the development of fisheries.

Future implications

Challenging times are facing nations like Fiji, which are attempting to develop their fishery resources for maximum benefit while undertaking to ensure their sustainability. The transition from subsistence to commercial and industrial fishery exploitation places more stress on the fisheries. The increasing number of fishers and their greater capacity will make the situation acute. Although the development of deep sea fisheries may help to reduce the intensity of fishing in inshore areas, the dominance of foreign interests in the exploitation of resources in the sector is cause for concern. It is unlikely that Fijian interests will dominate in this sector within the foreseeable future. There is a need for education to promote the importance of exploiting the resource in a manner that will enable future generations to enjoy the same resource that we are exploiting today.

The task of sustainable fishery management is made more difficult by the fact that the marine environment is being changed by the impacts of human activities and the reduced fish biomass. The preferential fishing demanded by the market places some species at greater risk. In addition, the impact of depleted fisheries on the ecosystem generally is uncertain. Thus the resources, their range and their nature are little known to people who are trying to manage them

(Veitayaki and South 1993; Slatter 1994). The figures used for management are approximations based on what people hope are reasonable assumptions and estimations. In the meantime, the business-as-usual approach continues in the hope that the current exploitation levels are within the capacity of the stocks to limit the impact of fishing.

The industrial fishery development in offshore areas is especially welcomed in Fiji because of the opportunities it provides to food provision and income earning. Offshore resources provide useful alternatives to intensively exploited inshore resources. The difficulty of establishing local markets for offshore fishery products and the problems associated with the need to extend fishing to offshore areas are related to traditional fishery resource-use customs. Unlike inshore areas, the offshore is open and the government is responsible for the management and control of all activities outside of customary fishing areas and extending outward to the edge of Fiji's EEZ. In these areas, enforcement of legislation is a necessary but costly exercise.

Maximum production is not the only way of attaining maximum gain. Improving post-harvest treatment and processing can enable people to maximise their gain and simultaneously protect their resource base by encouraging people to catch fewer fish and thus cause less disturbance to the marine environment. Reducing post-harvest loss is an aspect of contemporary fishing which is new to Fijian communities. Fijians traditionally did little of the processing they are now required to do by the commercial fishing in which they are involved.

The loss of traditional management arrangements currently experienced in Fiji is linked to the social changes taking place in traditional communities. Although the systems of resource-use of traditional communities are appropriate and effective, they have been quickly eroded and replaced by modern systems. There is a serious dilemma now in trying to save what is known of these rapidly changing systems of resource use. Current experience is showing how the useful elements of traditional resource use systems can be put to good use. The Customary Marine Tenure system for example, is a traditional management arrangement that is addressing the issues of open access characteristic most contemporary fisheries.

It is critical to understand fully the sociocultural situation affecting fishery use. Often, fishery projects that are planned elsewhere are imposed on people whose system of doing things is not well understood by those planning the projects. The lack of consistency among Fijian fishers in villages, the cultural factors that hinder commercial fishery operations and the people's lack of interest in certain fisheries are all related to traditional customs. Fijians need to be trained in marketing skills and fishery valuation.

Marine reserves and protected areas should be encouraged because of poor knowledge about marine habitats and organisms. Fishery resource management at the community level provides a workable unit for implementing this management concept. The chances of success will be better if the necessary scientific knowledge is made part of the system. The customary fishing areas are part of the people's heritage which they will need to manage.

A good system of education is required to improve the management of fishery resources. Modern scientific knowledge and data collection methods need to be disseminated through an effective education program that targets not only schools but all categories of users. Public education is as important as the development of curriculum for schools and tertiary education institutions. The proper use of fishery resources will demand commitment from all people and a good education system should be used to mobilise community support. Education is also critical to the acceptance of rational fishing in line with sustainable fishery use.

The traditional culture of fishery resource use is important to the sustainable utilisation of fishery resources in the future and should be taken into consideration when fishery developments are being planned. It is important to involve local communities in sustainable fishery development and to convince them through the use of good education programs. Fishery resources are important to the people and should be utilised in a manner that enables the people to enjoy the use of these resources now and in the future. For this purpose, Fijians need to employ all available fishery resource use culture to draw up effective methods for contemporary resource use; methods that allow maximum benefit and at the same time protect the resource base.

References

Cappell, A. and Lester, R.H., 1953. 'The nature of Fijian totemism', *Fiji Society of Science and Industry*, 2(1-5):59–67.

Carleton, C., 1983. *Guidelines for Establishment and Management of Collection, Handling, Processing and Marketing Facilities for the*

Artisanal Fisheries Sector in the South Pacific Commission Area, SPC/ Fisheries 15/WP.6, Noumea.

Cavuilati, S.T., 1993. 'Managing fisheries resources: the Fiji experience', in G.R. South (ed.), *Marine Resources and Development*, Pacific Islands Marine Resources Information System, Suva:35–62.

David, G., 1990. Strategies of reef resources exploitation in Pacific islands, the case of Vanuatu, in Proceedings: International Society of Reef Studies Congress, Noumea (unpublished).

Dolman, A.J., 1990. 'The potential contribution of marine resources to sustainable development in small island developing countries', in W. Beller, P. d'Ayala and P. Hein (eds), *Sustainable Development and Environmental Management of Small Islands*, UNESCO and Parthenon Publishing Group, Paris:87–102.

Fong, G., 1994. *Case study of traditional marine management system: Sasa village, Macuata Province, Fiji*, Field Report 94/1, Forum Fisheries Agency, Food and Agriculture Organisation, Paris.

Hviding, E., 1994. 'Customary marine tenure and fisheries management: some challenges, prospects and experiences', in G.R. South, D. Goulet, S. Tuqiri and M. Church (eds), *Traditional Marine Tenure and Sustainable Management of Marine Resources in Asia and the Pacific*, International Ocean Institute-South Pacific, Suva:88–100.

Iwakiri, S., 1983. *Mataqali of the sea: a study of the customary right on reef and lagoon in Fiji, the South Pacific*, Kagoshima University, Kagoshima.

Johannes, R.E., 1978. 'Traditional marine conservation methods in Oceania and their demise', *Annual Reviews Ecological Systems* 9:349–364.

——, 1989. 'Managing small-scale fisheries in Oceania: unusual constraints and opportunities', in H. Campbell, K. Menz and G. Waugh (eds), *Economics of Fishery Management in the Pacific Islands Region*, Proceedings of an international conference held at Hobart, Tasmania, 20–22 March 1990, Australian Centre for International Agricultural Research, Canberra:85–93.

Koroi, M., 1989. 'The sacred fish of Masomo', *Fiji Times*, January 28.

Kunatuba, P., 1983. *A report on the traditional fisheries of Fiji*, Institute of Marine Resources Technical Report, Suva.

Liew, J., 1990. 'Sustainable development and environmental management of atolls', in W. Beller, P. d'Ayala and P. Hein, *Sustainable Development and Environmental Management of Small Islands*, UNESCO and Parthenon Publishing Group, Paris: 77–86.

Ministry of Agriculture, Fisheries and Forests, 1994. *Fisheries Division Annual Report*, Suva.

——, 1995. *Fisheries Division Annual Report*, Suva.

Munro, J.L. and Fakahau, S.T., 1993. 'Appraisal, assessment and monitoring of small-scale coastal fisheries in the South Pacific', in A. Wright and L. Hills (eds), *Nearshore Marine Resources of the South Pacific. Information for Fisheries Development and Management*, Institute of Pacific Studies, Forum Fisheries Agency and International Centre for Ocean Development, Suva:15–54.

Ravuvu, A. 1983. *Vaka i taukei: the Fijian way of life*, Institute of Pacific Studies, Suva.

Ruddle, K., 1994. 'Traditional marine tenure in the 90s', in G.R. South, D. Goulet, S. Tuqiri and M. Church (eds), *Traditional Marine Tenure and Sustainable Management of Marine Resources in Asia and the Pacific*, International Ocean Institute-South Pacific, Suva:6–45.

Siwatibau, S., 1984. 'Traditional environment practices in the South Pacific—A case study of Fiji', *Ambio*, 13 (5–6):365–68.

Slatter, C., 1994. 'Food or foreign exchange? regional interests versus global imperatives in pacific fisheries development', in A.Emberson-Bain (ed.), *Sustainable Development or Malignant Growth. Perspectives of Pacific Island Women*, Marama Publications, Suva:123–30.

Tippett, A.R., 1959. 'The survival of an ancient custom relative to the pig's head, Bau, Fiji', *The Fiji Society*, 6(1–2):30–39.

Veitayaki, J., 1990. Village level fishing in Fiji: a case study of Qoma island, MA Thesis, University of the South Pacific.

——, 1995. *Fisheries Development in Fiji: The quest for sustainability*, Ocean Resources Management Program, Institute of Pacific Studies, Suva.

Veitayaki, J. and South G.R., 1993. Inshore fisheries in the tropical South Pacific—a question of sustainability, Paper presented at the 1993 Fisheries and Environment Beyond 2000 International Conference at the Universiti Pertainian, Malaysia (unpublished).

Veitayaki, J., Bidesi, V.R., Matthews, E. and Ballou, A. (eds), 1996. *Preliminary Baseline Survey of Marine Resources of Kaba Point, Fiji*, USP Marine Studies Technical Report 96/1, Suva.

Waqairatu, S., 1994. 'The delimitation of traditional fishing grounds—the Fiji experience', in G.R. South, D. Goulet, S. Tuqiri and M. Church (eds), *Traditional Marine Tenure and Sustainable Development in Asia and the Pacific*, International Ocean Institute-South Pacific, Suva:79–84.

10

Local hierarchies of authority and development

Kerry James

This chapter focuses attention on an aspect of culture that is frequently overlooked in development plans. Among the most enduring of a people's cultural traits are the customary patterns of authority that are upheld within families, households, and communities. The relations of authority in these basic social units are still adhered to by most village people and entail mutual responsibilities and obligations of respect, gifts and service.

The patterns of authority at the local level may be subtle and not easily discernible to an outsider. They may alter rapidly according to material circumstances and social contexts, but this does not mean that they cannot be understood. Given sufficient time, tact, and careful investigation, it is possible to identify the most influential and authoritative people in a community or in a particular situation.

Local knowledge is not immediately available to casual observers, however, and may entirely elude developmentalists and other outsiders who most need it but visit a country only briefly. Instead of eliciting local reactions to a proposed program, the overseas consultant or development expert is more likely to spend most of a limited official visit meeting top-level bureaucrats in the nation's capital.

Participatory development

If local-level developmental goals are to be pursued successfully, it is essential to identify the people of influence and authority, who can get things done or stifle efforts in the particular locality singled out for attention. This is especially true of programs which require a strong element of participatory development. A popular trend in recent years, participatory development is sometimes referred to as 'grass-roots' development or, somewhat more inelegantly, as 'bottom-up' development.

Politically, ideologically, and practically, such programs seem a good idea because they focus on the development of human resources and small amounts of working and fixed capital such as planting materials or livestock, fish nurseries, storage depots, boats, engines, refrigerators, or whatever is needed for the particular ventures with 'the poorest of the poor'. All too frequently, however, the loftiness of the original aim equals the depth of the subsequent disillusion when the schemes are found to have gone badly wrong: when they have failed to produce the desired results or, even worse, have produced pronounced negative social and economic effects that have left the poor people markedly less well-off than they were before.

At this point, recriminations are likely to occur and, in their disappointment, people look for likely causes to blame. In retrospect, everyone is wise. All too often, culture and tradition are the easiest and most convenient whipping boys that come to hand to explain a particular failure. At the very least, these concepts are so general and so abstract that no-one in charge need feel guilty of mismanagement. Most development literature, for example, alludes to the obligations of highly traditional people to others. These obligations are generally seen to be numerous, to compete for workers' time and effort and, in the end, undermine the goals of modern development.

For all the seriousness of the charges, there is disappointingly little analysis and few case studies recording the effect of such obligations on development projects. The 'family obligations' of people living in highly traditional societies remains a diffuse and general notion, of little analytic value. As remarked above, however, the very general nature of 'culture' and the assumptions derived from it can conveniently explain the failure of development projects.

Clearly, a prerequisite of the successful implementation of 'grass-roots' programs is first to find out local reactions. Instead of speaking generally about 'communities', it is possible to be specific and to identify precisely which people in the local community have the authority or informal influence to materially affect the progress and outcome of the developmental project, but these courses are rarely attempted.

People in proximity

People rarely engage with members of their entire extended family. Instead, they live and interact most closely with other members of their immediate household, and with members of other households to whom they are closely related who live nearby. Thus, it is the people with whom they live in close proximity, in their households and communities, who are usually the most important in terms of daily encounters, that involve activities as basic to survival as the sharing of food, productive labour, and equipment.

The relations of deference and respect, or of patron and client relations that can exist even within a family, are typically underplayed to facilitate necessary mundane cooperation and exchanges. In a small community, people's daily affairs are usually conducted with all the appearance of an easy familiarity between equals, being typically accompanied by banter, joking and laughter. The appearance of egalitarianism often belies the real situation and serves to check the personal rivalries and family feuds that can and do exist in villages. It should not be allowed to obscure the fact, however, that the relations between villagers are often delicately negotiated, handled with care and, at times, guarded zealously because it is at this level that their simple social and economic well-being or, at times of crisis, survival, most likely depends. The visiting expert's experience of people's lives at the local level, if imperfectly derived from logical deduction based on ideal statements about the culture as a whole, is generally partial, inaccurate, or non-existent.

Opaque communities and oblique communications

The sheer impenetrability of local organisation to short-term observers was brought home to me during a visit to Tonga. A team of agricultural developmentalists had made visits to two outer islands in order to gather people's reactions to proposed innovations. In particular, they wished to monitor women's reactions to the proposed changes and how the agricultural innovations might affect women or alter their ways of carrying out certain tasks. They had gathered together local people to discuss these matters but found that no-one would speak to them, let alone offer a frank opinion.

One of these consultants practically fell at my feet when he found I was an anthropologist: 'Thank God,' he cried, 'I have finally met someone who can explain what was going on!' During my years in the field, this reaction to my chosen profession remains unique. It is more usual for anthropologists to be greeted by developmentalists with hoots of derision or cool indifference. We are usually accused of either 'taking the people's part' in arguments over why projects failed to work, or of being fusspots who 'provide far too much detail' on issues about which the development people wish to be informed but not know too much. This is especially true of topics such as gender relations or the role of women in agriculture, which are included in their terms of reference—being, together with 'environmental issues', current aid donor buzzwords—but which do not interest, or overly concern the consultants.

In this case, however, the social scientist, namely myself, was meant to provide the key to the research dilemma immediately. 'Tell me why they wouldn't talk,' he continued desperately. 'Why, we even drew diagrams in the sand for them to illustrate the objectives of the project, but the people all sat there solemnly and would not utter a word in response.' I answered that I could not possibly say, because I had not been to those particular villages nor did I know the people who lived in them. That reply appeared to disappoint. 'But you've been in Tonga, you know the people and the culture!' Yes, to be sure, to a certain extent, I do, but not those people and not that local situation. I might have added that, by 1996, I am not sure that any people anywhere should respond to diagrams drawn for them in the sand.

To hazard a guess, however, the islanders' silence was probably because the people in question were waiting for their elders to speak first. If the elders had chosen not to speak—either because they did not understand the issues, or because they understood the issues and did not agree with the proposition but were not prepared to be so ungracious as to say so, or because they understood the issues, agreed with them and had nothing to say—or any one of a number of other possibilities; then, their junior relatives and others who were similarly inferior to them in the village structure would not speak before they did, without being asked by them to speak.

The silence did not necessarily mean that the local community did not have ideas about the proposed scheme, but it did suggest that the consultant team did not know how to tap into that local opinion. Tonga is, after all, a highly structured society where deference is customarily shown to village and family elders, the heads of extended families, *ulumotu'a*, the skilled and competent people, *ivilahi*, and the 'keepers of the land,' *tauhi fonua* who are the ones who should be looked up to in a local setting. 'Oh,' sighed the expert, 'if only we had had you with us on the team!' I only smiled modestly at this novel reaction.

Although it is currently the case that more provision for 'the social components' of a project and for social researchers is being made available on consultant teams, equally, I was aware that I might not have had any more success than the team in getting the village elders to speak if they did not want to. My only advantage would have lain in knowing where the difficulty most likely was located. In such a case, it might have been more advisable to have had someone originally from the village with the team, to explain the project to the islanders. But, then, in that case, the local response probably would have depended on how the erstwhile islander was regarded in village terms, and the leaders' estimation of the person and of the family that he or she represented. If there is any lesson to be learned from the consultants' discomfiture, it is that the total social situation within which the proposed development is to take place needs to be considered as part of the initial project proposal rather than added later as an afterthought, when it has presented itself as an obstacle to the achievement of the intended goals.

The total social situation

Too often the person singled out for particular development attention, such as a training program or workshop, is assumed to be a social isolate. This is far from the case in the Pacific. Most people in Pacific island cultures, although strongly individualist, have not acceded to the notion of individualism, if what is meant is the Western idea of 'bourgeois individualism', interpreted as encouraging people to act solely in their own interests and for the promotion of their own prosperity.

Islanders see themselves as part of wider groups. Their identity derives from the sets of social relations that define them in terms of the family or wider sets of relations based on kinship and locality. These relations are the ones that they value and need. This critical difference between the assumptions made by both aid donors and local project directors and the lived-in realities of those they try to develop can be illustrated by the efforts in Tonga in the late 1980s to help village fishing activities.

Tongan village fishing

Reflecting upon the problems encountered in the 1980s in the implementation of their fisheries schemes, a local fisheries expert concluded that the basic flaw lay in the initial project design that had failed to take into account the wider family situation of the men who were singled out for fisheries training and given bank loans to enable them to acquire fishing boats.

The assumption of a Western-style individualism was inherent, for example, in two major aspects of the schemes. First, the skills and training that were given to village men were those that were appropriate to people wishing to set up a small business, which the village men were not prepared to do. Second, the men were given training on the assumption that they were or would become solely commercial fishermen, which was also false. These unwarranted assumptions led in some cases to the failure of the men to repay the bank loan and the loss of the boat; or, in more extreme circumstances, to the breakdown of the men's extended family life, and damage to other relationships in the village. The expert told me

> Our mistake from the beginning was to overlook the family situation. The families that these trainees came from were really very well-balanced in the way that they get food to survive as they do, though poor. The man will spend four days or so in his garden while the wife makes handicrafts. On Saturdays, he goes fishing and sells fish and uses the little cash he gets to offset the costs of bully beef for Sunday lunch, and so on.

> Fisheries comes along with a training plan. The individual gets interested and after training he spends five days at sea. He does not grow and has to buy his food, if he can, from the market or his relatives. The pandanus leaves to assist the wife are missing. If he does well, he's OK. It eventually balances out and the family gets on.

> But most of them we destroyed, because the boat upset the balance. The family cannot manage the loan repayments and the boat is repossessed and he comes home again to nothing. In a few cases, not many, it has happened that the relatives may not recognise him [that is, want nothing more to do with him] after the things that have happened.

At first I could not believe the failure. We had bright guys come in to the training. We gave them a fishing lesson, explained the boat, the engine, how to manage money, and the training works well; they understand it all. Then, afterwards, they go back out to the villages with boats bought with a loan we structured from the Tonga Development Bank.

Before they joined the scheme, the men, usually in their 30s and 40s, are considered young in Tongan terms, no matter that they are married and have children of their own. They have hardly any status in the village. They just have a small fishing boat, or are hanging about and using other people's equipment for the occasional fishing trip. The family income is about T$45 a week, which then suddenly rises to T$1,000 a week.

We give them all the training in how to catch fish and nor is there a shortage of fish. But after about 8 months, we hear from the Bank, 'Oh, Sione, we have a problem with some of the fishermen: they are not repaying their loans, slowing right down.' I replied, 'What! These guys are loading tons and tons of fish!' After about a year, I found the reasons.

(1) The status of these guys just shot right up in the community because of the income they earned. Some had even become town officers. Their wives too: some were leaders of church groups or women's groups. Even their kids, during the Christmas holidays, would be made president of the basketball team. All the things like that. When you are the leader of something in a village, you are expected to do the most, give the most funds to support it, food, the basketball…

(2) So, they became the greatest member of their family. Even though young, they were looked up to by others. This too unravelled their effort and training, and helped to cream off their income.

(3) In some cases, the father was still alive and still making decisions for the family. Thus, in the village situation, someone else was taking over the decision-making for the venture, not the one who has been trained. This was fatal for the program and also led sadly to bad relations with the father who is the senior. One village man told me, 'My interest in fishing was started by my father. I got into it because he is a master fisherman. But when I got started with Fisheries, that is the last time he ever discussed fishing matters with me. Up to now, he still won't talk to me about it. I, being younger and his son, just took it for granted that I could go ahead [with my new ideas] without him and that is probably the biggest mistake as far as the family is concerned. If it had been my uncle, I don't think there would have been any

problem, but my father is a much harder worker and a harder man. He doesn't like anyone discussing his fishing grounds. When the subject comes up, that is the end of the story between us. We can discuss anything but not this. In Tonga, as you know, the father-son relationship is a very sensitive relationship, in any case, and this blew it. So, it is sad, but there it is.'

(4) The fishing men gave more to the church as a result of all the above changes of village status.

(5) The man still went to sea but, because so many people were asking him to lend them their kids' school fees and so on, he was defaulting on the loan repayments. In addition, other people were going out, the father, another son, a neighbour's boy, as crew or helpers or to earn money for themselves. So, he might go away for one week. But the family had already agreed to certain obligations to the community and church. His wife would say, 'While you were away, the Town Officer was asking for you because you had agreed to do something but you were not here. I think you should apologise.' So, the man would send the Town Officer a few fish to keep him happy or to help in the village meeting or whatever, which all added up. In some cases, we have ended up destroying whole families that we started out to help because the fisheries boat ended up destroying the family's balancing act. In short, we had the training program but what we should have done is to look at who the trainee is within the family and who has the big influence over this person.

We should include the wife and the church minister (*faifekau*) in the training, and tell the minister that after his loan repayment, the man has this amount of income left. He has a child still in secondary school, fees, food, clothes, and that we think this is the amount he can afford to give to the church. Can we ask you [the church minister] for your help? If he gives more than this amount [that he can afford], will you tell him in church that he is doing the wrong thing?

At this point the expert laughed heartily to himself at the thought that the *faifekau* would ever endanger church revenue by doing this, because, increasingly, his standing and prestige in the church depends on the amount of money that he can pull in. The fisheries officer, however, repeated, 'We should ask the *faifekau* and employ the whole family approach because Tongan villagers are not primarily commercial fishermen.'

The lesson to be drawn from this exercise is inescapable—the customary hierarchy of local authority should be acknowledged from the outset as part of the development situation. It can then consciously be built into the project frame as part of the social context in which development is to take place and the forces can ideally be harnessed in support of the developmental effort, rather than work against it.

As it is, local mores and patterns of authority tend to be overlooked until they emerge as major stumbling blocks to the success of the project. To say that a people's culture blocks their development makes a nonsense of both terms: culture and development. It suggests that people who progress do so without or in spite of their culture, and that the people embedded in culture get left behind. Culture and tradition may suddenly intrude in ways that materially affect outcomes when not incorporated in the development scheme, but this is due to the initial conceptualisation of the development schemes rather than immutable flaws inherent in the nature of culture, tradition, and development.

Possible solutions

First, clearly, developmentalists must find out more about the people they have designated to be key figures in the development situation. By their nature, actual social relations are not as static as ideal statements of cultural norms make them out to be, nor can they be extrapolated from these statements in any simple way. By its very nature, power is labile, ductile, fluid, and runs through the interstices of formal structures. It varies according to the material and human resources that are available at any one time, for a project to succeed. These resources may change very quickly over a relatively short period if a key figure decides to migrate, falls ill, or decides to concentrate on another activity. And the obligations of the trainee to his dependents should also be taken into account.

How might that be done? One idea is to build a database on all fisheries trainees. This approach may seem inimical to Western liberal ideas. Its intention, however, is far from sinister, and involves no more than the systematic recording, for the purpose of rapid review, of what is generally known about the household circumstances of the man who has applied for assistance. In this way, the fisheries officer can quickly get some idea of the numbers of able-bodied and skilled people who are in the household or work group, and are able to help with the project, and the number of dependents such as school children and aged parents, who cannot.

In 1987–90, Tongan Fisheries made an effort along these lines to collect relevant information from every village family involved in the training scheme: whether parents were alive and dependent on the family, if children were still at school or capable of and interested in working on the fishing project, the family's equity in house, land, or boats; its current expenditure and labour needs, whether it had other funds it could call upon, whether the wife worked, the other economic activities that the family members engaged in, how many days were spent on each type of occupation, and so on. It is possible to use the picture of the household which was built up in this way to judge whether a proposal for future assistance put forward is feasible in the light of the total family situation, and not judge it solely on the abilities of the one who has been singled out for training.

The aim is to reach mutual agreement with the applicant on what he needs to achieve his goals, which might be different from what he originally asked for. In this context, it must be remembered that the better-educated people from the village have usually left to enter government or private sector employment. The village sector is left with the least educated, who are then expected to carry out development projects, which are perhaps only effective in about 60 per cent of cases, or 60 per cent effective in any one case, because of the limitations imposed by education and experience, and by the family and community commitments and dynamics already discussed. In any event, someone other than the applicant for a bank loan or training with some insider knowledge should assess the situation. Ideally, of course, there would be an experienced anthropologist available to answer every question!

Aid donors, however, usually hold discussions only with their in-country representatives or with local bureaucrats. The assumption appears to be that any local person will know all that is required by virtue of his/her membership in the society at large, but this is far from the case. Bureaucrats from families who have worked for two or three generations in the nation's capital may claim origin and allegiance with far-away villages of which they have very little up-to-date knowledge because they rarely, if ever, visit them. Accordingly, they may give a very misleading picture of a local social situation or a sectoral activity within it. They may simply accept the aid donors' assumptions that people who fish are undeveloped fishermen, or that growers will become commercial farmers if only they are helped in particular ways, or go along with the donors' implementation schemes because that is the way the development projects are designed.

Instead, what is needed is a model of development that includes the realities of village life in which the development is intended to take place. When these realities are ignored at the planning stage, they are likely to emerge as problems in the fruition of projects. At this point, the development agents frequently blame extended family values as obstacles to development. This makes absolutely no sense to the people concerned because it is these sets of values that give their life meaning and upon which they depend in practical terms to survive as people and as families. After all, it is usually only for the sake of their families that they undertake progressive 'development' projects at all. If the traditional values, embodied in village and family relationships are left out of the development project calculations, modern development ceases to have a great deal of personal relevance to the subjects of development.

It is time for both developmentalists and the people they intend to help to leave aside the empty rhetoric of development and to 'get real'. Many people at the local level do not necessarily have the same development goals as their national leaders or the aid donors the leaders work with, but their aims are rarely sought or formally acknowledged, much less valued and respected. When both sides of the development equation are made clear, distorted no longer through official oversight or an over-eagerness to acquire particular forms of development aid, then both the developers and the people in whose interests the development is presumably being made will benefit. Substantial progress of a kind satisfactory to both is then more likely to take place. At present, the development process tends to involve a set of formal moves between aid donors, local bureaucrats, and local-level recipients and agents of change, in the course of which neither the appropriate personnel nor relevant grass-roots information is sought. This process of enquiry is time-consuming, not deemed necessary, and may even prove detrimental to the project design. As one Pacific island planner remarked, 'Yes, it's true: when we do a village project successfully, we tend to congratulate ourselves on having got the economics right; when we fail, we blame the culture and custom. We just put our failure right back on the poor people themselves!'

11

A paradox of tradition in a modernising society: chiefs and political development in Fiji

Robert Norton

This chapter went to press after the most remarkable parliamentary elections in Fiji's history gave victory to the People's Coalition, a loose alliance between the predominantly Indian Fiji Labour Party and two Fijian parties, the Fijian Association Party and the Party of National Unity, which massively defeated a coalition of the Fijian SVT and the Indian NFP, led by Rabuka and Reddy. For the first time Fiji has an Indian prime minister, Labour's leader Mahendra Chaudhry, who heads a cabinet with a majority of Fijian ministers. Rabuka was returned to parliament, but resigned to accept the chairmanship of the Council of Chiefs.

The defeat of Rabuka's government was caused mainly by an unprecedented political fragmentation among the Fijians. There was widespread disaffection over the failure of the government to improve living standards and economic opportunities, and resentment at Rabuka's personal role in the constitutional reform which many of this opponents denounced as a betrayal of the promise of his coups. One of the starkest ironies of the elections was the Labour Party's gain from Fijian ethnicist opposition to the constitutional reform to which the party had, in its universalist ideology, been so radically committed.

To some extent, Labour's victory also reflects the widening of a popular base of shared inter-ethnic interests at a time of growing anxiety and anger about economic conditions, and there is potential in these concerns for a strengthening of the party's multi-ethnic character. But Labour depends most on an unstable alliance of groups with contradictory agendas. Chaudhry must contend with the ever-present potential for ethnic conflict within his coalition on such sensitive matters as land reform where he aims to improve the security of the Indian tenants, and over rivalries for cabinet and other government posts.

Some aspects of the election aftermath reinforce my argument about the significance of the chiefs in contemporary political process. Fiji's president, Ratu Sir Kamisese Mara, refused a request by the Fijian Association Party, Labour's principal partner, that its own leader, Adi Kuini Speed (widow of the overthrown Dr Bavadra) be appointed prime minister. Chaudhry warmly acknowledged Mara's decisive influence in persuading the FAP to accept his leadership, and he sought to dispel Fijian anxieties 'about my intentions and those of my government' in a speech to a specially convened meeting of the Council of Chiefs. It was clear that Chaudhry viewed the occasion as crucial for strengthening the legitimacy of his leadership of the nation. In its fullsome rhetoric of respect, his address to the chiefs echoed that of Jai Ram Reddy, which had facilitated the constitutional reform. Chaudhry reaffirmed Reddy's 'assurances…that all communities…look to this great venerable institution for leadership and guidance in the good governance and well-being of our nation' (*Fiji Times*, 14 June 1999:22–3). He promised to protect and advance indigenous interests and to consult with the chiefs.

As chairman of the Council of Chiefs, Rabuka, still a potent icon of ethnic power and therefore well-suited for the office despite his lack of chiefly rank, will have an enhanced capacity to encourage Fijians to either oppose or cooperate with Chaudhry's government—at times to be a focal point of ethnicist resistance, and sometimes a mediator encouraging accommodation. In this respect Rabuka's new position may resemble that which leading chiefs have long taken in the national political arena. The crisis of expiring Indian farm leases, aggravated by Fijian resentment of the election outcome and threatening the national economic well-being, might prove to be his first challenge in this role. Some chiefs reacted against the Labour triumph by declaring that leases in their districts would not be renewed: 'Fijians have given up the political control of their native land. They are not prepared to give up anything else. They will now be reluctant to share with others' (Tui Wailevu, *Daily Post*, 23 June 1999).

A principle of shared national citizenship is a necessary condition for equitable development to meet basic human needs. In Fiji, the achievement of such a principle, still problematic nearly 30 years after political independence, must be based on the ideological and institutional management of deep ethnic difference. The centrality of chieftainship in framing Fijian ethnic identity has favoured this by constraining conflict with Indians and facilitating agreements for sharing land and political power. My theme refutes a commonly held view that the chiefs have been an obstacle to national integration.

Fijian chiefs and chiefly councils, as they were partly refashioned into 'neo-traditional' instruments of colonial rule, have been depicted in modernist academic discourse in terms of self-serving 'aristocratic' interests. Some writers have interpreted the military coups as primarily supporting the interests of 'the eastern chiefly élite' who stand in the way of unity among ordinary Fijians and Indians. These characterisations, mainly by political scientists, have misrepresented the social character of the Fijian élites who benefited from the coups (mostly commoners) and misled us about the place of chiefly leadership in shaping foundations for a nation state (Robertson and Tamanisau 1988; Lawson 1991; Sutherland 1992). While chiefs can certainly be said to have 'vested interests' (for example a privileged share in land rents), to focus attention on these will not illuminate the chiefs' significance in Fijian group and ethnic identities and in inter-ethnic accommodation. Anthropologists and historians have studied chiefs in the context of Fijian culture and administration (Nayacakalou 1975; Walters 1978; Sahlins 1981; MacNaught 1982; Kaplan 1988). They, too, have largely ignored the inter-ethnic context and some agree with the above characterisation of the chiefs (Howard 1991; Kaplan 1993). My discussion will focus on the paradoxical duality of modern Fijian chieftainship in both affirming and mediating the ethnic divide.

For indigenous Fijians today, the value of chieftainship is reinforced by its potency in symbolising an idealised traditional way of life in communal attachment to the land, in contrast with the often denigrated money-based modern lifestyles to which individuals and households are increasingly drawn. This contradiction has long been intensified by the profound ethnic divide. The Indians' superiority in commercial enterprise has both created economic opportunities for Fijians and provoked their resentment. The ethnic anxieties gave chiefs, and the state institutions empowering them, political strength, and significance as guardians of cultural identity, enabling them to keep their pre-eminence in leadership for many years after the introduction of the popular vote, often co-opting trade unionists and other potential challengers (Norton 1990). For all Fiji's economic modernity, its extensive urbanisation, and the marked predominance of commoners in leadership and administration today, the chiefs still embody the most potent cultural capital where matters of ethnic interest are seen to be at stake and for the legitimation of political leadership.

While chieftainship is the strongest expression of Fijian ethnic difference, it is always potentially accommodating, not antagonistic and excluding. Indeed, many Indians are disposed to view Fijian chieftainship favourably, because Indians need chiefs for the containment of ethnic conflict, no less than chiefs need Indians to shore up their popular relevance as the symbolic anchor of ethnic identity. To understand the part chiefs have played in the control of ethnic conflict we must link the culture and the development of modern political economy, for it is particularly in this linkage that chieftainship acquired its conciliatory function.

The national importance of the chiefs was underlined by an unprecedented event in the recent negotiations to reform Fiji's constitution. The principal Indian political leader was invited to speak before that bastion of Fijian ethnic identity and privilege—the Bose Levu Vakaturaga, the Great Council of Chiefs, comprising 50 Fijian chiefs from the 14 provinces. Jai Ram Reddy's address helped secure the chiefs' assent to a proposal agreed between Fijian and Indian politicians to change the post-coup constitution which heavily discriminated against the Indians. The proposal, later endorsed by parliament, will allow political representation in proportion to ethnic demography, a bi-partisan cabinet, and special powers for the Council of Chiefs.[1]

The Council of Chiefs is the strongest embodiment of Fijian ethnic identity and power, as a central presence in the nation. Originating in the assembly of chiefs who ceded their islands to the British Crown, it was formalised by the early governors to facilitate indirect rule and to select Fijian representatives for the colonial parliament. By the end of the colonial era its membership had been broadened to include commoner leaders who had emerged in modern contexts. After the army coup, it was remade in its old form as an almost exclusively chiefly council. Although the meetings are solemnly publicised to the nation as affirmations of indigenous tradition, there is also a modern corporate tone: important looking men in suits and ties assembling at Suva's main convention centre with their smart briefcases. There are a few women, several of the highest rank.

The Council is a forum where aggressively racial opinions are sometimes voiced, and national leaders sternly questioned. However, as part of the institutional framework of 'the Fijian way of life' it also provides direct and vicarious experiences, which, by enhancing Fijian convictions of political and cultural strength in relations with other ethnic groups, have encouraged acceptance of the concessions their leaders make to those groups. This strength embodied in the council stands in a balancing relation to non-Fijian economic advantages.

The invitation to Jai Ram Reddy to speak before the Council was organised by the then Prime Minister, Sitiveni Rabuka, who once expelled Reddy and his colleagues from parliament at gunpoint. Before introducing Reddy, Rabuka urged the chiefs 'to think of the other communities': 'International law has given us [Fijians] the right to self-determination…to administer our own affairs and to protect our interests…But equally under international law…we also have an obligation to look after the minority communities'. He called for 'a common vision of Fiji…united in our diversity…bound together by a commitment of love and care for each other…' (*Fiji Times*, 7 June 1997:2).

Reddy's speech began with a moving declaration of respect and unity: 'The grandson of an indentured labourer answers the call of the Bose Levu Vakaturaga…And together we keep an appointment with history…to put the final seal on a troubled era and to open a new chapter of hope'. He addressed his hosts as 'the chiefs not just of the indigenous Fijians, but of all the people of Fiji'. He spoke of how the ancestral chiefs had overcome their conflicts and laid the foundations for the modern nation in the Deed of Cession: 'Just as [they] were called to bind together a divided people…so is this great council…called upon again…to be a foundation of unity for the islands your ancestors set on the road to modern nationhood'. In suggesting the development of a 'partnership' between Indian and Fijian, Reddy assured the chiefs that 'we honour your place, and the place of your people, as the first inhabitants of Fiji…We seek not to threaten your security but to protect it…For in your security lies the basis for our own' (*Fiji Times*, 7 June, 1997).

The occasion was widely acclaimed in Fiji as a defining event, not just in the process of post-coup rapprochement, but for the larger quest to construct a political community reconciling the principle of indigenous primacy with multi-ethnic government. It affirmed the place of chieftainship in inter-ethnic accommodation, projecting for the national consciousness an image of complementarity and mutuality across difference.

Chieftainship and the control of militant ethnicity

The chiefs' approval of reform muted the voice of ethnic chauvinism. There were protest rallies by the 'Viti National Union of Taukei Workers' and the 'Indigenous Rights Movement', one speaker warning that 'the *lewe ni vanua* [the people of the land] will now turn against their chiefs, because they have betrayed the indigenous peoples' trust' (*Fiji Times* and *Daily Post*, 9 June, 1997). But the most significant feature of these challenges was that very few people took part.

The potential for a chauvinist challenge to his leadership had nonetheless inhibited Rabuka during his dialogue with Reddy. He swung repeatedly between ethnic and national visions, earnestly affirming a goal of power sharing, but later declaring he could only agree to change if it strengthened Fijian dominance. His popularity in the Fijian constituency remained based on his charismatic warrior action in pursuit of this power, but under the pressure for reforms, he has been trying to re-make himself as a national leader. As a commoner he has no basis of legitimacy for inter-ethnic 'bridging' actions, therefore he has had to rely on the chiefs to validate the compromise with Indian leaders, just as he depended on them to ratify his coup and secure his first regime, and to constrain the ethnic chauvinism inflamed by that crisis (Norton 1990). The Council of Chiefs later endorsed a new constitution and authorised the political party through which Rabuka has ruled.

At issue in all these episodes is the control of cultural capital, the discourses and relationships with which affirmations of ethnic identity can be made and manipulated. Discourses to rival modern chieftainship in the assertion of Fijian identity have usually remained marginal voices, despite stressful economic and social changes evidenced in urbanisation, rural land shortages, and local landowner protests, that might be expected to energise stronger expressions of ethnic militancy. A major reason for this is that chiefs remain firmly positioned in the hierarchical relationships of traditional groupings which continue to be at the centre of most Fijian social and cultural life (Norton 1993). The most progressive political group to challenge Rabuka has been careful to show its respect to chiefs. Although initially promoted as the party that would appeal to educated urban commoners on issues linking them with non-Fijians, it relies on traditional relationships and provincial loyalties for election campaigning. Prominent chiefs are among its most vocal leaders, and its commoner leaders have been quick to reprove Rabuka for insufficient consultation with the Council of Chiefs (Norton 1994).

What is most remarkable about Fiji is not that the popular interests shared across ethnic difference have yet to be given an effective political voice, but that antagonistic ethnic movements have not emerged more strongly than they have. The predominant pattern in the expression of ethnic difference and opposition has been an asymmetric complementarity and accommodation, rather than an antagonistic schism. Two factors have especially contributed to this. First, land sharing has been pivotal in shaping inter-ethnic relations at grassroots and national levels. It is an ongoing negotiable relationship, in which chiefs have played a major part. Second, the cultural logics and social forms of Fijian political life, centring on chieftainship, have constrained antagonistic ethnicity and facilitated conciliatory dialogue with Indian leaders.

The chiefs in the political economy of colonial Fiji

In the first 50 years of colonial government, many chiefs enjoyed power in a system of indirect rule which was designed to supervise Fijians in an administrative quarantine from the plantation economy. By the 1930s this system had been wound down, and the chiefs were marginalised in local government by the extended responsibilities of British district administrators (MacNaught 1982, Norton 1990). Yet it was at this time that chiefs began, under pressure from the colonial government, to assume a place in the management of the economy.

The Australian company controlling the sugar industry was re-making its plantation proletarians into smallholder peasants under contract to supply cane to the mills. After carving its own estates into thousands of tiny tenancies, the company relied on new farmers securing leases from Fijian clans. However, this movement clashed with a growing Fijian interest in cash cropping as the government began to encourage 'individualism…to fit the Fijian for competition with his Indian neighbour' (Fletcher 1932).

As Fijians exploited tenant vulnerability by encouraging bribes and threatening not to renew leases, colonial officials viewed their new 'land consciousness' as a threat to the Indian settlers (Barton 1936).

The company warned that 'any question of control of the land situation getting into the hands of the original owners must only end in calamity for all' (CSR 1934).[2] These concerns were reinforced by the English crusader for Indian welfare and friend of Gandhi, Charles Andrews, who concluded after his 1936 visit that many Indian farmers faced dispossession, and that 'the whole fabric of the sugar industry is in danger of collapsing' (Andrews 1936). The sense of urgency was intensified also by pressures from the Government of India in response to demands from Gandhi's movement.

The governor, wanting to avoid 'an imposed solution', was convinced that 'the problem should be faced…while the Fijians still…rely upon their chiefs to decide for them' (Richards 1937). Within months of Andrews' visit, he relied on the most influential chief, Ratu Sukuna, to persuade the Council of Chiefs, and the provincial councils, to allow government to manage the leasing out of clan lands not required for members' use. Sukuna preached to his fellow chiefs on the wisdom and morality of sharing land with the Indians from whose labour 'much of our prosperity is derived…The owner of property has an important duty to perform…Bear in mind the story of the talents: whoever utilises what is given him will be given more. He who fails to use what he has, will lose all…It is therefore the bounden duty of landowners to utilise what they possess for the benefit of all.' Sukuna urged an end to unethical practices that were damaging the morality and dignity of Fijians and their culture: 'The land can only be fairly leased if this is regulated by the government…We shall receive more rents for there will be no waste land. We will live peacefully with our neighbours…and we shall have dissipated causes of evils that are now giving us a disreputable name' (Sukuna 1936).

Sukuna warned the chiefs that if they rejected his proposal, 'our house will be forcibly put in order [from] without'. His success in winning their assent was hailed as a breakthrough for economic development, and the chiefs were praised for their 'act of loyalty and trust' and their 'statesmanlike attitude towards the general affairs of the colony' (Barton 1936:7). Sukuna was soon conceding that in the cane areas Indian interests should be paramount (Administrative Officers' Conference 1944). He had earlier insisted that 'the Indian community, having shown us the way, can hardly expect to continue to hold all the land in the sugar districts where the plough mints money' (Legislative Council Debates 1933:301).

The strongest expression of indigenous identity, chiefly leadership, had become a support for Indian prosperity. Central to this paradoxical link was the relationship the Deed of Cession had created between the chiefs and the British Crown, a bond of mutual commitment that established their collective authority in indigenous leadership, and, by binding the chiefs so strongly to the colonial state, helped to secure the Indians' position. On Sukuna's death, Vishnu Deo, the senior Indian political leader, lamented that 'the Indian community had lost a very good friend' (*Fiji Times*, 31 May 1958:1).

The potential conflict between the chiefs' decision and popular Fijian opinion is reflected in protests at the time by the exiled millenarian leader Apolosi Nawai 'The chiefs...have spoiled much of the land of their people and have given away many leases to Indians...All the good lands have been taken by Indians.' Now, with his release impending, Apolosi sent to his expectant followers a 'Proclamation of the New Era', announcing momentous events to come, including the destruction of 'the haughty chief'. He was confined to Suva and soon returned to exile.

The chiefs in inter-ethnic relations

For a brief time, the chiefs themselves were seen to pose the threat of disaffection. Their cooperation had become essential just as their status and authority had been greatly diminished, with some senior chiefs enduring a humiliating subordination to young European district officers. In this contradictory conjuncture, the chiefs' grievance was redressed by a new governor who worked with Sukuna to elevate their position, in a restored system of 'indirect rule'. In justifying this regressive move to the Colonial Office, the governor insisted that it was 'urgently necessary to broaden the base of Native collaboration'. He warned 'Fijians have political representation...but no direct responsibility or authority...If this does not produce irresponsible nationalism or racialism it will be surprising' (Mitchell 1943).[3]

Leading chiefs were placed in a stronger position in the state than ever before. The Council of Chiefs was made, in effect, a 'board of directors', controlling appointments to the Fijian Affairs Board. Sukuna became the first non-European in the colonial cabinet as executive head of a system of administration designed to confine as many Fijians as possible to a communal village life. The liberal philosophy of the 1930s had been reversed. When Sukuna was first appointed to the Legislative Council, colonial officials hoped he would help guide the Fijians in 'their transition to individualism' (Secretary for Native Affairs 1932). He now governed them with the conviction that they were 'still at heart subsistence villagers' (Norton 1990:46).

The new paternalism held contradictory meanings for the Fijian people. Many resented it for impeding free movement for work and residence. However, as Indian demographic superiority grew, and as the prospect of self-government loomed, the strength of the new institutions and of the chiefs in the state, gave them a reassuring symbolic importance. Indeed, it is one of the ironic twists of Fiji's history that the obstacles the Fijian administration placed in the way of Fijian economic advancement, helped to strengthen anxieties which gave the system value, as a framework and symbol of ethnic solidarity and political strength, against the perceived threat from the economically more successful Indians. For Fijians the postwar era was marked by a protective fusion of chieftainship, the state, and ethnic identity.

Yet in the context of inter-ethnic relations the chiefly élite assumed an identity as mediators and conciliators, no less than as ethnic boundary markers and rallying points of ethnic solidarity. This dual identity was encouraged by the new postwar colonial ideology. The empowering of leading chiefs as a 'corporate' ethnic élite governing a still largely segregated Fijian populace, occurred as the British Government remade its philosophy of rule, proclaiming a mission to encourage among colonial subjects everywhere a sense of national identity in preparation for self-government.

An annual holiday was introduced to celebrate the anniversary of the chiefs' gift of their islands to the British Crown. Until the 1950s this celebration was an affair between government and the Fijians. Now the occasion was to be commemorated 'not as a Fijian day, but as Fiji's day'. The Deed of Cession was made sacred as having secured peace and civilisation, marking the ancestral chiefs' commitment to the development of Fiji as a modern nation. Cession Day, Governor Garvey declared, was to be 'a focal point for the spirit of unity…[We] must think not as Fijians, Indians or Europeans, but as one' (*Fiji Times*, 29 September 1955:4–5, 6 November 1953:4). For the first time strong official efforts were made to inculcate in Indians a sense of belonging and importance (Administrative Officers' Conference 1953).

Chiefs in the Fijian Administration, or district officers in mainly Indian areas, assumed prominent roles in celebrations and festivals, and were drawn into relations with Indians as patrons or office-bearers in local social or sports clubs, or as chairmen of town boards.

Ties between mainly Indian organisations and Fijian chiefs became important as affirmations of the growth of a multi-ethnic society. There was, in these bonds, a sense of reconciliation between the 'foreign' agents of economic modernity and the élite custodians of an indigenous culture and political strength upon whose goodwill all ultimately depended. Both A.D. Patel and Vishnu Deo, the principal Indian leaders, agreed that Fijian interests should be paramount in government (Legislative Council Debates 1944:44, 1946:211, 1947:112, 1948:219). What most gave significance to the process of inter-ethnic bridging were the problems of land, which, while being a chronic source of ethnic tension, also encouraged negotiation and accommodation at both the local and national levels.

Thus it is another of Fiji's historical ironies that the immigrant Indians, emancipated from the ancient caste system, and developing an egalitarian society among themselves (Mayer 1973; Jayawardena 1975, 1980; Kelly 1991), were compelled by economic interests to come to terms with a new order of ascriptive difference and inequality—as dependent *vulagi* (guests) to their *taukei* hosts and patrons. For no other overseas Indian community did cultural and economic difference become the basis for an inter-ethnic system. The inequality in control of the means of production, and in associated forms of social deference, was offset by the material gains and by a conviction of cultural superiority. A contradiction soon emerged between the universalist egalitarian ideals adopted from Gandhi's movement for political agitation in Fiji, and the benefits accruing to Indians from the preservation of Fijian village 'communalism' within the framework of chiefly authority. Land leases were readily available and cheap to the Indian farmers and shopkeepers, to the extent that the *taukei* owners remained docile subsistence village folk little in need of money incomes, as most did until the 1970s. In the last decades of colonial rule, paternalistic Fijian administration was effectively a subsidy to Indian peasant welfare (and CSR company profits). Indeed of all overseas Indian populations descended from indentured workers, Fiji's has been one of the most economically successful (Subramani 1995).

The dual identity of leading chiefs as both ethnic and national figures is highlighted in the manner in which Sukuna is now revered on 'Ratu Sukuna Day' instigated by the Council of Chiefs several years after the army coups. The greatest chief of the colonial era is now exalted as a model of Fijian leadership for the national society, symbolising a way in which Fijian 'tradition' (or 'neo-tradition') might be incorporated into the core of a national political culture.

Sukuna represents the idealisation of high chiefs as figures of unassailable strength and dignity, representing and protecting Fijians, their land and culture in the modern world. Yet he also symbolises the role a chiefly leader should play in bridging the ethnic divide: 'Ratu Sukuna, the man who graced a nation. This man of noble birth carried out deeds with even greater nobility, without motive against any race in Fiji's multiracial society' (*Fiji Times*, 29 May 1995:1). On Sukuna Day in 1995, as public hearings for the constitutional review began, Rabuka's press statement intoned: 'The unity and sanctity of traditional Fijian society was always his first and foremost interest...But at the same time it was clear to him that Fijians would have to adjust to coexistence with other communities...All share a common wish to live peacefully...and to contribute to the development of Fiji' (*Fiji Times*, 29 May 1995:1).

A major outcome of the military coups has been a greater prominence of commoners in political leadership. The leading figures in Rabuka's government have been mostly commoners, and he has often displayed charismatic authority and skill in influencing decisions of the Council of Chiefs. Yet it is also clear that in the post-coup political process the chiefs have become more significant in the national domain. The part played by the Council in the recent constitutional reform highlighted this role, and the iconic Sukuna symbolically affirms it.

Three models for nationhood

Post-coup debate about how to make the nation revolves around three models or 'discourses'. At one extreme is the ethno-nationalist vision: an antagonistic and exclusionary ethnicity affirmed by some Fijian individuals and groups against Indians, such as the Taukei Movement launched for the street marches and violence that influenced the staging of the army coups. The proponents have typically been commoners. At the other extreme, a 'universalist' vision of equivalence among the citizens as workers, farmers, and consumers, is held by many leaders (mainly Indians) in the labour movement, by most of the Indian religious and political groups, some churches, and by some Fijians and others in the urban middle class. Its leading political proponent, Mahendra Chaudhry, was marginalised in the negotiations for constitutional reform, and another prominent advocate, Imrana Jalal, recently lamented that 'we still remain communities living side by side rather than with each other' (*Fiji Times*, 19 June 1997:7).

The prevailing model of the nation affirms an asymmetric complementarity linked with the role of chieftainship in the management of ethnic relations. The records of the Constitutional Review Commission show that most Fijian submissions did not express an 'antagonistic ethnicity', but a theme of accommodation and inclusion. They stressed the idea of a complementarity based on preserving Fijian political pre-eminence in some form. Although the petition of Rabuka's own party emphasised popular distrust of Indians and insisted on preserving *taukei* dominance, the Council of Chiefs declined to endorse it, and the party leaders themselves stressed that their document was a starting position from which compromise would be negotiated, as indeed it was.

Conclusion

The colonial legacy for ethnic relations in post-colonial Fiji has two dimensions. Most obvious is the reinforcement of the ethnic divide marked by persisting differences and inequalities in economy, culture, and social relations. In political life these differences have outweighed people's shared interests as workers, farmers, and consumers. The other colonial legacy, less recognised, is the one with which the post-colonial political process has now strongly reconnected: cultural codes and social structures that facilitate mediation and accommodation across difference.

The colonial rulers encouraged the development of a chiefly élite enjoying a privileged position in the state and embodying core values of indigenous Fijian culture. Yet chiefly political privilege has not inevitably been equated with Fijian ethno-nationalism. On the contrary, the formation of the chiefly élite facilitated the growth of a national political economy, and inhibited potentials for antagonistic ethnicity. The significance of the chiefs in the national political process has been their paradoxically dual position as, on the one hand, ethnic boundary markers and rallying figures in the occasional affirmation of indigenous Fijian solidarity in opposition to Indians, and on the other hand, as mediators of that division, reconcilers of the conflicting demands of ethnic and national arenas. This accommodation was favoured precisely by the manner in which Fijian ethnic identity and leadership were constituted from the late colonial period on the basis of the privileged relation between chieftainship and the state.

Of the four principal chiefs who dominated the Council of Chiefs and Fijian political leadership after Sukuna's death, only Ratu Sir Kamisese Mara survives. Both he and the late Ratu Sir Penaia Ganilau played a crucial part in moderating the impact of the Taukei Movement and the military coups. Elected political leadership is now dominated by commoners or people of relatively low traditional rank. Yet the chiefs, particularly as the Council of Chiefs, still hold considerable power as the most potent source of legitimacy for the policies and actions of leaders and as holders of prerogatives in the state under the reformed constitution. They will control appointments of the president and vice-president, and of nearly half the seats in an upper house where they will hold veto power.

Of course, the circumstances of ethnic relations today are very different from those in which the forms of Fijian leadership and ethnic identity I have been describing were shaped. The inter-ethnic role of the chiefs was linked with a pattern of complementarity supported in large part by a substantial ethnic separation in economy. There is now an increasing competition for jobs, land, and other economic resources. A critical question for Fiji's future is whether the chiefs will continue to act as conciliators, or whether, as this competition intensifies, they will align with the aggressively ethnicist styles of leadership they have in the past helped to subdue.

Notes

1   The reforms introduce some common roll seats, complementing a majority of communal seats, as well as allocating the latter roughly in proportion to ethnic demography. The offices of President, Vice-President and Prime Minister will no longer be reserved for Fijians (Parliament of Fiji 1996, 1997; Lal 1997). Several factors pushed the leaders towards an accord. Rabuka must nurture a stagnating national economy dependent on the resources of non-indigenous people and foreign investors. Since the coups, one in seven Indians have emigrated, to the great detriment of all Fiji. On the other hand, this exodus helped give Fijians a demographic edge that emboldened their leaders to agree to changes that will allow an Indian share in government. Further inducements were the wish for readmission to the Commonwealth and pressures on human

rights issues from major foreign aid givers and trade partners. While all these factors were important, the rapprochement was enabled by features of Fijian leadership discussed here.

2 By 1934, 4,600 farmers were tenants of Fijians, and 4,100 were company tenants (Lal 1992:100).

3 Sukuna's ambivalence toward the British began with his rejection on racial grounds when as a young Oxford student he tried to enlist for World War I. At the height of his career he united with Indian leaders against discriminatory legislation, had a close friendship with a leading Indian critic of colonial rule, and was sympathetic to striking Indian cane farmers. Continuing official anxiety about Fijian loyalty is revealed in Governor Freeston's urgent request to London for funds to rebuild the leading Fijian school. He warned that dissatisfaction 'was reaching such a pitch as to threaten the longstanding Fijian loyalty to government…Further procrastination will have disturbing political consequences' (Freeston 1949).

References

Administrative Officers' Conference, 1944. Fiji National Archives CSO files, FSO/104.

——, 1953. Fiji National Archives F4/3/7-5.

Andrews, C.F., 1936. *Report to Government of Fiji, May 1936*, CO83/215, 85038/36. AJCP Reels 4168 and 4169, PRO London.

Barton, L., 1936. Acting Governor Luxon Barton to Secretary of State for Colonies 31/10/1936, PRO London CO83/215/15.

CSR (Colonial Sugar Refining Company Ltd), 1934. General Manager, Sydney, to Governor of Fiji 23/2/1934. PRO London CO83/207/9.

Fletcher, M., 1932. Governor M Fletcher to Secretary of State for Colonies 26/1/1932, PRO London CO 83 196/7.

Freeston, B., 1949. Freeston to Secretary of State for Colonies 12/1/1949, Fiji National Archives CSO files, F28/225.

Howard, M., 1991. *Fiji: Race and Politics in an Island State*, University of British Columbia Press, Vancouver.

Jayawardena, C., 1975. 'Farm, household and family in Fiji Indian rural society (Part 1)', *Journal of Comparative Family Studies*, 6(1):74–88.

——, 1975. 'Farm, household and family in Fiji Indian rural society (Part 2)', *Journal of Comparative Family Studies*, 6(2):209–221.

——, 1980. 'Culture and ethnicity in Guyana and Fiji', *Man*, 15:430–450.

Kaplan, M., 1988. Land and sea and the new white men: a reconsideration of the Fijian Tuka Movement, PhD thesis, Department of Anthropology, University of Chicago.

——, 1993. 'Imagining a nation: race, politics, and crisis in postcolonial Fiji', in V.Lockwood, T.Harding, and B.Wallace (eds), *Contemporary Pacific Societies*, Prentice-Hall, New Jersey, 43–54.

Kelly, J., 1991. *A Politics of Virtue: Hinduism, Sexuality, and Countercolonial Discourse in Fiji*. University of Chicago Press, Chicago.

Lal, B., 1992. *Broken Waves: a history of Fiji in the 20th century*, University of Hawaii Press, Honolulu.

——, 1997. 'Towards a united future: report of the Fiji Constitution Review Commission', *Journal of Pacific History*, 32(1):71–84.

Lawson, S., *The Failure of Democratic Politics in Fiji*, Clarendon Press, Oxford.

MacNaught, T., 1982. *The Fijian Colonial Experience*, Pacific Research Monograph No.7, Australian National University, Canberra.

Mayer, A., 1973. *Peasants in the Pacific*, Routledge & Kegan Paul, London.

Mitchell, P., 1943. Sir Phillip Mitchell to Secretary of State for Colonies 15/4/1943, 16/7/43. PRO London CO/83 236/15.

Nayacakalou, R., 1975. *Leadership in Fiji*. Oxford University Press, Melbourne.

Norton, R., 1990. *Race and Politics in Fiji* (second edition),University of Queensland Press, St Lucia .

——, 1993. 'Culture and identity in the South Pacific: a comparative analysis', *Man*, 28(4):741–59.

——, 1994. 'Ethnic conflict and accommodation in post-coup Fiji', in G.Hage, J.Lloyd and L.Johnson, *Pluralising the Asia-Pacific* (Volume 3 of *Communal/Plural*), Research Centre in Intercommunal Studies, University of Western Sydney, Sydney: 43–64.

Parliament of Fiji, 1996. The Fiji Islands—towards a united future, Parliamentary Paper No 34 of 1996, Report of the Fiji Constitution Review Commission.

——, 1997. Report of the Joint Parliamentary Select Committee on the Report of the Fiji Constitution Review Commission, Parliamentary Paper No 17 of 1997.

Richards, A., 1937. Governor Richards to Secretary of State for Colonies 30/12/37, PRO London CO83/222/8.

Robertson, R., and Tamanisau, A., 1988. *Fiji: Shattered Coups*, Pluto Press, Sydney.

Sahlins, M., 1981. 'The stranger-king', *Journal of Pacific History*, 16(3):107–32.

Secretary for Native Affairs, 1932. Secretary of Native Affairs to Colonial Secretary 5/7/1932, Fiji National Archives, CSO CF38/1.

Subramani, 1995. *Altering Imagination*, Fiji Writers' Association, University of the South Pacific, Suva.

Sukuna, R. L., 1936. Ratu Lala Sukuna to Council of Chiefs, Bau 31/10/36, PRO London CO83215/15.

Sutherland, W., 1992. *Beyond the Politics of Race: an alternative history of Fiji to 1992*, Political and Social Change Monograph 15, Australian National University Research School of Pacific and Asian Studies, Canberra.

Walters, M., 1978. 'An examination of hierarchical notions in Fijian society: a test case for the applicability of the term 'chief'', *Oceania*, 49(1):1–19.

12

Development and Maori society: building from the centre or the edge?

Shane Jones

The basic question in this chapter on Maori development is whether the rebuilding of Maori society should proceed from the rejuvenation of tribal membership rolls, or from other forms of organisation. The debate is a complex mixture of cultural nationalism, separating commerce from community, battling mainstream antagonism and discovering whether the trickle-down theory can overcome growing political dissatisfaction.

New Zealand has a population of approximately 3.5 million people. They are predominantly *pakeha*, of European extraction. The next largest group are the Maori, descendants of the original Polynesian settlers, who comprise almost 12 per cent of the total population. Their ancestors signed the Treaty of Waitangi, which was entered into between the chiefs on behalf of their tribes and the British Crown in 1840.

The Treaty is a bilingual document, having been written initially in English then translated into Maori by the Anglican missionaries. It contains three articles, each of which has been the subject of great disagreement between successive generations of Maori and the Crown. The first article ceded sovereignty to the Crown. The word 'sovereignty,' however, was not translated clearly. Rather than using the ancient Polynesian word *mana*, a transliteration, *kawanatanga* (*kawana*, from English 'governor') was favoured. The latter, a term used by the translators of the Bible to describe the status of Pontius Pilate, did not convey the concept of handing over powers of ultimate political authority.

The second article recognised Maori ownership of natural resources and guaranteed the continued authority of the chiefs. The precise extent of this authority was not however outlined. It was seen as a threat to the sovereignty of the Crown and, not surprisingly, disappeared from the political framework. The ownership by Maori of land and natural resources was soon weakened once the European settlers had increased in numbers and the Crown had a large enough military presence.

The third article accorded to Maori the rights and privileges of British subjects. This however was of limited relevance because the actual Treaty was not incorporated into the domestic law of New Zealand and was ruled as having no legal status. At the time of the signing of the Treaty, New Zealand was overwhelmingly under the control of the Maori chiefs, but as each decade passed, immigration increased and the Maori soon became a minority. As European settlers arrived and possessed the resources of the countryside and ocean through a host of means ranging from war through to legislative fiat and free transactions, the pressure grew to create a system of government which was controlled by settler society rather than colonial governors.

This was achieved with the Constitution Act 1852, which led to the creation of a legislature and the establishment of a system of government where authority for law-making was based in New Zealand as opposed to being exercised through the Queen's representative. During this period where there was a transfer of political power from the Crown to the settler-dominated legislature, the Maori chiefs continued to assert the importance of their relationship with the distant British Crown. They continually pointed to the founding document, the Treaty of Waitangi, as the protection of their rights and authority over their people and resources. Their entreaties, however, fell on deaf ears. As each decade passed they were encouraged to take the matters up with NZ governments, as they were seen as issues of domestic policy. Needless to say the tribes suffered further and within 20 years after the signing of the Treaty of

Waitangi over 45 million acres of the country had passed from Maori ownership. The appetite for land continued unabated. Throughout the 1800s the pressure exerted on Maori to yield their resources was constant. Wars were fought, and as payment for services, the colonial soldiers received land.

As in any frontier economy the largest profits went to those who speculated on the land. The distinction between legislator and land speculator was virtually nil. To aid the land alienation process a special court, the Native Land Court, was created in the 1860s. Its purpose was to convert customary title into a form that was recognisable in terms of British-based tenure law and alienable. It was a devastating and cost-efficient way of completing the process of alienating tribal land, and by the turn of the century less than 10 per cent of the land base of New Zealand was left in Maori ownership. The Maori population sank perilously low at this time, declining to a mere 40,000. This led commentators of the day to conclude that Maori were indeed a dying race. Poor health, constantly high infant mortality rates, decrepit housing, insufficient land resources, grossly inadequate educational opportunities and a general marginalisation rendered Maori vulnerable. Despite this, however, the Maori rates of participation in both the World Wars was very high. In each war Maori made very significant contributions and were formed into distinctive organisations, the most notable being the Maori Battalion of World War II.

The socioeconomic status of Maori has continued to be a blight within New Zealand. During the 1960s and 1970s an enormous shift took place as entire rural hinterlands were emptied of their Maori populations. The growth of New Zealand manufacturing, the wool boom and a general positive performance of the economy meant there was a great need for labour within the cities. Attempts to develop Maori land-holdings were not adequate to meet the rising needs of the population. Fishing was not an option as the capital barriers were substantial, licenses were difficult to procure and the law did not recognise the existence of Maori customary fishing rights. The writing was not only 'on the wall' but within the bureaucracy as well, as government officials encouraged and facilitated the urban migration of Maori. Unfortunately the infrastructure within the cities could not cope with the arrival of such large numbers of Maori. Although housing was eventually made available it was often located in areas where there were no other services. The support networks of the extended family were not able to cope, and problems followed.

The vast majority of the Maori population no longer speak the language, the family structure has eroded to a point where approximately 50 per cent of Maori children are brought up in single-parent families and a larger proportion are being raised by parents or care-givers who receive welfare benefits. Subsistence on a marginal rural resource base has been overtaken by welfare dependency.

During the 1970s Maori (primarily *rangatahi*, young people) begun to publicise through protest action the poor socioeconomic status of Maori and they focused on the Treaty of Waitangi. The Treaty, after years of neglect and dismissal by governments became an icon for Maori aspirations. Within Maori society it had never been forgotten. For mainstream society however its status had been severely diminished. Successive generations of New Zealanders had been fed a diet, through the education system, of the 'happy go lucky Maori' and the inevitability of assimilation. The low social status of Maori and their marginal economic status was never critically analysed or understood by educators in terms of the abandonment of the Treaty of Waitangi.

During the 1970s and 1980s, as the Treaty became more the object of political activism and social commentary, the political parties slowly adopted resolutions requiring that the Treaty be recognised and grievances concerning the historical loss of tribal resources be investigated and settled. The judicial system could not satisfactorily respond to the Treaty as it did not have legal status. The route forward was inexorably political. It was an extraordinary development that a seemingly obscure, colonial artifice, a 'toothless' document, should influence the economic and political agenda of governments in the final years of the twentieth century.

In 1975 the Labour government established a special Treaty of Waitangi Tribunal to hear claims from Maori as to how the principles of the Treaty had been violated through legislative action or policy. It was given powers of recommendation but could only consider claims arising from actions after 1975. In 1985 when the same political party became government again, after many years in opposition, it went further and enabled the Tribunal to hear grievances stemming from the time that the actual treaty was signed. This effectively served up the entire colonial history of New Zealand for inspection at the end of the twentieth century.

At the time these changes were taking place, the New Zealand system of government and the economy went through a rapid series of reforms. Vast areas of the government were restructured into commercial and non-commercial enterprises. The former became state-owned enterprises under a statute known as the State Owned Enterprises Act. Telecommunications, forests, hotels, railways, shipping companies, energy supply companies and a host of other operations were either corporatised or sold outright. Virtually every sector of the economy was restructured. Unemployment grew markedly, and Maori were the principal casualties.

In a macroeconomic sense New Zealand has undertaken a series of reforms that has captured the attention of international economic policymakers. It is quite incongruous that this economic liberalisation has taken place at the same time as the historical grievances of Maori have been given legislative space to grow. In terms of socioeconomic status, Maori fortunes have plummeted as the reforms have set in. Whether a process focused on historical events can address contemporary socioeconomic problems for Maori remains to be seen. The publicity surrounding the historical Maori claims has grown enormously. The dislocation from the structural adjustment programs implemented by recent governments has caused anger and resentment towards Maori and their claims under the Treaty of Waitangi, the implication being that the Maori are enjoying a separate and privileged treatment.

History: retribution or recovery?

It is interesting to note that as the historical grievances have been examined by the Waitangi Tribunal, Maori have endeavoured to weave together several development strategies. First they have sought to affirm the primacy of Maori as *tangata whenua*, the original people, the indigenes. To do this it has been necessary to draw on oral testimony which reinforces pre-Christian beliefs and stories about the creation of the world, the order between people, environment and the universe. This has given greater exposure to traditional Maori cosmology and served as an introduction for younger Maori of their ancestors and their *kaupapa*, foundation beliefs. It serves to boost the *mana*, the sense of power, status and prestige, inherited from the ancestors and the gods.

In terms of development this process of affirmation is likened to a rite of passage, giving development strategies a root against which colonialism can be measured. Not suprisingly it also easily becomes an ideological tool. For the more politically inclined it is wielded as evidence of the degrading and destructive legacy of British imperialism. Maori identity must be refashioned or rearranged to give absolute primacy to the pre-colonial ideas and concepts of belonging, place and achievement. Given that these are impossible to know, there is an broad scope for interpretation.

For those who wish to see the growth of the market economy and its stress on personal responsibility, the importance of being *tangata whenua* is principally about property. After all, how can one enjoy primacy unless there is a set of rights outlining that which you hold primacy over, and that which ought to be kept well beyond the grasp of collective power? In this view, the magico-spiritual notions are personal beliefs and tolerable providing they do not inhibit the growth, exchange or trade in property.

Whether there is virtue in either of these two views cannot be settled here. Rather it is to illustrate that the development debate is saddled with having to resolve the deep feelings of sadness and resentment that Maori have been denied their historical place. Their history over the past 150 years has been the victim of a conspiracy of silence. Through inattention and an unwillingness to depict the causes and impacts of historical resource loss accurately there is now a well of scepticism.

The hearing of evidence as to how the ancestors were militarily overcome, forced to yield their resources and then reduced to constant poverty, is both a relief and a burden. For many it is an overdue recognition of what actually took place as New Zealand *pakeha* sought to make their place. The moral force of the Treaty of Waitangi was overridden; the Maori were not the authors of their own demise. When the Crown acknowledges that indeed much of what took place was in direct contravention of the Treaty, it is often regarded as vindicating the stance taken by the ancestors and affirms that they were not inferior. The *mana* of the ancestors remains intact. Having achieved that, it is appropriate to move from grievance mode and into development mode.

Such a process, however, becomes a burden if the current generations of *pakeha* are held responsible for every crime or historical error towards the Maori. With the restoration of *mana* the spirit of retribution creeps in. In a quantitative sense it is neither possible nor necessarily desirable to force current generations to recompense Maori for historical wrongs fully. Obviously it is unfair that the Crown allowed the Treaty to be violated and that Maori have lost the majority of their resources. The notion of fairness however is double-edged. Current generations of *pakeha* are adamant that they should not bear the brunt of the costs of colonialism.

The burden becomes evident when development is seen as synonymous with 'selling out' one's heritage. It is easier for many to maintain a sense of grievance against the Crown because this conveys an air of righteousness. It is also far more comfortable than taking responsibility for trying to move on from a heavy chapter of history, especially when any move may be condemned by future generations and will most certainly be criticised by a sizeable chunk of the current generation. Setting out to honour one's ancestors and salvaging their aspirations through retrieving the Treaty is often only a short distance from descending into a spiral of victim mentality.

From the centre or the edge?

Rights are social constructions and must be accompanied by countervailing duties. Their nature and character is altered as the circumstances impacting on the holders and the resource change. The original rationale of entitlement may remain but the extent to which that rationale can be satisfied is not set in stone. Rather it flows, and it is inevitably in conflict with expectations or the needs of the various groups that may have interests in the entitlement.

Given the primacy accorded to culture and its central importance in defining the modern identity of Maori, it is not surprising that there has been a growing interest in revitalising the identity and the operational capacity of the tribes. These are sociopolitical forms of organisation that were recorded as being in existence at the time of the Treaty of Waitangi. It is asserted that the rights that were lost in the process of colonisation were vested in the tribal collectivities. The losses may have been suffered by individuals and their personal circumstances may have been blighted, but the repository of the rights is the collectivity. It is asserted that by doing this, the integrity of the culture is safeguarded and the identity of the individual is assured, along with their tribal patrimony. In practice this means that the capital to be transferred by the Crown, as a consequence of the historical claims being satisfactorily settled, is to be vested in corporate bodies representing the tribal membership. Given that one can never renounce one's tribal membership it is envisaged that this type of arrangement will sustain the existence of the tribe.

The challenge, however, arises when theory meets reality. The Maori population is overwhelmingly urbanised. It is by no means clear that a majority of Maori are regularly involved in tribal affairs. The tribes are rooted in certain territories, virtually all of which are rural, with an occasional urban presence. If there happens to be a city or large town within their boundaries, it is difficult to maintain contact with the full membership of the group.

The importance of the settlement of historical grievances is bound up with the affirmation of *mana* and the transfer of capital. Development cannot be sustainable if *mana* is not left intact. It represents the link with the past, both ancestral and divine, the roots of identity, as reflected in the well-known saying, *He purapura i ruia mai i Rangiatea, e kore au e ngaro*—A shoot planted in Rangiatea, I will not be lost.

Capital is a means to an end. As we proceed with the historical grievance settlement process, it is apparent that the end has more to do with sustaining the ancestral legacy, to ensure that future generations of Maori are well-adjusted in their culture. Increasingly added to this, is the notion of being competitive in the economy. To this end the debate about resource endowments looms large. The capacity of these endowments, however, in actually changing the material well-being of Maori depends on the quality of management. As Maori emerge from a prolonged period of poor education, suspicion of mainstream institutions, in particular the justice system, and poor socioeconomic status, the management of the capital flowing from these tribal settlements is a difficult issue.

In addition, the national census statistics show that 25 per cent of the population of Maori descent do not know their tribal affiliation. This is perhaps not surprising given the historical pattern of resource loss and the marginal position which tribes have had in terms of economic activity. Very few have been able to offer material assistance to their members. However, within the development model, flowing from the settlement of historical grievances, tribes are given an important role. Not only are they seen as being the body to receive assets but also the body to distribute the benefits, and this is a problem if significant numbers of the potentially eligible group are not known or have lost contact with their tribal kin and the administration.

This problem is currently before the courts in New Zealand as organisations formed to advance the interests of Maori based in the cities, are challenging the exclusive authority of the tribal bodies to deliver resources and fulfil development programs. The urban bodies wish to be included in the list of organisations eligible to receive assistance from the Treaty of Waitangi Fisheries Commission—a body formed to hold, administer and distribute resources to Maori from the multi-million dollar fisheries settlement completed with the Crown in 1992.

The urban organisations do not doubt the existence of Maori tribal bodies or their importance. They are, however, adamant that the Maori population is dynamic and institutions need to change to service the needs of Maori. In their view the needs of city-based Maori will not be met by traditional tribal bodies. They view the settlement of historical grievances as being primarily to compensate individual Maori and to assist them break out of dependency. To do this there need to be programs that are tailored to meet their needs, based on a very good understanding of their actual situation and the capacity to work closely with them.

A further view is expressed by those who do not favour the allocation of resources to tribal bodies because of human capital constraints. In their view the transfer of resources to Maori from the historical grievance process should be dedicated to building up large corporations with growing capital bases. The funds should be dedicated to meeting growth targets, maintaining technology advances and investment in people through a dividend policy that sees them engaging in further education and training. This is regarded as a centrist approach and is criticised as undermining the cultural identity of Maori. By not treating the tribe as the primary body for the vesting of resources, it is regarded as a 'sell-out'. The Waitangi Tribunal has crystalised its thinking into a development model known as the tribal endowment thesis. It promotes the notion that all tribes require a critical mass of resources, a resource base that ensures all its members are able to learn tribal history and receive assistance for education and business development. An estate that they and their descendants can call their *turangawaewae*, a place to stand and celebrate their roots, a home away from the cities, and a place where each generation renews its ties with the past.

For fear of losing readers with too much detail it is important that several points are stressed here. Cultural politics cannot be underestimated. A particular model may make sense in a strict corporate, commercial sense. If, however, it is seen as weakening the capacity of the tribes to actually take possession of resources and engage in the development of those resources, it is likely that conflict will ensue. By and large the tribes are seen as being the legitimate bodies to advance the interests of Maori in terms of land-based historical settlements. In a linear sense they are the inheritors of the rights and resources denied to their forefathers. They are and will be handicapped for some time to come, however, as there are simply not enough skilled people from within their own ranks to fill the management responsibilities. This is only a temporary problem and will change as young Maori graduate, gain experience and take a place in the development of their own assets. Given the limited contact that the corporate world has had with Maori it will take a long time before the two worlds discover how to make their way together.

By and large the resources being returned to Maori lock them into the operations of the economy. The fisheries grievance was settled by assigning cash, share and fishing property rights (individual transferable quota) to Maori. The aspiration of the Maori leadership is for assets that generate immediate commercial returns, that can then be made available to the population in the form of dividend payments. The current leaders are very suspicious of the concept of investing to create work, although it is apparent that the greatest problem in Maori communities is unemployment. The model of the subsistence economy is not applicable to Maori today. The welfare dependency syndrome is relevant. Although the pressure is great to alleviate these problems, there are no major initiatives emerging from the historical grievance process to respond specifically to welfare dependency. By and large this is seen as a matter of personal responsibility and government action, and Maori urban authorities receive resources from the government to do this type of work. The tribal administrators, however, assert that if government cannot fix the problem, the tribal bodies will have greater difficulties, with their limited resources. Unless such problems are resolved, the amassing of assets and wealth under the name of tribal development may end up being of dubious benefit.

The distribution of resources is a question that Maori have only begun to address in the context of the historical grievance process. It is most certainly a critical issue. Unless the structure of Maori society is changed there will be no significant developments, notwithstanding the examination and laying bare the body of nineteenth century colonialism. Effecting a change to the structure of a society requires major investments in education, Maori are perhaps the most vulnerable in this regard.

Sustainability: fiat or ethic?

The Resource Management Act 1991, is the principal planning and management statute in New Zealand. Its purpose is the sustainable management of natural resources. More recently the Fisheries Act 1996, has been enacted with a similar provision. In each of these acts the notion of 'sustainability' is directed primarily at the natural environment. Social considerations are not given a prominent position, although economic issues of efficiency, and compliance costs of regulation, are an important consideration.

These statutes do, however, give status to *kaitiakitanga*, a term that is interpreted by the legislation as meaning 'the exercise of guardianship, in relation to a resource, including the ethic of stewardship based on the nature of the resource itself'. *Kaitiakitanga* derives from the word *tiaki*, which means to foster, to preserve and to protect. The prefix *kai* with the verb indicates the agent of the act. A *kaitiaki* is a guardian, conservator, foster parent, or protector. The suffix *tanga* added to the noun means guardianship, fostering, conservation and protection. In relation to environmental management *kaitiakitanga* is regarded as an ethic. It does not involve Maori having authority over natural resources independent of the statutory regime, but the incorporation of Maori terminology into the statutory lexicon has been seen as a triumph for Maori environmental values. It allows Maori to require formal environmental decision-makers to take into account a wider range of interests when natural resource decisions are made.

The pursuit of sustainability through improved environmental decision-making represents an interesting situation for Maori. Sustainability is associated with the imposition of limits to growth. The problem arises when these limits are measured and then imposed on Maori developments. More often than not, Maori communities will stress that they have a better approach to the protection of the environment than *pakeha*. This is often met with disdain by the members of the environmental movement, who quickly point out that large numbers of birds were wiped out by Maori prior to the arrival of *pakeha*. The application of the principles of sustainability is quickly overtaken by a political debate as to whether Maori resource-use decisions should be subject to legislative provisions. There have been cases where Maori have sought to mill native timber, which is a particularly scarce resource and an important habitat. Earlier generations of pioneers milled the vast majority of the native forests.

Current Maori landowners assert that they should be permitted to use their resources to improve the parlous socioeconomic status of their communities. In their view it is an equity issue. Why should they bear the full costs of retaining the final vestiges of the flora and fauna? There has been a range of formal responses, including the establishment of a fund to compensate forest owners. The level of milling has dropped off considerably. The conundrum, however, remains. In order for Maori to pursue the development of such resources they must run the gauntlet of public opprobrium. If the Crown agrees to compensate them for lost opportunity they are likely to be branded as carpetbaggers, but if they proceed to mill the resources, they are attacked as brown capitalists using the ethic of sustainability to suit their personal circumstances.

The conservation estate, those resources administered by the Department of Conservation under the Conservation Act, 1987, is the new theatre of conflict. This is where political debates between the environmentalists, tribes, tourism operators and the Crown are taking place. As the historical claims process gathers pace, the pressure to open up the conservation estate and transfer parts of it into Maori ownership grows. The majority of environmentalists view the estate as sacrosanct. For the Crown, however, it is of mixed importance, as not all of it is of high conservation value.

For Maori it has a range of values. It is a source of valuable material for arts and crafts. It also the location of many of important sites that represent identity, and the resting place of the ancestors. In addition, it is of economic value as a location for tourism. Such agendas for development are seen as a threat to sustainability. The environmentalists frequently criticise the Maori conservation agenda as being primarily driven by commercial motives. The tribes in response insist that they have been fine stewards of their resources and the public need not have any concerns. The debate about the conservation estate take places in many cases because there are precious few other blocks of economic resource which can be used to recompense the tribes for historical loss. The other resources such as the exotic forestry plantations developed by the Crown over the twentieth century have been sold as a part of the restructuring of the national economy. The former farms developed by successive governments have been corporatised, and are administered as state owned enterprises. This incenses the environmental constituency, who see the conservation estate as having to bear the freight of Maori development aspirations.

This is a reasonable fear given the pressure on Maori leaders to create employment for their people, but the employment potential of the conservation estate is very limited. In fact many of the resources likely to be included in the Treaty of Waitangi settlements, including the fisheries settlement, are not capable of generating great numbers of jobs. The pressure on the conservation estate to yield employment opportunities is likely to force owners to consider projects that are threatening to environmentalists. Redressing historical resource loss may result in asset transfers; such transfers of resources, however, will require ongoing sustainable management. There will not be a separate regime for the tribes to manage their resources as they see fit. Decisions will be made and bound by the standards contained in the Resource Management Act and associated planning schemes.

As Maori adopt more of a corporate approach to the organisation and development of their resources, the costs of sustainability will begin to bite. This has already begun to take place within the fishing industry. Maori shareholders are increasingly uneasy about the depletion of fish stocks. Their concerns, however, are not easily translated into management action. Competitors are not obliged to follow suit and desist from fishing in certain areas or for certain species. The fishing techniques are capital intensive, the markets are fickle and the margins are tight for the owners of fishing assets. Inevitably the fishing activities of large companies are a threat to customary and non-commercial Maori fishing. This is unavoidable as the fisheries cannot cope with the expectations of the recreational sector, as well as those of commercial investors. The resource, like all fisheries, is continuing to decline. Maori custom might advise a reduction of effort but the commercial costs may require an intensification of effort. In this sense the injunction of sustainability has an impact on Maori in an orthodox, commercial, sense as well as a customary sense. This is a consequence of attempting to redress historical claims by transferring assets which require participation in industries which have been viewed with scepticism by Maori in the past. The commercialisation of customary resources has been the outcome of the developments flowing from the Treaty of Waitangi settlement process, bringing about the accelerated involvement of Maori in the economy after many years of marginal participation. Maori leadership is opposed to a development process that does not have Maori at heart, and eventually driving it—but the process is international and highly competitive.

Conclusion

Maori development is framed by the terms of the Treaty of Waitangi reconciliation process. It is the process where there is a transfer of resources, ostensibly to settle the historical wrongdoing of colonial governments, but also to improve the resource base of Maori and thus strengthen their capacity to participate in the economy. The task is premised on the notion that Maori had rights that were in existence prior to the arrival of the British. Those rights were not respected by the Crown after the Treaty was signed. The task now is to give economic force to those rights through the transfer of resources, and greater recognition of the importance of Maori language and culture.

Separate political development is not on the political agenda. While there is support for the settlement of historical grievances, and an economic transfer of resources is countenanced, the purpose is to integrate Maori further into the mainstream of the economy. The sentiments of nationalism are given expression through language and culture rather than through the creation of institutions of self-government. The desired result appears to be economic prowess and cultural cohesiveness. Political development is mediated through a set of regular parliamentary elections where Maori are integrated into mainstream political parties.

Culture and language is being restored after long periods of neglect. Social change has altered the character of Maori identity and now poses questions that are more akin to those of inner urban areas in the United Kingdom or the United States, than those associated with traditional societies reeling from the impact of outside culture. This impact has taken place as Maori have declined to a low status in their own country. The recovery of status is emerging through the settling of historical claims—a process that requires considerable political skill and a capacity to compromise.

The agenda for development debates within Maori society is rooted in the political process. It rests uneasily on assumptions about the effectiveness of market-led economic reforms as a basis for improving the position of Maori in the labour market, tribal enterprise development and the distribution of resources within Maori society. Discussions on how to address welfare dependency echo with voices and ideas that come directly from the United States. At the same time the relentless push for Maori identity through the promotion of the

Treaty of Waitangi, indigenous culture (at a time when MTV and CNN beam into virtually every house), and language retention, reflect a need for adaptation in the models for economic development, to capture the full range of Maori ambitions.

13

Culturally and ecologically sustainable tourism development through local community management

Richard A. Engelhardt

The question of how traditional cultures, in whole or in part, may be mobilised for economic and social development, without culture itself being destroyed in the process continues to be a major concern. After ten years of grappling with this issue during the World Decade for Culture and Development, and four successful years implementing projects to this end within the framework of the *Vaka Moana* program, our specific task now is to recommend to UNESCO not only how to continue the *Vaka Moana* program, but how to use experiences here in the Pacific to move the debate on culture and development to the next higher plane of policy, and to expand its application into action which penetrates deeply into our societies and sets an example throughout the world.

As the Director-General of UNESCO frequently reminds us, the twin pillars of UNESCO's mission—like that of all of the agencies of the United Nations system—are peace-building and development. Tourism is a factor in both. The spectacular rise in travel and tourism is one of the most significant changes in world trade in the second half of the twentieth century, generating more than US$3.5 trillion in gross output a year and providing employment for well over 150 million people. Travel and tourism now account for 10 per cent of all world commerce. And nowhere in the world is tourism bigger business than in Asia and the Pacific. The World Travel and Tourism Council estimates that regional revenues which amounted to US$805 billion in 1995 will grow at an annual rate of nearly 8 per cent over the next decade to reach US$2 trillion by the year 2005.

If UNESCO's ethical values are to be heard in the debate on sustainable development in the twenty-first century, tourism is one of the key industries where we must take an informed stance. To do so we must analyse the effects of tourism on society critically and evaluate its potential to contribute positively to the development of the cultural life of the world's communities. The Pacific island nations must find a place at the forefront of this debate, for the small and environmentally fragile countries in this region are some of the most susceptible in the world to both the negative—and positive—effects of tourism.

Tourism is a demand-driven industry inspired by the need of people to experience something different from their daily lives. Tourists travel to new places to see something cultural, historically significant or naturally beautiful, to experience new and alternative ways of perceiving the beauty and the richness of the world, through the eyes of other cultures. In short, they travel to seek, learn and experience the world's heritage.

On the supply side, the major stimulus for the development of tourism is economic. Tourism is often praised by economic planners as a labour-intensive, undifferentiated-service industry, requiring marginal start-up capital investment. Thus tourism ranks as a favourite development tool in less developed areas of the world with a large, unskilled labour pool. One also often hears that tourism is both 'environmentally-clean' and 'culturally-benign', fostering communication and understanding among peoples of different cultures, but what is the reality? Can unskilled, uneducated labour really be absorbed into the tourist industry? Who actually profits from the money tourism generates? And, as the numbers of tourists increase exponentially every year, what exactly is their impact on local cultures and the environment? These are questions to which we do not yet have clear-cut answers for the region and which need to be carefully researched.

Tourism has brought a measure—sometimes a great measure—of wealth and economic development, at least to certain areas and to certain individual and business concerns. However, experience in Asia has shown that the rapid and unregulated growth of tourism in recent years has also been responsible for massive environmental destruction; for ruthless land expropriation; and for the exploitation of society's most vulnerable groups: ethnic minorities and young children who have the misfortune to become embroiled in the sex trade or forced to work as beggars on the fringes of affluent tourist resorts.

Not least among a nation's assets endangered by indiscriminate tourism are the historic monuments and ancient landscapes of the region's cultural heritage. These are fragile old structures which have a limited tolerance to the stress caused by visitors, their tour buses and their garbage. A heritage site has zero tolerance for thieves who wish to take home with them a piece of the monument as a souvenir.

Like rainforest, mangroves and coral reefs, the cultural heritage of Asia and the Pacific may be exotic and seductive attractions for both foreign and domestic tourists, but their carrying capacity does have its limits. Unless this limit is respected and visitors to these sites managed carefully, the sites will quickly deteriorate. Their demise will mean not only the loss of some of the most sacred, spectacular, historic and scientifically important places on earth, it will also mean the end of the tourist industry based on these cultural and natural treasures.

It is painfully obvious that the exponential tourism growth of the past four decades cannot continue indefinitely. There are limits to this growth imposed by the absolute carrying capacity of a tourism site. When this limit is reached, the site must either be closed to the public or will be degraded beyond repair. In either case, the site is lost to tourism. In the rush to provide expanded facilities for the rapid increase of mass-marketed tourism, the authenticity and integrity of indigenous traditional culture is all-too-frequently sacrificed. Ironically, it is precisely the authentic traditional culture and customs that tourists, both domestic and foreign, expect to experience when they visit a heritage site.

When there is an attempt by the tourism industry to expand the carrying capacity of the cultural or environmental resources of an area, these efforts typically take the form, not of conservation, but of promotional activities where complex cultural heritage is simplified, homogenised, packaged, and, in the end, trivialised for the quick and easy consumption of the tourist.

I will present two possibly successful models of culturally sustainable tourism development. However, mine is nevertheless a cautionary tale. Tourism presents a viable option for Pacific island states to participate in the global economy, but only if this option is carefully considered and, if taken up, even more carefully regulated.

Tourism and cultural preservation

Discussions on the growth of tourism are always lively, and because they draw points of view from different sectors—archaeological, commercial, anthropological, architectural, even political—these debates have not always resulted in clear or harmonious points of convergence. The battle line is drawn between those who wish for the economic opportunity and development of the area at whatever cost, and those who would preserve or conserve culture and environments in a pristine state.

Tourism and preservation may appear to be strange bedfellows, but with proper management a synergy can be developed. Sustainable tourism can bring improved income and living standards for local people. Tourism can revitalise local culture, especially traditional crafts and customs. It can stimulate the rural economy by creating demand for agricultural produce and, through infrastructure development projects, it can inject capital into rural areas.

Informed and expert tourism also has the potential to play a vital role in the preservation of the cultural heritage of a nation. Maintenance and preservation of cultural heritage can lead to increased awareness of, and pride in, history and civilisation. Tourism can also help preserve and develop national culture by providing a wider patronage for handicrafts and traditional performing arts. UNESCO's concern therefore is to promote the development of cultural tourism, not as an end unto itself, but as a tool for the preservation and enhancement of a society's culture, its physical and intangible heritage, and its environment.

This reassessment of the purpose of tourism development may seem to be a radical approach, but it gives an invigorating sense of purpose and direction to sustainable tourism development and to the tourism industry as a whole. It makes good economic sense. If the cultural and environmental resources on which tourism is based are not conserved, the industry cannot be sustained. It is also good public relations strategy for the tourism industry to be seen as pro-culture and pro-environment, which, indeed, it surely must be if it is to survive.

The specific role of UNESCO in this realignment of the tourism industry is to encourage linkages between community development and heritage preservation, through local effort, public-private partnerships and by strengthening, through training, local-level endogenous capacity in heritage preservation and management. In this way we attempt to promote the essential role of culture in development, recognising that cultural traditions and practices provide the most stable basis for sustainable social and economic development.

To make tourism a viable tool for cultural and environmental conservation, several issues will have to be addressed and improved

- information for the potential tourist (promotion)
- quality (authenticity) of tourism products and sites (interpretation)
- conservation and management of sites with respect for a site's carrying capacity. This will require that the tourism industry cooperate with and work under the guidance of professional conservators
- financing, so that the increased needs of the sites in terms of maintenance and presentation which tourism demands are able to be met from the profit revenues of the tourism industry, not from dwindling public funds
- endogenous planning, indigenous management, and profit-sharing by the affected local community.

Two case studies, from Vietnam and Laos

Hue, Vietnam

I will start with Hue because it is a more straightforward type of site and because I want to dispel any notion which I may have mistakenly conveyed that local community empowerment is the panacea to all tourism development issues. All development issues are management issues embedded in a matrix of power at the family, village, tribal, national, regional and global levels. Tourism is no different and the failure of sustainability from which so many tourism development schemes suffer is caused precisely by the failure to reconcile the interests of all stakeholders.

Hue is the former royal capital of Vietnam. Inscribed on UNESCO's World Heritage List in 1993, it was the subject of a priority international safeguarding campaign by UNESCO from 1994–95. The purpose of this campaign was to restore the site and the traditional culture associated with it, not only by conserving the physical remains but also through the revitalisation of Vietnam's intangible cultural heritage which had been trivialised by colonisation, discredited by political ideology and decimated by war.

The challenge in Hue has been to take a rather decrepit, although emotionally significant, cultural heritage site and to bring it back to life by re-discovering the crafts, sciences, tools, materials, but also the landscapes, music, food, activities, art and poetry which were associated with it. This also is a challenge familiar in the Pacific with its rich, but sometimes eroded, heritage of intangible culture. The challenge for tourism development at Hue and at many sites in the Asia Pacific region is the same: how to keep what is sacred, sacred; how to retain or revitalise the richness, complexity and creativity of the traditional performing arts; how to maintain cultural authenticity and communicate an appreciation of this to the visitor—both foreign and domestic—privileged enough to experience it.

At the present time, tourism in Hue is still small-scale and manageable, but it is expanding quickly. As part of UNESCO's campaign to safeguard the site, and with the help of students from the Hue University, the local business association undertook econometric studies to address the potential contribution of cultural tourism to the rehabilitation of the socioeconomic life of Hue.

Based on the results of this study, a year-long series of training workshops was conducted for both public and private sector players interested in developing tourism at Hue. These workshops targeted a wide spectrum of stakeholders: land developers and hotel entrepreneurs; local historians and students looking for employment in the tourism industry; cyclo drivers and souvenir vendors; even handicapped street people who formerly begged for alms outside the monuments and temples.

The workshops resulted in a detailed tourism development management plan that was compiled for the guidance of everyone. The specific provisions of this plan were re-debated at length by the local and regional People's Committees then adopted and sent to the Prime Minister for promulgation as policy.

In outline format, the Hue Plan for Sustainable Tourism Development, makes the following statements with regard to financing, zoning and integration of living culture into a heritage site tourism development plan.

Finance. Although heritage conservation is not incompatible with sustainable tourism development, there must be a well thought-out plan that is used by all actors as the basis for this development, if the concerns of heritage preservation are to be given due consideration. Following a well thought-out master plan can, in fact, lead to the reinvigoration of traditional cultures by creating new audiences (that is, consumers) for traditional culture and offering the possibilities of financing this cultural revival with tourist revenues. In outline,

- an overall development master plan incorporating both preservation and development concerns is required for the guidance of all
- sustainable cultural tourism implies increased investment to maintain and/or invigorate the cultural resources on which tourism is based
- financing for the necessary increases to investment in culture can and should be found within the profit margins of the tourism industry
- innovative public-private partnerships can be established to link conservation efforts to sustainable tourism development.

Zoning. Although an increase in visitors to a site can bring economic benefits, the increase in the number of people is in itself problematic because of the additional stress it places on the already fragile monuments. Therefore it is important to determine and respect the limits of the carrying capacity of each monument, site or facility. Consequently,

- there is an upper limit to the number of visitors a historical/cultural site can receive at any one time without the site suffering permanent degradation or damage
- strict zoning and land-use regulations must be put in place and scrupulously enforced in order to preserve the traditional environmental context of the historical monuments and sites
- integrated, inter-agency planning is essential both at the national and the local level if the twin goals of heritage conservation and sustainable tourism development are to be successfully achieved.

Integrating living and historical culture. It is both desirable and possible to expand both the carrying capacity of a site and the touristic interest of a site by integrating intangible culture with the physical heritage. A lively local culture of dance, theatre, poetry, painting and even food, all encourage a visitor to stay longer in the area and give the visitor a greater depth of understanding about the traditional local culture. Research documentation and training are necessary in order to ensure that the authenticity of these intangible cultural traditions is scrupulously preserved. In brief

- cultural tourists are seeking a high-quality, informed and authentic cultural experience
- in addition to the historical monuments, traditional vernacular villages, rural temples and the natural environment, are also of particular interest to the visitor and form part of the unique 'cultural landscape' of a site
- investment in training and human resource development in the performing and other traditional arts is, therefore, good tourist economics
- personnel, drawn from the local community and thoroughly trained in the presentation of a cultural site and its maintenance, are crucial to the successful development of cultural tourism as a sustainable business.

The Vietnamese tourism development plan for Hue shows that conservation and preservation of cultural heritage through cultural tourism depends on the combined efforts of the different stakeholders. A strong government policy on cultural tourism and heritage preservation is important, but this must be accompanied by a commitment at the local level to ensure that policy is carried out. Cooperation among institutions and agencies involved in tourism is also needed to bring finance and state-of-the-art expertise to this effort. The contribution of the mass media and the education system are also vital in increasing the awareness of the entire local population concerning the importance of preserving historical building and archaeological sites.

Luang Namtha, Lao PDR

Although Laos is a landlocked country, it presents many development analogies to Pacific island states in terms of its isolation, small population, low GDP, a regional approach to development based on historical ties, trade and migration routes, and intimate links between its natural environment and culture. Laos, like some of the Pacific states, is, according to the United Nations, also one of the world's 'least-developed economies'. A crucial aspect for policy formulation in Lao PDR is the way in which culture and the natural environment are interlinked. Forty per cent of the land is under forest and these forests are home to 68 different ethnic groups.

Recognising the wealth of this heritage, the Lao government has made a commitment to the preservation of its cultural heritage and natural environment. However, a single-minded, country-wide commitment to the preservation of tropical forests and rivers in their pristine state is not a viable political option for Laos. The imperatives of poverty alleviation and economic development dictate that the natural environment be put to economically productive use. The task for policymakers is to accomplish this on a sustainable basis, with a minimum of environmental degradation and in such a way as control of the environment remains in Lao hands.

The biggest asset of developing countries is often their beautiful natural landscape and unique, living traditional culture, therefore governments frequently seek to market their countries through tourism as an immediate way to earn foreign exchange. Laos has also chosen this option.

With the opening of the Lao PDR to international and inter-regional tourism, there are increasing internal and external pressures on the national and local tourism authorities to approve and invest in a wide variety of tourism products and to improve the infrastructure to support the growing tourism industry. However, a too rapid expansion of the cultural and ecotourism industry without adequate regard for the carrying capacity of the environment, or without a mechanism for providing the funds and technical expertise for the required increase in conservation, will prove devastating both to the ecotourism industry and to the cultural heritage of Laos.

Urgent assistance is required to ensure the creation of a sound tourism investment policy, which guarantees that a major percentage of the economic benefits earned by tourism stay within the country and are applied in ways that directly benefit the population of that country. Without this assistance in economic policy formulation, grass-roots community empowerment will have little long-term effect.

There is an urgent need to enhance the capacity of Lao tourism planners and authorities to handle this situation in a proactive way, and to create mechanisms for the direct participation of communities affected by increased tourism in order to bring economic benefits, safeguard the environment, and maintain cultural and spiritual values intact.

The challenge presented to UNESCO by the National Tourism Authority of Laos was to assist the national authorities to meet these needs by developing sustainable 'ecotourism' in the 24 'national bio-diversity conservation areas' which together comprise fully one-quarter of the total land area of country. This daunting task was complicated by the fact that all of the 24 conservation areas are home to significant numbers of minority tribal peoples, some of whom have been identified by UNESCO as having among the most endangered cultures of the world.

'Ecotourism' is a term loosely used by the tourism industry to connote organising tourist activities around visits to natural scenic locations and visits to villages of the local inhabitants. Usually this appellation is merely politically-correct advertising copy, disguising the all-too-familiar exploitation of people and environments by mass-based tourism.

However, 'ecotourism' also has the potential to be a significant development activity, in which case its proper implementation is considerably more complicated than taking tourists for a hike in a forest or diving on a coral reef. The Ecotourism Society's 1992 definition of ecotourism is 'purposeful travel to natural areas to understand the cultural and natural history of the environment, taking care not to alter the integrity of the ecosystem, while producing economic opportunities that make the conservation of natural resources financially beneficial to local citizens.' The 1995 Australian National Ecotourism Strategy defines ecotourism as 'tourism that involves education and interpretation of the natural and cultural environment and is managed to be ecologically sustainable.'

UNESCO assistance to Laos—co-financed by the government of New Zealand and by the first-ever grant to UNESCO by the International Finance Corporation—consists in fostering the articulation of an endogenous tourism management plan. A plan based on traditionally evolved practices of land use and stewardship, and consideration of criteria and the commercial viability of private investment. The goal is to ensure that local cultural communities can continue to manage their environments sustainably and in accordance with established traditional practices while simultaneously developing their economic potential through ecotourism.

The participants of this project and its beneficiaries are

- Lao authorities at the provincial and district levels whose position at the regional is equivalent to national level forestry, cultural and tourism offices and who have been assigned the task of developing tourism in their regions
- the local communities who live in and around these protected areas targeted for tourism development, especially ethnic and cultural minorities, youth, women and local culture specialists
- Lao and foreign investors who wish to invest in commercially viable ecotourism projects in an environmentally and culturally sustainable way.

Project activities emphasise the sustained economic development of natural and cultural resources by planning and promoting environmentally sound and culturally appropriate ecotourism, which is community based and ensures that any benefits will be shared with the affected communities through the generation of employment and other economic opportunities. The involvement of local communities in decision-making and the distribution of economic benefits is essential to achieve long-term sustainable development in the area.

To this end, endogenous models of cultural and ecotourism development, based on traditional community land management practices—to the extent that they continue to be sustainable—and technical expertise from the natural and cultural conservation sciences have been developed in northern Lao PDR. The models are now being tested and evaluated in one particularly vulnerable and protected area bordering China and Myanmar: Luang Namtha.

The criterion used to evaluate the models is their success in attaining non-subsidised, commercial viability, providing local employment opportunities and contributing to raising the standard of living of the people of the area to comparable national levels, contributing to their long-term welfare and allowing them to maintain the integrity of their social and cultural traditions.

The models developed in Luang Namtha hopefully will be applicable to cultural and ecotourism development in the other protected areas of the Lao PDR, with modifications to fit local environmental, cultural and developmental conditions. These models will serve to guide both public and private sector investment in this industry, leading to job creation in rural areas, enabling local communities to participate in the management and conservation of their natural and cultural resources for the sustainable development of tourism and other economic sectors.

Conservation problems at world heritage sites

The results of a recent survey of conservation problems at World Heritage sites attribute the major problems to unmanaged tourism development and the resultant degradation of the environment of the site.

The conclusion is that sustainable culture/tourism equates to the safeguarding of the cultural and natural environment on which this tourism is based. Unfortunately, standard models of tourism development in many areas of the region remain volume-oriented, driven by macroeconomic considerations, and by a private sector which indiscriminately pursues mass tourism with little regard for culture, ecology and social values.

Carefully planned, managed and controlled tourism that services and enhances heritage preservation is an attractive alternative and can be economically profitable if the following objectives are maintained

- use of the country's cultural and natural resources to stimulate the development of a tourism industry which will play a significant role in national economic growth
- development of tourism as a tool in the conservation of the country's cultural and natural heritage and the preservation of the complex linkages between culture and environment
- enable tourism related to the country's cultural and natural heritage to prosper without damaging that heritage or engendering social problems
- development of tourism in a manner that keeps control and operation in the hands of local peoples and allows local peoples to reap the fruits of the business.

Community participation in the planning and implementation of a tourist development plan is essential. This will serve to mitigate the negative social aspects which mass tourism brings and to provide guidelines for appropriate tourist behaviour in historically important but culturally fragile sites. Community involvement in the planning of social activities focused on its cultural heritage will also enrich the cultural calendar with fairs, festivals and theatrical performances for the enjoyment and education of not only tourists, but local residents as well. When local people are active participants in all of these activities they will develop a personal stake in the development of long-term sustainable tourism through the conservation and maintenance of the authentic cultural heritage of their community.

Cultural heritage is not a static relic from the past. It is the very basis of development. Cultural values determine the priorities a society sets for its future economic and social development. Plumbing the wisdom of human cultures we can find the inspiration and the courage to manage the complexity which challenges the region, to realise the aspiration to diversity and to create new forms of solidarity for future peace and prosperity.

Conclusion

I began with a reference to the need to develop specific recommendations for the continuation and development of the *Vaka Moana* program. I hope that my remarks have suggested to you some ideas in this regard both with regard to sustainable cultural tourism development and with regard to the promotion of effective local community management of cultural resources. I cannot presume to advise you on the future of *Vaka Moana*, but I can suggest three general areas of action that might be appropriate in regard to sustainable tourism development.

- There is a need to elaborate regional, national and local guidelines for undertaking cultural impact assessments; such assessments should be required by law prior to the approval of each (tourism) development activity.
- There is a need to undertake national inventories, including surveys and maps, of all immovable physical cultural heritage and sites—and to determine their visitor carrying capacity—with a view to their long-term protection within the framework of the 1972 UNESCO World Heritage Convention, and other appropriate international, national, local and customary conservation instruments.
- There is a need to develop, where they do not already exist, instructional modules for teaching regional, national and, especially, local heritage in the formal school system. With special reference to tourism development, there is a need for teaching school-leavers in non-formal situations with the particular aim of training and licensing local heritage expert guides and resource persons.

14

Tourism and culture: a sustainable partnership

Levani V. Tuinabua

In the Pacific, and certainly in Fiji, tourism has been stigmatised as the industry that trivialises sacred traditions, brings us drugs and immodesty and destroys culture. In instances where these have occurred tourism cannot, and should not, be held totally responsible for these changes as it is only one of numerous influences and forces that brought them about. It was not the sole factor. Indeed, when one takes a closer look at tourism, it is actually contributing to the preservation of culture.

Increasingly, tourists of today are shunning enclave holidays. These are holidays where they are whisked from the airport to a resort to hibernate for a week or so before they are whisked back to the airport for the journey home. Today's tourists want to see and get to know the country in which they are holidaying. They want to meet the people, eat what they eat, experience how they live, and get to know their culture.

Against this background, tourism destinations are developing new products to satisfy this demand. Even a regional organisation like the Tourism Council of the South Pacific has not been immune to this trend. Between 1989 and 1994, we were heavily involved in efforts to expand and diversify the products available to tourists in the South Pacific.

In Fiji, we were involved in the development of the Tavuni Hill Fort near Sigatoka as a tourist attraction. One old man from a nearby village tells how the hill fort was founded. In the late eighteenth century, there was a dispute within the Tu'i Pelehake family in the village of Alaki in Mu'a, Tonga. A member of the family, Maile Latumai, decided to leave for Fiji and, during the trip, he saw Kadavu and Serua but did not go ashore. He did go ashore at Korotogo on the Coral Coast, and, after moving around a little, he finally settled at Tavuni. Today, Maile's descendants, called the Yavusa Noitoga, live in a number of villages around Tavuni Hill Fort.

The Tavuni Hill Fort is a cultural heritage site, representative of the links between Fiji and Tonga. This site was chosen not only because of its cultural attributes but also because it is close to the Queens Road and in a high-density tourism area. These factors will facilitate tourism and the commercial viability of the venture. Many of the historical and archaeological sites along the Sigatoka Valley have all but vanished due to agriculture or housing developments, but tourism has contributed to the preservation of the Tavuni Hill Fort.

Some time ago, a lad from Kabara or Fulaga (two islands of the Lau group renowned for carving) built a Fijian canoe, a *drua*, and sailed it to Suva intending to use it for short cruises in the harbour. The cruises were popular, but the tourist industry in Fiji was in one of its cyclical recessions and tourists were not coming to Fiji, let alone Suva, and the innovative venture folded. But it is another example of tourism's role in the preservation of culture.

Coupled with a desire to be more meaningfully involved in the tourism sector, the development of modern day tourism has resulted in the mushrooming of small, family-run and 'value for money' lodges. Through tourism establishments like these, the tourist has the rare opportunity to live our culture. He eats what we eat, does what we do—particularly for farmstays—and sleeps like we sleep. Last month, I attended the first ever Solomon Islands National Tourism Conference, which was followed immediately by an ecotourism conference. At tea one morning, I was delighted to hear a Solomon Island lady explaining with pride how she prepares local dishes for her tourists and how her guests devour them. In this case, tourism is contributing to the preservation of our culture. After all, food is an indispensable part of South Pacific culture.

Although Frank Hilton is reported to have said that the three most important factors for a hotel are: 'One, location; two, location; and three, location' tourism is not an industry constrained by the presence of infrastructure and utilities (although of course, it is tremendously beneficial if these facilities are available). This makes hotels and resorts a very mobile industry. They can be located throughout a country. Indeed, sometimes the more inaccessible a resort is, the more exclusive and expensive it gets—mainly because it can claim to provide privacy in these days of cameras with telephoto lenses! Because hotels are able to move, workers are not always forced to uproot themselves from the social and cultural environment in order to obtain employment in the tourism industry. This is one more way in which tourism supports the preservation of culture.

One eight-unit boutique resort off the coast of Vanua Levu does this and more. The management has employed two or three teams of neighbouring villagers. Each team is employed for two weeks or so before it is sent back to the village and a new team is engaged. Through this approach there is an obvious distributional benefit as many more people are employed at the resort, and because each team is not permanently employed, the sociocultural dislocation is not so great.

A stretch of white sandy beach edged by swaying palm trees is no unique attribute. It looks the same whether it is in the Caribbean, Mauritius or in the South Pacific. Similarly for five star resorts, cruise ships, and colourful, romantically named yet deceptive cocktails. If you ask the tourism industry of the South Pacific, they will say that what sets the South Pacific apart from all the other tropical and maritime destinations are the South Pacific peoples and cultures. Where else in the world can one experience the captivating sways of a Tahitian *tamure* or the serenity and grace of a Tongan *taualunga*? Where else in the world can one experience the myriad of colours and costumes of traditional Papua New Guinean outfits? Where else in the world can one experience the raw challenge of a Pentecost dive or the pomp and precision of a Fijian *yaqona* ceremony? The examples go on and on.

These can only be experienced in the South Pacific. These are what set our region and peoples apart. In tourism, we call them our 'unique selling points'. Without them, we are no longer unique. Without them, we are like any other tropical holiday destination. The preservation of the region's culture means the maintenance of our unique selling points in the tourism industry. The preservation of our cultures is a prerequisite to a sustainable tourism industry in the region.

15

Vaka Moana—a road map for the South Pacific economy

Hana Ayala

The long-term impact of UNESCO's World Decade for Cultural Development 1988–97 is shaped by the timeliness of this endeavour. As an antidote to the globalisation megatrend, which is often marked by cultural homogenisation, the World Decade has encouraged interdisciplinary and inter-agency approaches that emphasise the rich contributions of cultural diversity to resource conservation and the sustainable growth of a progressively globalising economy. I believe that there exists, in the target regions of Mundo Maya, Silk Road, and *Vaka Moana*, an outstanding opportunity to align the Decade's spirit and achievements with the economic aspirations that the regions' governments increasingly entrust to the promise of tourism. The ever stronger heritage orientation of international leisure travel resonates remarkably well with the heritage bias of the World Decade, notwithstanding differences in motivation, humanistic for UNESCO, and business-oriented for the tourism industry. The boom in heritage tourism gives a forceful economic connotation to the World Decade's legacy and sets the stage for shifting the focus of its implementation from correcting economic development to driving it. My proposal for employing *Vaka Moana* as a catalyst for the South Pacific economy provides a sequel to the World Decade that would accomplish this shift in focus.

The paradigm of international ecotourism

International tourism and international ecotourism are irreversibly merging. The majority of international leisure travellers are 'soft' ecotourists: 'ecotourists' because of their demand for an authentic and enriching experience of nature and culture as well as their willingness to contribute to conservation, and 'soft' because of their overwhelming preference for high standards of accommodation, service, and security. Market data from Central America fully confirm this trend. 'Hard' or 'pure' ecotourists, who are willing to sustain low comfort levels and utilise minimal facilities, represent only a small number of tourists who visit the region's protected areas, and their proportion diminishes every year (Ashton 1993).

It is not just the accommodation element of heritage-centred tourism that entails a great amount of investment, in terms of both capital and technical expertise. The interpretive infrastructure poses no less of a challenge. International leisure travellers have increasingly higher expectations of the quality of information concerning the nature and culture of their destinations, regarding both the content and presentation (Ayala 1995a). This contrasts sharply with the common, but false belief particularly widespread among governments and developers in island countries, that nature—or other heritage-based tourism—is an excellent way to attract tourists with little initial capital expenditure (Bookman 1994).

Cooperation is emerging as another challenge for heritage destinations. Evolution, history, ecology, and other relationships that bond natural and human ecosystems allow the tourism industry to combine multiple destinations into heritage themes whose aggregate identity and eminent marketability enhance the heritage value of each participating destination. As international leisure tourism progressively redefines itself into heritage tourism, competition unfolds among national and regional heritage packages. The World Tourism Organization (WTO) supports this idea through its involvement in some fifty countries across Europe and Asia that participate in the Silk Road project as a new destination (WTO News 1994). This composite destination is not to be travelled all in one trip, but lends a powerful heritage context to any sub-destination, be it a gateway city of Tashkent or Istanbul, or a nature reserve in China's Xinjiang (Tang 1991). The same principle applies for Mundo Maya, the umbrella theme that spans a splendid cultural and landscape heritage across five Latin American countries, and for Paseo Pantera, a multi-country initiative that envisions the proposed Central American Biological Corridor as the backbone of the Central American heritage product.

The more international tourism transforms itself into heritage tourism, the less viable and manageable it becomes as a sectoral activity. The international tourism and hotel industry needs access to knowledge about the destination's nature and culture in order to provide interpretive guidance for the heritage experience. Generating such knowledge is not within the industry's expertise. It is, however, within the industry's capacity and business interest to mobilise others to generate such knowledge. Further, the resources that support the heritage experience and, thus, decisively condition the business value of the tourist enterprise are not owned or managed by the industry, but by indigenous peoples and conservation authorities among others. That confronts the industry with the need to engage in partnerships to guarantee product quality, which opens a major—so far largely untapped—opportunity for indigenous and local people to benefit from international tourism by assuming responsibility for sustainable resource management. When cultural experience derives from intangible attractions, such as sacred values, rituals and beliefs, the indigenous or local management of the experience in the presence of tourists helps ensure the viability of the tourist enterprise, since it greatly increases the tourists' satisfaction and sense of participation (Sofield 1991).

The proliferation of national and regional development plans that single out heritage tourism as a new priority for economic growth, creates a unique circumstance for realising the potential of international tourism and the hotel industry to become, globally, the strongest sponsor of conservation. This scenario pertains to both natural and cultural conservation. The prospect of transforming the industry into an important benefactor of research on natural and human ecosystems is attainable because of the boom in heritage tourism. The value of such research is not limited to tourism, but spills over into agriculture, education, health, and other sectors of the host country's economy. There are already examples of conservation and research patronage undertaken by the tourism industry, motivated by the business reasons of investment protection and marketability, and they keep increasing throughout the world. However, no country or region— including the heritage regions of Mundo Maya, Silk Road, and *Vaka Moana*—has yet launched a strategy to systematically implement the tourism-destination partnership.

A national or regional strategy that strives to fashion heritage tourism into the engine of a viable economy must be realistic about the visitor volume that can be generated by both the scope and the goal of such a strategy. The emphasis for accommodation and interpretive infrastructures, at the level of a country or a region, must be on planning, design, and management solutions that will transform the volume of visitors into a resource for conservation and sustainable development, while effectively zoning tourists through experienced management. A national or regional master plan that adopts these principles would acquire the capacity to attract tourism and hotel projects that could deliver what the industry now endorses as the formula for high-quality, high-profitability tourism: namely, environmental and cultural sensitivity (Shundich 1996).

I claim that ecotourism is the new direction in which all heritage-oriented tourism will have to embark if it is to become prosperous and competitive in the twenty-first century. Natural, cultural, and archaeological tourism divide heritage tourism according to the specific character of the heritage resource or according to the special interests of travellers. Ecotourism is a value-based term that stresses the mutual interdependence of heritage conservation and sustainable valuation in the quality of the experience. The location or the type of the heritage resource that supports the ecotourism experience should be secondary. As a value-based term, ecotourism should also bring together the natural and cultural dimensions that are closely interwoven, both in the tourists' interests and interests of maintaining the spiritual, conservation, and research importance of many heritage attractions.

Vaka Moana: beyond the world decade

According to its guiding principles, the *Vaka Moana* program has been launched in response to the Pacific people's growing awareness of the need to maintain and further develop their heritage, and to promote economic development that will be based on the conservation and careful use of the region's resources. These principles could equally well be used to define the optimum course for leading South Pacific tourism into the century in which the winning strategy is the ability to compete globally while nourishing resources that are meaningful locally. This convergence of goals is a compelling reason for fashioning *Vaka Moana* into a flagship project for the continuation of the World Decade within the framework of regional development strategies.

This argument is also persuasive because of the scope and seriousness of the concerns it addresses. While great importance has been attached by Pacific island governments to service-sector activities, led by tourism, the island countries lack the capital to develop tourism infrastructures and products (Hall 1994). The network of protected areas across the region is only rudimentary, considering the diversity and uniqueness of the region's heritage, and it is ill-funded. It is beyond the financial and human resource capabilities of existing agencies to deal with the very large number of areas that deserve immediate attention for their conservation value (Tourism Council of the South Pacific 1990). A conservation strategy that seeks to remedy the current situation will have to fully engage the beliefs, values, and activities of the Pacific island cultures that have been associated with the island environments for thousands of years, and whose lifestyles continue to be based on the land and the sea (Helu-Thaman 1992). No region matches the South Pacific island region in its potential for shattering ecotourism's narrow definition as nature travel. The national and regional benefits of the South Pacific tourism industry will depend on the ability of heritage tourism to appreciate, and alert the visitor to the blurring of natural and human ecology in the unique setting of each island ecosystem. This appreciation must be underscored by economic incentives directed at the local communities and conditioned on the sustainable utilisation of both the islands and their marine environs. Further, nowhere there is a more urgent need than in the South Pacific to pool the region's resources and aspirations to make tourism a long-term contributor to the individual countries' well-being. This island region must establish itself as a heritage destination in its own right in order to combat the physical remoteness of the South Pacific islands from the major tourist-generating markets of Europe and North America. It must take on the predominantly multi-destination mode of long-haul leisure travel that becomes the rule in heritage tourism, and recognise the need to mitigate against the relatively high cost of travel to the region through the product's quality, complexity, and immunity to imitation.

Vaka Moana possesses an outstanding potential to become the unifying theme and the source of a strong identity, appeal, and propensity to grow for the regional tourism strategy, which, in turn, would become the main sponsor and executor of the interdisciplinary, intercultural, and inter-agency mission of *Vaka Moana*. However, such a strategy will only be suitable, and economically sound, for the South

Pacific island region if it is devised as a tourism-cum-conservation strategy that systematically enhances cultural integrity and cross-cultural understanding. The ecological and cultural fitness of such a strategy will also be conditioned on its ability to shift from 'raw material' to 'value-added material' of the region's heritage product.

The common premise in heritage tourism is that the natural and cultural attractions ('raw material') exist and that tourism development means very much what it meant before, that is, adding infrastructure to accommodate the tourists and generating employment in servicing the tourists. Yet a tourism strategy centred around heritage experiences creates novel economic opportunities for making conservation profitable, for revitalising local traditions in concert with present-day needs, and for advancing research into multiple fields dealing with natural and cultural resources.

I identify three core steps of the value-adding process, in the context of creating a master-plan for heritage tourism. The first step is to define the multi-layered dimension of the destination's heritage. A site's heritage can often be connected with natural and cultural themes that are meaningful within the size of a country, or even a region. It might go back in time and link tangible attractions to intangible legends or beliefs. Therefore heritage product development should be approached as a dynamic process in which cooperation is essential. Heritage themes do not just enhance the complexity and interest of the tourist. They are valuable tools of cross-reference for a destination that will entice return visits, that will make naturally or culturally sensitive areas an integral part of the heritage experience with no excursion traffic, and that will provide a channel for spreading tourism-generated benefits—particularly those of conservation sponsorship—beyond areas that are suitable for tourist visits.

The second step is to equip the heritage resources with conservation guarantees. The tourism and hotel industry has a solid business reason to invest in conservation to make it effective in protecting the attractions that are now vital to the tourist enterprise. To maintain its investment, the industry needs the support of a pro-active and well-enforced conservation strategy. I would argue that the global megatrend of heritage tourism creates an unprecedented opportunity—particularly in developing countries—for launching and sustaining national and regional conservation strategies, with the backing of the tourism and hotel industry's investment in management.

The third step is to make provisions for continuous diversification and upgrading of the heritage experience. In heritage tourism, the experience of the heritage resources is the central pillar of tourism. The heritage experience is, in turn, catalysed by interpretation. A forward-looking plan for experience management should identify universities and research institutes willing to share the knowledge they advance about the natural and cultural resources in return for funding for future research, and invite indigenous people to share their cultural knowledge regarding reciprocal benefits from the tourism industry. This would offer long-term protection of the uniqueness and educational value of the heritage product.

It is in implementing these three steps that the cross-sectoral benefit, long-term success, and sustainability of heritage tourism will be decided for any country that makes the development of this industry a national priority. A tourism-conservation-research master plan I developed in concept for Panama illustrates this argument (Ayala 1997). It is within this three-step process of value-adding that *Vaka Moana* could be transformed into the propeller for the tourism-driven economy of the South Pacific islands in the twenty-first century.

Defining the multi-layered dimension of the South Pacific heritage

The South Pacific island region has had difficulty connecting with the international boom in leisure travel. Much of the blame is put on the airlines that tend to overfly the traditional stop-overs, and on the competition from new resorts in Queensland, South East Asia, and elsewhere (Bywater 1989). I would place at least as much blame on the homogenised image of 'paradise,' echoed by many of the South Pacific islands and their resorts, making these tourist island paradises mutually interchangeable and not so different from tropical paradises much closer to home. Reversing this image is a precondition of the viability of the national and regional tourism industries in the South Pacific.

The region's outstanding cultural diversity is being increasingly discovered by tourism marketing, although little of this 'discovery' is reflected in tourism planning. What has remained virtually overlooked in bringing tourism to the South Pacific economy is the daunting diversity of the island ecosystems within individual countries and across the region. Focusing just on the islands of eastern

Fiji, a 1974 pilot project co-sponsored by UNESCO, the United Nations Fund for Population Activities (UNFPA) and the government of Fiji, disclosed remarkable ecological diversity within the traditional categories of high-volcanic and low-lying islands (UNESCO/UNFPA 1983). A follow-up study called Fiji an 'ecological theatre' since it alone exhibits many of the different stages of evolution in the South Pacific islands (Bayliss-Smith *et al*. 1988).

Webs of evolutionary, ecological, and cultural linkages of outstanding conservation and research importance pervade the South Pacific island ecosystem and are definable and meaningful on a multiplicity of spatial levels throughout the region. They lend themselves to the development of heritage themes that would alert the world, and the region itself, to the South Pacific's one-of-a-kind heritage identity that encompasses multiple heritage assets worthy of the World Heritage recognition. My own field research leads me to claim that Fiji's natural heritage alone comprises examples that, together, could measure up to all four categories of criteria used by UNESCO to determine natural sites for the World Heritage List. Yet, as of June 1997, neither Fiji nor any other South Pacific island country featured a single World Heritage Site.

The multi-layered valuation of the region's heritage according to themes would also allow the richness of cultural associations that envelop many island ecosystems to be addressed, in both tourism and conservation planning. A landscape that conforms to the definition of a natural landscape in its physical features, is more often than not a cultural landscape in the South Pacific, in view of its ties to the indigenous people's identity. It embodies the term 'associative cultural landscapes,' that UNESCO has chosen for the newest category of the World Heritage Sites, 'justifiable by virtue of the powerful religious, artistic, or cultural associations of the natural element rather than material cultural evidence, which may be insignificant or even absent' (Rossler 1994). This is a category that deserves prominence in establishing the region's World Heritage values because it connects landscapes and seascapes of superlative natural beauty and interest to the spiritual life of the South Pacific peoples.

I propose that the criteria for identifying World Heritage Sites be further broadened. Two or more sites, regardless of their 'natural,' 'cultural,' or 'associative cultural landscape' classification, could share World Heritage recognition on the basis of the evolutionary, ecological, or cultural relationships that bond them together and that are integral parts of their heritage value. The South Pacific island region is uniquely endowed to pioneer this concept of sites based on themes, which would introduce a dynamic dimension into recognition by World Heritage and would stimulate the spirit of cooperation that is at the heart of UNESCO's mandate.

The concept of multi-layered, cross-national valuation of heritage resources in the context of developing regional foundations for heritage tourism, resonates with *Vaka Moana's* goal of reinforcing the links between Pacific peoples through a better knowledge of their common characteristics. It results in economic ramifications for this and the related goal of involving all peoples of the various island countries of the Pacific Ocean, including those from non-independent countries.

Equipping the region's heritage resources with conservation guarantees

Global analyses now suggest that the fast rate at which entire habitats—from reefs to tropical forests—are being destroyed is becoming more important for determining risks of extinction than the present rarity of a species (Sisk *et al.* 1994). These findings are also relevant to the South Pacific island region. Estimates suggest that, at the current rate of log extraction and exportation, Papua New Guinea's timber will last only ten years more. Similarly, all reserves of lowland rainforest in the Solomon islands will be exhausted in less than a decade (Wallace 1996).

As Trevor Sofield (1992) states, though environmentalists have condemned logging operations, they have offered only idealism without cash. The solutions must be realistic about the region's development needs and be aware of the cultural and ecological clash between the western-style concept of a national park and the intimate relationship between the activities and lifestyles of the South Pacific peoples and their countries' natural environment. If ecotourism is to become the industry that makes the environment worth conserving, while promoting sustainable development, it has to generate a monetary benefit for the land-owning groups that outweighs the short-term financial gains from logging and other unsound land uses (Young 1992).

Conservation must become an integral part of a nation's entire development process, but that can only happen if the South Pacific governments and land-owners cease equating ecotourism with small budget, small scale, rough-it tourism. The reality is that all heritage-oriented tourism is evolving into ecotourism, very rapidly in the field of marketing and steadily in respect of planning. In both marketing and planning, the driving force is the great marketability of the ecotourism philosophy; in the latter, the driving force is also the business imperative of protecting and enhancing heritage attractions to ensure quality and immunity to competition.

A thematic, multi-layered disclosure of the outstanding diversity of the region's heritage is the foundation for bringing conservation and development into a partnership. It offers a platform for a bold step the South Pacific island countries could take jointly by making conservation patronage a passport for all incoming tourism and hotel projects. The high profile that conservation sponsorship increasingly carries in the international tourism and hotel industry also encourages the use of regional heritage themes as instruments for extending the sponsorship benefits to places that are currently disadvantaged in their ability to attract tourism but that possess heritage resources of global significance. For example, while the occurrence of violence and diseases, such as malaria, hinders tourism development in parts of Melanesia, it does not mitigate against the prestige that the patron of the relevant countries' outstanding heritage would receive in any part of the region.

The effectiveness of this approach would correlate directly with the consistency of its implementation. This, in turn, needs a serious commitment by the governments to programs of public awareness, education, and, importantly, a network of tourism and conservation authorities at both the national and regional levels. In an economic perspective that is based on heritage tourism, the objective of the Tourism Council of the South Pacific (TCSP) is to foster regional cooperation in the development and promotion of tourism which is inseparable from the conservation goals of the South Pacific Regional Environment Program (SPREP) and the South Pacific Biodiversity Conservation Program (SPBCP). This claim can be supported by studies already undertaken within the region that appeal to the TSCP and SPREP to increase their contacts for mutual benefit (Tourism Council of the South Pacific 1990:3). Other studies point out that, despite the SPBCP's regionally-defined mandate, its program activities have been largely site-specific and further hampered in their effectiveness by a lack of support for biodiversity conservation from local communities (Reti 1995).

Developing the foundations of a tourism industry that derives momentum from the heritage resources, must include the economic foundations of conservation. Conservation of natural resources, but also cultural conservation that would motivate indigenous and local people to keep their sociocultural systems alive and evolving. In the South Pacific, the natural and cultural integrity of potential ecotourism sites depends on provision for sustainable utilisation by the Pacific islanders of the ecosystems with which they are bonded through ecology or association.

Fortunately, there is a planning-management model at hand: UNESCO's biosphere reserve. The value of the model is in its emphasis on integrating conservation with the promotion of scientific knowledge, skills, and the human values needed to support sustainable development. The 'Seville Strategy,' resulting from the 1995 International Conference on Biosphere Reserves in Seville, has further enhanced the desirability of introducing the biosphere reserve concept throughout the South Pacific. The Seville Strategy's emphasises the 'human dimension' of biosphere reserves that brings together cultural and biological diversity within the inter-generational perspective of benefits of sustainable development (UNESCO 1996).

In the South Pacific, I recommend delimiting areas that contain multiple heritage cores interrelated by heritage themes of national and regional significance for UNESCO's recognition as biosphere reserves. All of the region's future World Heritage Sites should be among those cores. Such a multi-layered approach to biosphere reserve development across the region would be conducive to mobilising the region's human capacity to foster sustainable development through cooperation, while paying tribute to the region's ecological and cultural complexity. As of now, Atoll de Taiaro in French Polynesia is the only biosphere reserve in the South Pacific island region.

The thematic approach addresses the priority that UNESCO's Man and the Biosphere program (MAB) now gives to consolidating the networks of biosphere reserves. It proposes an original solution to accomplishing a shift from specific sites to larger territories, and a possible scenario for setting up what the MAB program has coined 'regional units of sustainable development' (Azcarate 1993). Azcarate notes that putting in place such units will also imply recourse to new economic mechanisms, notably financial ones (1993:21). This is where underwriting the regional strategy of sustainable development by a regional tourism-cum-conservation strategy carries financial security.

And this is where *Vaka Moana's* goal of resource conservation for the benefit of the peoples of the region can be reinforced by a business perspective on development without eroding the region's cultural identity.

Providing for diversification and upgrading of the heritage experience in the region

The Seville Strategy assigns great importance to the role of biosphere reserves in developing two sets of knowledge: one based on scientific research and supported by monitoring, training, and education, the other based on popular knowledge. When used in a complementary fashion, these two sets offer a powerful tool for achieving and managing sustainable development, particularly suitable for many island countries (UNESCO 1994). Simultaneous development and integration of these two sets of knowledge is also a priority concern for heritage tourism, particularly in the South Pacific where the quality of tourism needs to be addressed urgently. A complex interweaving of shared values linking people to the land, the skies, and the sea (Helu-Thaman 1992:27), makes conservation and accessibility of the time-tested knowledge of indigenous people indispensable for the hidden spiritual dimension of the region's heritage incorporated into the tourist experience. The diversity of the region's nature and culture, the high degree of endemism, the intricacy and complexity of bonds—some of which have unparalleled evolutionary and ecological significance—within and between the natural and human ecosystems, make modern research crucial for the valuation of the region's heritage through heritage tourism.

Knowledge may well be the single most persuasive reason for bonding the tourism-destination partnership across the South Pacific island region, on the basis of reciprocity of benefits. The industry's business motivation to invest in a knowledge-mobilising partnership is strong, given that the complexity, authenticity, and educational value of the tourist experience are at stake—the very qualities that progressively drive international leisure travel.

Interpretation, through which both sets of knowledge will be channelled into the heritage product, can also serve as an effective zoning tool. The idea of zoning is integral to the biosphere reserve concept, and is increasingly used in managing national parks and other protected areas world-wide. However, the way in which tourism has been brought into the zones buffering the protected cores has not been very successful in reconciling the number of tourists with the goals of conservation and sustainable development. The confinement of accommodations, particularly of larger hotels and resorts, to a zone outside nature reserves, World Heritage Sites, and other types of protected areas, is typically controlled by the consideration of the least intrusive or the least undesirable location for development that can service the incoming visitors. The accommodation facilities of the outer zone are expected to send their guests to inner zones to participate in ecotourism experiences (Ashton 1991).

The boom in heritage tourism makes this premise increasingly unsustainable and one that threatens, by sheer numbers, the integrity of the sensitive inner zones. In order to delimit and develop the zone to accommodate the bulk of the tourism, infrastructure ought to seek to maximise opportunities for interpretation—mediated contextual access at the expense of physical access (Ayala 1996b). The foremost objective ought to be to enhance the zone's capacity to retain the bulk of the visitors, without compromising the quality of the heritage experience. Consequently, views accessible from any prospective development site, combining scenic and interpretive qualities, should be given as much attention as the site's carrying capacity for the infrastructural projects, since the views will greatly condition the site's capacity for the management of the experience. Maximising contextual access and minimising physical access is the formula for tourism development that adheres to the spirit of the Seville Strategy. It fits the island region where success and sustainability of the tourism-driven economy are dependent on tourism's ability to bring the region's many superlative—but ecologically and culturally highly-sensitive—ecosystems under the umbrella of a heritage product, without subjecting them to tourist traffic.

I have already developed the concept in a greater detail for Fiji, with a special emphasis on developing a master plan for the growth of Fiji's resort industry to become a catalyst for Fiji's heritage product (Ayala 1995b, 1995c). Fiji has an important role to play in activating the region's transformation into a flagship heritage destination, because of its already established position as a gateway country to South Pacific tourism, and as the main seat of the University of the South Pacific. I view and treat the University in my proposal as the main stakeholder in developing the indigenous modern-knowledge partnership under the auspices of heritage tourism (Ayala 1995a:44).

The road ahead

The South Pacific island region must have a clear, cross-nationally endorsed action plan for heritage valuation in order to capitalise on the tourism and hotel industry's business interest in investing in the management of tourist experiences. This would conserve heritage resources, spread the tourism-generated benefit to the grass roots level, and help sponsor research. It will best serve the region if characterised by hierarchy and synergy. Hierarchy not in a political sense, but in the sense of highlighting the evolutionary and ecological bonds among the region's heritage resources, and their cumulative value for tourism, conservation, and research. Synergy should yield an alignment of commitments to natural and cultural conservation, and bridge the goals set for conservation and development.

Heritage themes, defined—with help of existing knowledge of the region, traditional as well as modern—on multiple spatial scales within and across the South Pacific island countries will provide the platform for bringing tourism, conservation, and sustainable development into an alliance. The thematic assessment of the region's heritage will back a thematic development of the region's conservation network, as well as proposals for the World Heritage recognition of the South Pacific's most remarkable heritage assets. The establishment of 'staging areas' will catalyse tourism planning in parallel with conservation planning that will be meaningful not only in the spatial sense but also, and primarily, as settings capable of supporting interpretation-mediated heritage experiences that cover much greater areas than tourists will visit. This will allow ecologically and culturally sensitive island environments to be set aside in a systematic fashion and region-wide, without depriving them of the benefits the tourism and hotel industry. An invitation for a prestigious sponsorship of the heritage attractions within both direct and contextual access will introduce each staging area to the investors. Where the biosphere reserve approach is applied, and either honoured by UNESCO's recognition or just used as a planning-management concept, the staging areas will become parts of the outer zones and executors of the biosphere reserve concept at the level of experience management and its funding. Since the implementation of the biosphere reserve concept will echo the thematic, multi-layered structure of the tourism-cum-conservation strategy, it will also facilitate the achievement of *Vaka Moana*'s goal of promoting widely disseminating all forms knowledge, both traditional and scientific across the region.

Vaka Moana has been conceived and carried out as an ongoing program seeking the recognition of cultural, spiritual, and social values in the development process. It is this dynamic quality that places *Vaka Moana* in the heart of an economic development strategy that must continuously nourish the region's unique cultural identity if it is to triumph through heritage tourism.

References

Ashton, R., 1991. 'Trend and problems in ecotourism', in *Proceedings of the 1991 World Congress on Adventure Travel and Eco-Tourism*, The Adventure Travel Society, Englewood:22–31.

Ashton, R.E. and Ashton, P.S., 1993. *An Introduction to Sustainable Tourism (Ecotourism) in Central America*, USAID, Regional Office for Central American Programs, Guatemala City.

Ayala, H., 1995a. 'Ecoresort: a 'green' master plan for the international resort industry', *International Journal of Hospitality Management*, 14 (3/4):351–74.

——, 1995b. 'The international resort industry, heritage conservation and sustainable development: towards an unprecedented partnership', *Insula—International Journal of Island Affairs*, 4(1):32–47.

——, 1995c. 'From quality product to ecoproduct: will Fiji set a precedent?', *Tourism Management*, 16(1):39–47.

——, 1996a. 'Resort ecotourism: a paradigm for the 21st century', *The Cornell Hotel and Restaurant Administration Quarterly*, 37(5):46–53.

——, 1996b. 'Resort ecotourism: a master plan for experience management', *The Cornell Hotel and Restaurant Administration Quarterly*, 37(5):54–61.

——, 1997. 'Resort ecotourism: a catalyst for national and regional partnerships', *The Cornell Hotel and Restaurant Administration Quarterly*, 38(4):34–45.

Azcarate, T., 1993. Speech published in *The Biosphere Conference: 25 years later*, UNESCO, Paris:18–21.

Bayliss-Smith, T., Bedford, R., Brookfield, H., and Latham, M., 1988. *Islands, Islanders and the World*, Cambridge University Press, Cambridge.

Bookman, S., 1994. 'Perspective on ecotourism in island development', *Insula–International Journal of Island Affairs*, 3(1):19–21.

Bywater, M., 1989. 'The Pacific islands', *International Tourism Reports*, 4:70–99.

Hall, C.M., 1994. 'Ecotourism in Australia, New Zealand and the South Pacific: appropriate tourism or a new form of ecological imperialism?', in E. Cater and G. Lowman (eds), *Ecotourism: A Sustainable Option?* John Wiley, Chichester:137–57.

Helu-Thaman, K., 1992. 'Ecocultural tourism: a personal view for maintaining cultural integrity in ecotourism development', in J.E. Hay (ed.), *Ecotourism Business in the Pacific: promoting a sustainable experience*, Environmental Science, University of Auckland, Auckland:24–29.

Reti, I., 1995. 'The South Pacific biodiversity conservation program', K.R. Miller and S.M. Lanou (eds), *National Biodiversity Planning: guidelines based on early experiences around the world*, World Resources Institute, Washington, DC:125–27.

Rossler, M., 1994. 'Tongariro: first cultural landscape on the World Heritage list', *The World Heritage Newsletter*, 4:15.

Shundich, S., 1996. 'Ecoresorts: dollars, sense and the environment', *Hotels*, 30(3):34–40.

Sisk, T.D., Launer, A.E., Switky, K.R., and Erlich, P.R. 1994. 'Identifying extinction threats', *BioScience*, 44(9):592–604.

Sofield, T., 1991. 'Sustainable ethnic tourism in the South Pacific: some principles', *Journal of Tourism Studies*, 2(1):56–72.

——, 1992. 'The Guadalcanal track ecotourism project in the Solomon Islands', J.E. Hay (ed.), *Ecotourism Business in the Pacific: promoting a sustainable experience*, Environmental Science, University of Auckland, Auckland:89–100.

Tang, M., 1991. 'Evaluation of the tourist resources of the northern Silk Road, Xinjiang', *Chinese Journal of Arid Land Research*, 4(4):329–37.

Tourism Council of the South Pacific, 1990. *Guidelines for the Integration Of Tourism Development And Environmental Protection in the South Pacific*, Suva.

UNESCO, 1994. *Island Agenda: an overview of UNESCO's work on island environments, territories and societies*, UNESCO, Paris.

——, 1996. *Biosphere Reserves: the Seville strategy and the statutory framework of the world network*, UNESCO, Paris.

UNESCO/UNFPA, 1983. *The Eastern Islands of Fiji— a study of the natural environment, its use and man's influence on its evolution*, Orstom, Paris.

Wallace, C.P., 1996. 'Pacific paradox: isles in despair', *Los Angeles Times*, March 16:A1, A34, A35.

World Tourism Organisation News, 1994. 'The Silk Road: creating a new tourism destination', 5:2–3.

Young, M., 1992. 'Ecotourism—profitable conservation', in J.E. Hay (ed.), *Ecotourism Business in the Pacific: promoting a sustainable experience*, Environmental Science, University of Auckland, Auckland:55–60.

16

Vaka Moana—the ocean roads

Mali Voi

The debates and discussions which laid the foundations for the UN's World Decade for Cultural Development had their origins in Resolution 27 of the 1982 World Conference on Cultural Policies, Mexico City, which declared that '…culture constitutes a fundamental part of the life of each individual and of each community, and that, consequently, development—whose ultimate aim should be focused on man—must have a cultural dimension.'

In 1987 the General Assembly of the United Nations resolved that the period 1988 to 1997 would be the World Decade for Cultural Development and that the responsibility for implementing the Decade would be given to UNESCO. Subsequently, the twenty-fourth session of UNESCO's General Conference invited member states to implement, at national, regional and international levels, significant activities and projects drawn up along interdisciplinary lines. Among the large-scale projects that were developed in response to this invitation were the Integral Study of the Silk Roads; the Iron Roads of Africa, The Baroque World Project, Roads of Faith Project, The Maya World Project; The Slave Route and The Memory of the World and Latin America-Caribbean 2000.

Vaka Moana

The Pacific member states' somewhat belated response was the *Vaka Moana* project, which grew out of discussions at the July 1991 sub-regional consultation meeting of the Pacific member states. The meeting asked the New Zealand National Commission to initiate moves to seek funding for a regional project using the Pacific Ocean as an integrating theme. *Vaka Moana* was one of the possible titles canvassed at the meeting, and the one that was eventually agreed upon. *Moana* is the common word for 'ocean' in all the Austronesian languages of the Pacific and *vaka* is the common word for 'canoe', the vessel developed for the exploration and settlement of the whole region. In many Pacific languages *vaka* also connotes a social group linked by tradition of common descent and migration. *Vaka Moana* thus evokes a host of associated meanings, those linked with groupings for a common purpose as well as those associated with wide-ranging exploratory sea voyages—enterprise, daring, trade, wide kinship links, intimate knowledge of star navigation and marine development together alongside land use.

It was decided that the project should have the following broad goals

- the reinforcement of links between Pacific peoples through a better knowledge of their shared historical roots and common dependence on the ocean
- the promotion and dissemination of all forms of knowledge, both traditional and scientific, concerning the sea, the land and their resources
- the conservation, management and appropriate uses of these resources for the benefit of the people of the region
- the promotion of all forms of art bearing upon the common theme of the sea
- the involvement of all peoples of the various islands of the Pacific Ocean, including those from non-independent countries.

The New Zealand National Commission took a draft resolution (DR 315) to the October 1991 UNESCO General Conference, seeking support for the draft program and budget for 1992–93 of a major regional project entitled *Vaka Moana*, to be implemented during the period 1994 to 1997. The resolution invited the Director-General to support the project from UNESCO program funding, to provide technical assistance for the establishment of a sub-regional committee to undertake the preparation of a plan of action for the project, and for the mobilisation of extra-budgetary funds, to consult with other United Nations organisations within the region with a view to obtaining their co-operation in planning and implementing the project.

This resolution was supported by all the Pacific member states at that time (Australia, Cook Islands, Fiji, Kiribati, Papua New Guinea, Tonga and Western Samoa) as well as by France. Solomon Islands, Niue, Nauru, Marshall Islands, and Vanuatu, which have since become member states, also gave their support to this resolution.

The response from the UNESCO secretariat was most positive and supportive, and the New Zealand National Commission then lodged a participation program request for US$15,000 at the end of 1991, to be used for detailed planning for the *Vaka Moana* project. That request was granted, and a further US$20,000 was allocated to the UNESCO Apia office was also earmarked for *Vaka Moana*, bringing the total allocation to US$35,000. This money was basically to get the project mobilised in the Pacific.

During this period the nature and scope of the program was further developed and refined. Antony Hooper, then a member of the New Zealand National Commission and the originator of the *Vaka Moana* proposal, suggested a three-part program: the first would deal mainly with linguistic scholarship, archaeology and biological anthropology; the second would consist of cultural matters such as the re-establishment of links for the discussion of genealogies, traditions, and the re-enactment of canoe voyages. The final development aspect of the project would cover predominantly the economic importance of activities in the areas of sea resources and tourism, taking note of the concerns regarding conservation.

The Hon. Russell Marshall, as chair of the NZ National Commission, worked ceaselessly on the organisational aspects. He not only sought views of academics, arts and cultural administrators in New Zealand, but he also reached out to the UNESCO national commissions and Pacific member states and regional organisations such as the Forum, the South Pacific Commission, the South Pacific Regional Environmental Program and the University of the South Pacific. He ensured that all the UN agencies based in the Pacific were also informed and consulted about the program.

The *Vaka Moana* working committee

At the consultative meeting of the Pacific member states in February 1991, a working committee consisting of a representative of each of the geographic ethnic groups was formed: Australian Aboriginal and Torres Strait Islanders, Melanesians, Micronesians, and Polynesians. The committee was to be assisted by both Australian and New Zealand national commissions. Further conceptualisation of the project also took place during the Pacific Arts Symposium which was held in conjunction with the 6th Festival of Pacific Arts in Cook Islands. Between the 1991 meeting in Rarotonga and the Apia meeting in May 1993, there were a number of consultative meetings held with various regional and national organisations. The Apia Meeting of May 1993 finally decided on the activities to be included in UNESCO's program and budget for 1994–95. A decision was also made to expand membership of the working committee to include representatives from the University of the South Pacific and the South Pacific Commission, the Secretariat members of the UNESCO Apia office and a staff member from the World Decade for Cultural Development in Paris. The coordination of the whole project was to be done from the office of the regional adviser for culture in the Pacific—the Pacific member states being fairly confident at that point that the Director-General, Mr Federico Mayor, would fulfil the promise that had been made to appoint a cultural adviser for the Pacific states in due course. During the general conference in October 1993 in Paris, the Pacific member states agreed on a number of regional participation programs which were duly lodged for consideration.

I was appointed culture adviser for the Pacific member states, and took over the responsibilities of coordinating the project. In December 1993 the program was really launched, in the sense that the *vaka* had a 'house and caretaker', a place which disseminated information about it and coordinated its activities coordinated. A work plan was endorsed at this meeting, and the working committee now constituted itself as the board of *Vaka Moana*.

The dilemmas of *Vaka Moana*

Russell Marshall predicted funding difficulties from a very early stage of the program. This project was specifically conceived to address the peculiarities of the Pacific situation, but these had to be addressed in the context of the world's contemporary development concerns and the consumer society. *Vaka Moana* encountered not only funding constraints but also negative attitudes from the larger countries towards the small size and populations of the island countries involved. From the beginning of the *Vaka Moana* experience it appeared that those that had the financial resources and who would receive little assistance from the project were not particularly interested in the noble philosophical directions of the Mexico Declaration—even if they were fully endorsed by the United Nations. A perfect example of a mismatch of endorsing a decision on the one hand and doing something else on the other.

The Pacific is a vast ocean and the islands are scattered over almost one-third of the surface of the earth. Such a scattered nature presents not only communication problems to island people but also hampers coordination. Then there are also the difficulties presented by the 1200 or so different languages of the region, not to mention the English, French, and Spanish that Pacific peoples have to learn in order to communicate with each other. Only a handful of Pacific countries have internet facilities, and some of them have only just installed facsimile connections. They rely very heavily on airmail services, which are often very slow. The telephone facilities mostly exist but then tariffs are usually very high. Airline services in many islands are either unreliable or the schedules are such that a two-day meeting can involve participants in five to seven days away from work. In addition, the costs of accommodation in many of the Pacific islands are high and therefore the idea of rotating collaborative meetings is very much restricted to one or two venues.

In addition, innovative programs such as *Vaka Moana* cannot expect much help from small and already overburdened public services. In many countries, one person has to carry responsibilities for two or more regional activities. For example, the director of the museum in several of the countries is also the chief adviser to the government on national cultural policies, and carries out all the administrative tasks of both positions. In a four-window organisational structure, this person may have the following policy functions: decision-making; consultation; implementation and evaluation! Then, over and above all these 'national' duties there are also the competing demands of regional organisations. In the culture sector, such demands may come from the quadrennial Pacific Arts Festival, or from regional participation programs which involve meetings of the heads of cultural agencies, or training programs on aspects of museum or heritage management—and others matters as well.

There were some initial misunderstandings as to the nature of *Vaka Moana*. Many of those who read the brief information flier thought that it was only concerned with canoes and the sea, and thus of no direct interest them. More than this, many of them were either too shy to request more information or else they were too busy with their routine duties to try to understand this new idea of addressing development from its cultural dimension. Even within the circle of those who employed in 'culture' (culture administrators, museum managers, cultural centre managers) there were those who saw this new concept as a threat to the institutions under their control. Why should they be interested in activities that might be seen as money-making activities? After all these are not supposed to be the functions of their institutions. Their respective states are responsible for providing them with annual grants to run their affairs. Even within the culture institutions there was some opposition even though the public funding for their institutions has been dwindling over the years.

The program has also had to face the traditional hard-nosed economists who regard the idea of considering development from cultural dimensions as so much grandiloquent academic hanky-panky rather than a practical economic reality. It was also claimed that *Vaka Moana* was too ambitious. For example, many potential donors, the World Bank included, have heavily criticised the traditional land tenure system of Papua New Guinea. What such people tend to forget is that their notion of development is based on the belief that when a nation becomes materially rich, its people all have a high standard of living, but even in the rich OECD countries, and particularly in their cities, we find that there is an increasing proportion of their populations that are either dispossessed or excluded from the mainstream activities of their societies. The second problem is that investors generally want quick returns on their investment, and will go to great lengths to achieve them. Many potential donors to *Vaka Moana* were put off by the fact that they could see no direct pay-offs for themselves.

The wider Pacific values about the use of natural resources need to be taken into account with regard to land and land tenure systems in the Pacific. There are merits in some of these values. For example the harvest of oysters that grow on mangrove roots is regarded as an inferior 'second rate' practice by anyone on the Aroma Coast of Marshall Lagoon District, Central Province in Papua New Guinea. Instead, in particular among the male population, they encourage fishing at the reefs near the open sea, saying that this is what 'true fisherman' do. When one seriously examines this traditional value system, there are obvious scientific merits in encouraging the people not to harvest oysters from the roots of mangrove trees. In most circumstances, the roots would be cut, as an easier task than carefully extracting the oysters, and the damage inflicted on the trees would lead to environmental degradation. Giving in to the commercial demands of the consumer society in this way would interrupt the life cycle of fish breeding and lead to the depletion of the source of sustainable supply of fish, which is the local people's daily protein source.

There are many traditional values, throughout the Pacific, which the indigenous people have come to espouse on the basis of centuries of practical observations on the interactions between themselves and the natural world. The results of these observations have become accepted as an integral part of their daily living. In short, the basis for sustainable development is a holistic approach to the relationship between nature and man. This is a common thread running through Pacific belief systems. For example, when Foua Toloa conducted his research into the traditional marine management practices of Tokelau (funded by the *Vaka Moana* program) he found that to be a good and reputable fisherman there, one needed to be knowledgeable in natural sciences, astronomy, marine biology, and seasonal changes, as well as social, political, economic and cultural matters. This situation is in marked contrast to that in industrialised societies where universities encourage and promote specialisation and the compartmentalisation of knowledge.

This is to give an illustration of the fact that any attempts to 'tailor-make' developmental packages elsewhere and impose them here, will not work. Therefore it calls on higher learning institutions to re-think and re-design their courses of studies to have broad-based training programs and develop thinkers rather than emulating thinkers.

By the same token it may be worth mentioning the introduction of the so-called value-added goods and services tax to a number of Pacific island countries. This policy may work in countries where about 95 per cent of the working population is in the formal sector. In such situations one can argue that the consumers should pay taxes on what they consume, and that may be one way of penalising excessive consumerism. However, in many Pacific island nations only a very small proportion (around 15 to 25 per cent) of the working population is in the modern sector. This sector has been paying income tax to support the state and its services. Now it is also paying value-added goods and services tax. In practice this small sector has been milked yet again to contribute to the consolidated revenue.

These are some of the not so obvious aspects of the Pacific Island societies. To these it may be added that there are still strong kinship systems in the Pacific that work as a social security net for the unemployed, retirees and old-age care. Any 'development' must framed from within Pacific island cultural dimensions if these developments are to remain viable.

Conceptual development

One of the original aims of the *Vaka Moana* program was to promote an understanding among Pacific peoples of their common heritage and unique accomplishments. The intention was to accomplish this through studies of history and migrations which would be published for use in schools and other educational institutions in the region. The aims were in fact very similar to those of the leaders in the late 1960s when they requested the South Pacific Commission to consider the establishment of a regional gathering in which their cultural identities as Pacific Islanders were recognised and promoted. The response to this was the establishment of the South Pacific Festival of Arts, the first of which was held in Suva in 1972. Like all organisations, it grew, changed and adjusted to the changing circumstances of the Pacific. The South Pacific Festival of Arts is no longer called by its original name. The name is now the Pacific Festival of Arts and it is governed by the Council of Pacific Arts and managed by a board.

The *Vaka Moana* program has evolved in a somewhat similar way, with each of its separate projects and activities being allowed to adjust to circumstances and assume a life of its own. The project on traditional marine management may be taken as a case in point. The project drew some criticism on the grounds that it was not preceded by a proper academic research plan, and that the research itself was done not by an ethnographer, but by a marine biologist. However, traditional knowledge in Tokelau is shared only among family members, and the project managers took the view that the validity of the project's findings in this case could be assessed only by the members of the society concerned. A satisfactory assessment was duly made in this way using the local kinship system before the results were passed to a team of technical experts to decide how the knowledge might be used, while giving due recognition to the owners. This method of operation was preferred because in many cases foreign researchers were, and still are, given either incomplete or inaccurate information. The consequences have been misrepresentations of factual information at the local level.

In his unpublished research, Foua Toloa, himself a Tokelauan, observed that the practice of traditional marine management is only an aspect of a whole body of knowledge that one must master before the status of master fisherman is earned. Such knowledge includes a wide range of subjects: reef structure (inshore, reef fringe, open sea etc); seasonal changes; traditional lunar calendar; land animal and plants behaviour; celestial knowledge; economic and political structure of Tokelau society. This may give the impression that Tokelau demands that a fisherman be 'jack of all trades and master of none', but the issue is really one of specialised and partial education versus general education—general with the view of understanding the total system before practicing a particular sector of the whole body of related knowledge.

A similar approach has also been made in regards to the *vaka* (Youth to Youth Health Canoes) project that was established at Marshall Islands in 1996. In this project the youths are taught the whole process of canoe-making from the tree to its construction; sailing and navigational skills and canoe maintenance. The tourism industry is also brought in through a hotel offering tourists canoe trips involving the youths.

The framework of a project consists of three principal parts. The first is the expressed need of the local people themselves as a group: they must make a decision on a project or activity that they know they are able to carry out within their existing system. Second, the project should be designed to ensure that it involves a gainful economic activity so as to sustain itself. Third, where change to an existing way of life is envisaged, careful planning is recommended with the view to minimising disruptive elements in the community and internalising development as a growth factor to an adjusted way of life.

The original ideas of the *Vaka Moana* program have continued to guide its project or activity planning. There are, however, added dimensions which are consistent with the philosophical directions of the World Decade For Cultural Development, wherein Pacific member states choose to explore the option of addressing developments from a cultural dimension. However, this philosophical direction—addressing development from a cultural dimension—remains difficult to grasp because different people have their own perceptions of culture. The word has been used in different ways, and definitions abound in literature. This is why the implementation of the *Vaka Moana* program was initially very difficult. Its location within the culture sector did not help either, since many people (including some from learned educational institutions) immediately assumed either that it was culture specific, because of its location for planning and implementation, or canoe-related because of its title.

Most people in the Pacific probably associate culture with songs and dances, performing arts, painting, books and crafts, but on a different level, culture is also characterised in terms of creativity, intellectual activity and abstract thinking. Still other definitions of culture see it in very wide-ranging terms including behaviour peculiar to *homo sapiens*, and material objects used as an integral part of behaviour. Or again, in much more specific terms, culture consists of language, ideas, customs, codes, institutions, tools, techniques, works of arts, rituals, ceremonies—and so forth.

Just as individuals differ, so does their culture. For this reason the *Vaka Moana* program did not attempt to come up with tailor-made projects or activities for the people to do. Rather it allowed the creative impulses of people to come up with projects or activities within which they were better able to express themselves. This process encourages and rekindles self esteem, particularly among youth in the contemporary urban situation, where an increasing proportion have been excluded from meaningful participation in the life of their respective societies in the Pacific.

There are two definitions of culture that this writer prefers, the first being that of Raymond Williams in *Culture and Society*, which consists of four jointly applicable meanings

- a general state or habit of mind, having close relations with the idea of human perfection
- a general state of intellectual development in a society as a whole
- the general body of the arts
- a whole way of life, that is material, intellectual and spiritual.

This last meaning is the one that this writer prefers. Culture is, and can be, both general and specific. It is general in the sense that it covers all aspects of human life as it is lived in collective groupings, sharing many common things. But it is also specific because individuals have both peculiar and particular make-ups that may not necessarily be shared in common, and these are as important as things that are shared in a group. This 'double nature' makes culture difficult to hem into a rigid definition. Instead, culture ought to be perceived as dynamic, growing and adjusting through time, space, circumstances, and people.

The second preferred definition of culture is the one that laid the foundations of the World Decade for Cultural Development. This was the definition proclaimed at the World Conference on Culture in 1982. It adds a further dimension to Williams (1958), although it corresponds quite closely to the fourth aspect of his meaning.

> [Culture] comprises the whole complex of distinctive spiritual, intellectual and emotional features that characterize a society or social group. It includes not only the arts and letters, but also modes of life, fundamental rights of the human being, value systems, traditions and beliefs.

Buried in this declaration is a holistic view of all human activity, involving certain steps of change or development. 'Change' and 'development' are used interchangeably as both terms involve a new stage or event, or moving from one point to another. To move onto a new stage, it is necessary for the existing stage to provide the foundations for the new. The movement is a continuum, from 'here' to 'next'—not imposed from outside but suggested and adjusted and accommodated endemically.

Description

Vaka Moana, the 'ocean voyaging vessel' is an initiative that has come from the peoples of the Pacific. Although it came into being as a direct response to the UN's World Decade for Cultural Development, now, as the Decade ends, it has emerged as more than just a UNESCO program. It has become a symbol of the collective yearning of the peoples of the Pacific to retrieve, and retain their identity as gifted and unique human beings.

The intention of the planners of the *Vaka Moana* program, however, is that it should address a broader range of activities, including the study of traditional and contemporary cultures, the reinforcement of traditional links, the conservation of resources, traditions, and economic development based on careful use of the region's resources. Fundamental to the philosophy of both the World Decade for Cultural Development and the *Vaka Moana* program is a commitment to the recognition of cultural, spiritual and social values in the development process.

Development objectives

The intention of the program is that it will lead to
- a better understanding and appreciation of the cultural heritage and diversity of the Pacific peoples
- the development of cultures and attitudes which build on that heritage while taking advantage of contemporary technologies and opportunities
- a greater understanding of, and tolerance for, the values, practices and attitudes of others.

Operational goals

The *Vaka Moana* program has the following operational goals
- the reinforcement of links between Pacific peoples, the principal resource, through a better knowledge of their common historical links and dependence on both the ocean and land
- the promotion and dissemination of all forms of knowledge, both traditional and scientific, concerning the sea and the land resources
- the conservation, management and appropriate use of these resources for the benefit of the peoples of the region
- the involvement of all peoples of the various island countries of the Pacific, including those from non-independent countries
- the preservation of their individual and as well as collective identities as the people of the Pacific.

Outcomes

- Craft revival
- Culturally relevant education programs
- Revival of *vaka* building and sailing skills including the teaching of traditional celestial navigational skills

- Strengthened language and oral traditions
- Promotion of art and craft industry in new markets
- Community fulfilment
- Increased international awareness of Pacific cultures
- Better records of cultural knowledge.

Central themes

- Peopling of the Pacific
- Linguistics, archaeology, anthropology
- Migrations
- Trade routes
- Re-establishing links.

Culture and tourism

- Ecotourism
- Marketing and promotion of the cultural tourism.

Culture and Science

- Marine resources
- Medicine
- Technology.

Contemporary Pacific societies

- Traditional and contemporary
- Economics
- Political and other structures
- Cultural pluralism
- Law and society
- Communications
- Religion.

Culture and education

- Archives
- Museums
- Libraries
- Mother tongues
- Cultural Centres
- Craft techniques

- Oral history and traditions
- Arts education
- Heritage sites.

Culture and environment

- Land and sea uses
- Belief systems
- Recording of traditional land and sea resources management.

Resources

Funding is being sought from various sources, to be used for activities under the *Vaka Moana* program within the following categories

- Research and publications
- Education and training
- Cultural events
- Conferences, seminars and workshops.

References

Williams, R., 1958. *Culture and Society, 1780–1950,* Harper and Row, New York.

17

Afterword: after the World Decade

Russell Marshall

I want to begin with a few general remarks about Aotearoa and its place in the Pacific. In many respects the New Zealand *pakeha* response to Maori and Pacific Islanders has come a long way in the last 20 years. There is, consciously and subconsciously, a sense that we are enriched by the relationships which have built up in that time. An ever-growing proportion of *pakeha* New Zealanders are now relatively closely connected with Maori or, increasingly, with Samoan and other Pacific island communities. I do not have the most recent census figures, but my educated guess is that close to 20 per cent of our population now identify themselves as Maori or Pacific Islander. The figure for those who do not see themselves as Maori but who have some Polynesian strand in their *whakapapa* would be somewhat higher.

Nevertheless, from time to time I am still suddenly made to realise that we have some way to go before we can genuinely claim to be of the South Pacific. In my own recent political experience, New Zealand's response to the coup in Fiji in 1987, and the unilateral attempts to break an agreement with Samoa over immigration quotas in 1989, were salutary reminders of the strength of lingering Europeanness. Nevertheless, one of the better foreign policy decisions made by Australia and New Zealand in recent years was to shift from the electoral group known as Western European and Others, to Asia

Pacific in our UNESCO membership, thereby recognising at last that our future interests were more likely to be influenced by our geography than by the history of 80 per cent of the population. It is a diplomatic move which we have yet to make at the United Nations itself.

Vaka Moana was the Pacific states' response to the opportunity offered by the World Decade for Cultural Development, a UNESCO program which began in 1988 and comes to an end this year. At the meeting of Pacific representatives in Auckland in 1991, Antony Hooper proposed the development of a coherent Pacific program, with a central unifying theme. The idea was to take advantage of the funding offered through the World Decade, to make a positive practical and philosophical contribution for the Pacific in this field.

As stated by Epeli Hau'ofa in an earlier chapter, it is the ocean which unites and connects us. As I recall it was Malama Meleisea who made the same point to us as we set out on this journey six years ago. The Auckland meeting resolved to make navigation its general theme, and adopted the title *Vaka Moana*. At that time the best known World Decade project was the Silk Roads, and discussion was just beginning on the possibility of an African Iron roads project. We therefore added a subtitle—the Ocean Roads.

Support in principle for a Pacific program was given at the 1991 session of the UNESCO General Conference, and a *Vaka Moana* board was finally established in 1993, comprising one representative from each of Melanesia, Micronesia, Polynesia, and one from the Aboriginal and Torres Strait Islands communities. Representatives of the Australian and New Zealand National Commissions, the University of the South Pacific and the South Pacific Commission were co-opted. Jackie Lewis Harris of the St Louis Museum was added to the board at the 1994 meeting. Mali Voi became the executive officer when he was appointed to the Apia office as cultural adviser at the end of 1993.

From the beginning of 1994, UNESCO funding has come through the Participation Program and the Regular Program for a variety of projects, most of them arising out of a brainstorming session at the establishment meeting in 1993. Mali Voi has already referred to several of them. Others include the heads of cultural agencies, who hold their second meeting in Suva next week. Samoa arranged some opportunities for craftspeople to exchange experience and practices, as did Te Waka Toi in New Zealand. *Vaka Moana* initiated a week-long seminar on traditional navigation at the beginning of 1996, a gathering which brought together scholars, navigators and boat builders. Comprehensive short-wave radio coverage of the l996 Festival of Pacific Arts, funded by *Vaka Moana*, was broadcast out of the Apia office. Since October 1995, Radio New Zealand International has been broadcasting a weekly 15-minute short-wave program on culture in the Pacific, a program which is now rebroadcast in nine Pacific countries.

Earlier this year the Intergovernmental Committee for the World Decade resolved that funding arrangements would be made to provide ongoing support for five projects, most of which developed in the latter years of the Decade. Funding for these projects will now come from within the framework of the general and mainstream part of UNESCO's program and budget.

Vaka Moana is one of the five projects, and tentative indications are that between US$60,000 and US$100,000 will be set aside in the Regular Program for two years from January 1998. We should be able to expand this sum by using the Participation Program. This program entitles member states to apply for funding for several projects in the two years, though culture has to compete in the process with education, communications, science and social science.

Previous authors have already made reference to the report of the World Commission on Culture and Development, a commission chaired by former United Nations Secretary General Javier Perez de Cuellar, *Our Creative Diversity*. It is already clear that the general philosophy of this report is to form the basis of UNESCO's cultural program for the foreseeable future.

One of the original members of the Commission was Lourdes Arizpe, then the director of the Institute for Anthropological Research at the National University of Mexico, and former president of the International Union of Anthropological and Ethnological Sciences. In July 1994, Madame Arizpe left the Commission to become the assistant director general for culture at UNESCO in Paris, effectively the head of UNESCO's cultural program. She effectively then became the chief executive officer for the Commission, and from the latest draft budget and program document (C/5) it appears that she regards the De Cuellar report as the basis of UNESCO's cultural programs in the future. Reorganisation of the cultural sector staff framework also points to an intention to adopt the general thrust of the report.

This is not the place to spend much time on what this means for the organisation's cultural direction. The New Zealand National Commission and our culture sub-commission have spent some time working through the report, and reflecting on what it means for us and for the Pacific member states. Our impression is that the report and the likelihood of its implementation augur well for the kind of priorities we want to set. Our immediate challenge is to trawl through the C/5 document (the program and budget for 1998–99) to find other sources of extra funding and general support.

In our view, *Our Creative Diversity* reflects an intention to move away from a Eurocentric approach to culture, development and heritage issues, and a move towards greater support for intangible heritage issues and programs. For instance, the international agenda at the conclusion of the report, includes a challenge to UNESCO and the UNDP to 'take the lead in assisting countries to formulate new human development strategies which preserve and enrich cultural values and ethnic heritage'.

The essential orientation of *Our Creative Diversity* presents us with a clear opportunity to secure financial and moral support for Pacific-sensitive policies. The rather extraordinary cluster of meetings in Suva involving UNESCO in a range of cultural discussions and workshops is, I hope, an encouraging straw in the new wind which is now blowing.

Thirteen years ago, Dr Langi Kavaliku and I took part in the ceremony to open the UNESCO office for Pacific states in Apia. At that time, there were five members of UNESCO in the South Pacific (and it *was* the South Pacific). Today there are fourteen, with only the Federated States of Micronesia and Belau of the independent states in the Pacific not yet members, and we are hopeful that the Federated States will join us this year. As a sub-region, we are also now seeking to forge closer links with the French territories in the region, French Polynesia, New Caledonia and Wallis and Futuna. A number of our activities involve Tokelau, and eventually we should find ways to engage the people of American Samoa, Guam, the Marianas, Rapanui and, of course, Hawaii.

Over the last few years we have found that we can succeed in securing attention for this part of the world by working together. The fact that Tonga could beat off Vietnam for a place on the Executive Board in 1993 and that Samoa came within a handful of votes of beating Pakistan for a seat in 1995 confirmed our collective strength, not least to ourselves. In the way in which the United Nations system operates, our fourteen or so votes give us a rare opportunity to flex some muscle.

In the recent evaluation of the sixty or so UNESCO field offices, the Apia office was in the top five for its effectiveness and management. Edna Tait and her colleagues deserve a good deal of credit for the energy with which they have transformed the office and are implementing their programs over the last eighteen months.

During the most recent meeting of the Executive Board in Paris, the deputy director-general, Mr Badran, took the initiative to start preparation for a meeting to be called Audience Pacific, to take place during the general conference later this year. The initiative came out of a conclusion on his part that UNESCO has so far done less than justice to its Pacific member states. We are to have a three-hour opportunity to present ourselves and our list of priorities to a range of senior staff members, and to start a process in which UNESCO will give greater attention to member states of the Pacific.

I have gone through these tangible indicators of the present UNESCO climate to illustrate my belief that we have an unusual opportunity to use the services of a major United Nations agency for the benefit of the region. Ultimately, our greatest strength is our own people, but I am not at all averse to making the most of others' resources. A partial reimbursement, perhaps for all the fish they have taken!

Although we keep singing the praises of *Vaka Moana* to UNESCO secretariat staff in Paris, and we have had some success in securing support for the overall program, the reality is that since 1993 we have run a series of largely unrelated and *ad hoc* activities, many of them one-off. My major hope is that out of our reflections will come some philosophical basis from which we can develop a more coherent strategy for UNESCO's cultural activities in the Pacific, and perhaps some tentative indicators for the kind of activities which we might develop over the next five years or so. What follows is a short list of possible activities.

- the discussion showed that the idea of some kind of Pacific Cultural Arbitration system had considerable support. To that we added one suggestion that the idea was also worth taking up on a larger stage, and another, that we might also give some consideration to the drafting of a national bill of cultural rights for reference to governments in the region.

- There was an indication from the head of the Apia office that she was already working on an expansion of the Associated Schools Project and that she was attracted to the notion that there could be some connection between the ASP project and the promotion of World Heritage sites.

- It may appear to be cynical to do so, but we might as well capitalise on the Director General's particular interests. For instance, to advance proposals which fit comfortably within his Culture of Peace, and to promote greater intersectorality with the Communications, Education, Science and Social Science sectors. We should also capitalise on the good personal connections which we now have with the ADG for Culture and her senior officials.

- Now that at last we have had the chance to spend three days giving some serious consideration to the broader issues and realities surrounding or undergirding Culture and Development, I would like to think that we could make some provision for some other similar opportunity for reflection in three or four years' time.

- We need to keep offering support for projects which feature both contemporary and traditional dimensions of cultural issues.

- In the 1970s, UNESCO began a project which sought to locate and to describe as many as possible of the artefacts and *taonga* from New Zealand and the Pacific Islands. In the case of New Zealand material alone, well over 10000 items are known to be in European and North American collections. Much of the material was collected by Cook and his colleagues and the French explorers of the late 18th and early 19th centuries, with the result that there are some items which pre–date anything found in collections kept in Pacific museums. The first of the New Zealand museums were not established until the 1860s. Apart from the catalogue of artefacts in Australian collections, the project was never completed. Much of the ground work has been done, though there is still a great deal more to do. I hope that under *Vaka Moana* we can finish the task, and make available around the region on CD ROM and through other vehicles the details of what is where.

- The Communications sector of UNESCO provides for assistance in the fields of endangered languages, archives and oral history. Incidentally, I was rather surprised to see that in the recent publication on endangered languages, there was a map showing the endangered Western European languages, but not one of Melanesia. The recent establishment of the Memory of the World project, in which Australia has been closely involved, seeks to identify the world's significant documents and to register them in a way somewhat similar to the World Heritage list. National Archives in New Zealand has proposed the inclusion of the Treaty of Waitangi and the list of names of women who signed the 1892 petition seeking universal franchise, a petition which led to the world's first provision for votes for women. There is considerable capacity in all these elements of UNESCO's programme for the Pacific to receive assistance.
- The Navigation workshop which took place in Auckland last year produced some further ongoing activity, and I hope we can continue to support that.
- Hana Ayala's paper on Tourism and Culture and the ensuing discussion open up another package of interesting possibilities.
- It would be good for the programme and for the region as a whole if we could find some ways to lift the profile of *Vaka Moana*. A significant first step might be to persuade at least one head of government to find a way to put the broader issues of the fundamental importance of culture and tradition on the agenda for a Pacific Forum.

In summary, since 1993 we have made a beginning. The growing strength of this region's relationship with UNESCO and UNESCO's own current changes in direction within the Cultural sector give us an unparalleled opportunity. I think we are ready to seize that opportunity.